Bereavement Narratives

Bereavement is often treated as a psychological condition of the individual with both healthy and pathological forms. However, this empirically grounded study argues that this is not always the best or only way to help bereaved people. In a radical departure, it emphasises normality and social and cultural diversity in grieving.

Illustrated by recent research, *Bereavement Narratives* explores the extent to which dead loved ones may retain a social presence in the lives of survivors and how bereavement interacts with other agendas to shape peoples day-to-day experience and sense of identity. As such, it presents a perspective that does justice to the complexity of each, while contributing to a broader picture of bereavement that reflects the increasing fragmentation and multiculturalism of British society.

By focusing on the way people make sense of their worlds, this book expands current thinking on the nature of the continuing bonds people forge with dead loved ones to reveal a discourse of care and reciprocity, the role of deathbed accounts in people's ongoing relationships and the way the dead may gain a presence in the interview situation. Drawing attention to the profoundly social nature of grief, it considers the practical implications this has for supporting bereaved people.

This book is an innovative and invaluable read for all students and researchers of death, dying and bereavement.

Christine Valentine is a researcher and teacher at the Centre for Death and Society, University of Bath. She is currently based at the University of Tokyo comparing bereavement in the UK and Japan.

D0322162

Bereavement Narratives

Continuing bonds in the
twenty-first century

Christine Valentine

Routledge
Taylor & Francis Group

LONDON AND NEW YORK

First published 2008
by Routledge
2 Park Square, Milton Park, Abingdon, Oxon OX14 4RN

Simultaneously published in the USA and Canada
by Routledge
270 Madison Avenue, New York, NY 10016

Routledge is an imprint of the Taylor & Francis Group

Typeset in Times New Roman by
Swales & Willis Ltd, Innovation Centre, Exeter, Devon
Printed and bound in Great Britain by
TJ International Ltd, Padstow, Cornwall

British Library Cataloguing in Publication Data
A catalogue record for this book is available from the British Library

Library of Congress Cataloging-in-Publication Data
Valentine, Christine, 1949–
   Bereavement narratives: continuing bonds in the 21st century/
   Christine Valentine
        p. cm.
   1. Bereavement—Great Britain.   2. Bereavement—Psychological
aspects.   I. Title.
   BF575.G7V35 2008
   155.9′370941—dc2   2008003292

ISBN 10: 0–415–45729–7 (hbk)
ISBN 10: 0–415–45730–0 (pbk)
ISBN 10: 0–203–89336–0 (ebk)

ISBN 13: 978–0-415–45729–3 (hbk)
ISBN 13: 978–0-415–45730–9 (pbk)
ISBN 13: 978–0-203–89336–4 (ebk)

To the continuing bond with my father

Contents

Acknowledgements

This book could not have been written without the help and support of others. It therefore represents a joint project, to which I have the privilege of putting my name. In particular I would like to acknowledge my debt to the 25 bereaved individuals who supplied the material for this book, but must remain anonymous. I would like to thank them not only for their generosity in agreeing to give their time to be interviewed by me, but also for the trust and frankness with which they shared their experiences.

I am indebted to Glennys Howarth who played an integral role in the development of both the theory and the methodology on which this book is based. In addition to the benefit of her experience and expertise, I am especially grateful for her faith in me and the way she helped me to see the wood for the trees. I would like to acknowledge the support of Jane Batchelor, in reading drafts and supplying a fresh perspective.

I am very grateful to Tony Walter for sharing his wealth of experience with me through many stimulating conversations. His thoughtful and constructive suggestions enabled me to further clarify my findings and the nature of their significance and contribution to the bereavement literature, as well as come up with a title for the book. I would like to thank Allan Kellehear, Jenny Hockey and Dennis Klass, whose support and encouragement were instrumental in creating the opportunity for me to publish my work.

Last, but not least, I would like to thank Grace McInnes, my commissioning editor, for her positive and encouraging response both in word and deed to my initial proposal and her speed and efficiency in securing me a contract to write this book.

Introduction

This book takes a social look at the experience of bereavement as it reflects the norms, values and beliefs of contemporary British Society. Illustrated by recent research, it explores the extent to which and the variety of ways in which dead loved ones may retain a significant social presence in the life of survivors and how bereavement interacts with other personal agendas to shape people's day-to-day social experience and sense of identity. By focusing on the way people make sense of their experience, as revealed by the interview narratives of 25 bereaved people, this book expands current thinking on the nature and role of the continuing bonds people forge with their dead. It highlights how the continuing significance of the dead in the lives of the living revises what most people understand as the boundaries between the living and the dead. Drawing attention to the profoundly social nature of grief, it considers the practical implications this has for supporting bereaved people.

In order to appreciate the implications of the experiences my interviewees shared with me, my research and the approach I took must first be placed in context. This introductory chapter therefore provides a brief overview of the ways in which the academic study of bereavement has so far been tackled. First it traces a significant shift in perspective from an individualised, to a more social understanding of grief, highlighting the implications of taking a more social approach. Then, it considers the way such an approach has informed the theoretical and practical investigation on which this book is based. It concludes with a brief outline and rationale of the way the book is structured.

The academic study of bereavement

During the twentieth century, Western approaches to the study of bereavement have been shaped by the scientific rationality associated with modernity to represent grief as a condition of the individual psyche (Stroebe *et al.*, 1992; Hockey, 1996a; Valentine, 2006). Reflecting a social and cultural context of liberal democracy or secular society of private individuals, psychological studies of bereavement have focused on defining the symptoms of grief and identifying its 'healthy' and 'pathological' forms (Lindemann, 1944; Parkes, 1972; Parkes and Weiss, 1983; Stroebe and Stroebe, 1987). Such observations of the individual 'grief reactions' of Westerners, mainly widows, have formed the basis of universal theories, which take little account of ethnic, cultural and individual diversity.

Though originally intended as descriptive, these theories have provided the substance of the prescriptive stage models of bereavement used by many bereavement counselling services (Small, 2001). Such models have obscured the more reflective, tentative and nuanced approach of theorists in attempting to convey grief's inner turmoil, to represent grief as a measurable, predictable, controllable condition. For example, Worden's 'tasks of mourning' (1991), a popular basis for bereavement counselling, include: accepting the reality of the loss; working through its pain; adjusting to life without the deceased; emotionally relocating the deceased and moving on with life. Rather than 'the discovery of the meaning of what has been lost in all its ambiguity, ambivalence and complexity' (Craib, 1998: 166), such an approach neglects the extent to which grief is socially shaped and inhibits any real understanding of the individual, social and cultural complexity and diversity of the way people grieve.

Demonstrating the diversity of responses to death around the world, anthropologists have highlighted the profound social shaping of bereavement (Goody, 1962; Boas, 1911/1965; Evans-Pritchard, 1972/1937). Yet a preoccupation with the 'exotic' aspects of pre-modern societies and a cultural determinism has failed to capture the complexity of the way people actually experience bereavement in their lives. Rather, observations of mourning behaviour have been interpreted as evidence to support universal theories of the function of death ritual, such as promoting social solidarity or representing the dominant values of society (Durkheim, 1915; Radcliffe-Brown, 1964; Huntington and Metcalf, 1979).

However, more recent anthropological and sociological perspectives have drawn attention to the increasingly diverse and fragmented nature of contemporary Western societies. Studies are adopting a more interactional view of society in which individuals make sense of their world through negotiation with each other (Hockey, 1990; Bradbury, 1999; Riches and Dawson, 2000; Francis *et al.*, 2005). As noted by Hockey (1996b), the complexity and diversity of contemporary British society poses a challenge to any attempt to represent the way the social reality of bereavement comes to be experienced and lived out on a day-to-day basis. We can no longer approach people's experience and understandings in terms of generalities and overarching explanations, either those that take the 'individual' and a 'common humanity' as a starting point or those that prioritise 'society' and its structures. As indicated, in the former case the experience of bereavement is understood in terms of what is normal and pathological and in the latter, a collective framework of meanings.

This book seeks to demonstrate how the social reality of death and bereavement within contemporary Britain is both characterised and constructed by a diversity of meanings and world views (Hockey, 1996b: 47). It draws attention to the way people use available cultural scripts to construct and express meanings that are particular and personal to them. Such discursive activity reflects a meeting of people's different agendas, both internally as well as externally, to create a tension through which social reality is generated. This process calls into question any straightforward relationship between society's structures and individual agency. Rather it reveals the complex and creative interplay between individual and cultural resources, the human capacity for agency in difficult situations and the way people act on the basis of meaning.

By taking a discursive perspective it becomes possible to gain access to the interface between internal and external realities through the medium of conversation (Small, 2001: 41–42). This approach represents a significant challenge to the way the scientific paradigm has drawn a distinction between private, inner experience and outer observable behaviour. Rather, in focusing on the way people talk about their experience, it reveals the separation of the inner world of consciousness from the outer world of what is said and seen as a social artefact. It highlights the way the human encounter with death and loss, and indeed any aspect of the social world, is constructed in the present, through social interaction to allow a very different picture from that presented by models and prescriptions of grief to emerge. This perspective is raising questions about the nature of reality and the production of knowledge, as well as how society supports bereaved people and treats its dead members.

An increasing use of qualitative, interactive methods in relation to small-scale, exploratory studies has allowed researchers to enter the social world of participants to reveal the experience of death and bereavement as integral to life rather than a condition to be treated. This is not to minimise the extreme pain, suffering and disruption the loss of a loved one may generate. Rather, following the current trend in the field of health and illness, it is to focus on the way and the extent to which such suffering 'becomes embodied in a particular life trajectory' (Kleinman, 1988: 31). Thus there can be no 'formula' for grief since how people grieve cannot be separated from the way they live the particularity of their individual lives.

The focus of study has thus shifted from the 'symptomology' of the 'grief reaction' to the utterances of self-reflecting individuals to capture the overlapping aspects of the experience of death and bereavement (Hockey, 1990; Bradbury, 1999; Hallam *et al.*, 1999; Hallam and Hockey, 2001). In contrast to traditional methods in which the researcher remains separated from the field of study, a more inclusive focus and engaged stance is revealing the way bereavement experiences may incorporate dying, death, mourning, memorialisation, religion, spirituality, ethics, practical and legal issues. It has revealed the limitations of the dominant psychological model in which 'healthy' grieving entailed severing ties with deceased loved ones in order to move on in life. A more socially sensitive perspective has drawn attention to the variety of ways in which people may maintain their relationship with dead loved ones and the dead continue to influence the lives of the living. Such a perspective has raised questions about the nature of social identity, and of society itself (Hallam *et al.*, 1999).

Far from conceptualising grief as a task of internal adjustment to the 'reality of death' in order to return to normal functioning, such an approach calls into question the strict separation between life and death. Instead it recognises how people's relationships with their loved ones may survive the life–death boundary, the focus being placed on how bereaved people make sense of, and manage, the changed

nature of their relationship with deceased loved ones. Bereavement is thus con-
ceptualised as an ongoing process of negotiation and meaning-making (Neimeyer,
2001) to offer a focus of study that allows us to ask questions about the nature of
human attachment and sociality (Klass, 2006).

The concept of 'continuing bonds' was originally coined and presented by Klass,
Silverman and Nickman as a new model of grief (1996). It has now replaced
'severing ties' as the dominant academic discourse, to beg two important questions.
First, how can we avoid the danger of creating a new orthodoxy, thus marginalising
those who do not wish to retain ties with their dead (Small, 2001: 35; Klass, 2006)?
Second, to what extent does this academic shift reflect the experience of lay people
for whom continuing bonds may be far from a new discourse? Indeed continuing
bonds are well represented in popular culture, through music, in memoriam notices,
on gravestones and in letters of condolence. The interview narratives on which
this book is based reveal how contemporary continuing bonds are flourishing,
taking highly idiosyncratic forms rather than being grounded in traditional or
religious structures. Of course, these recent interviews cannot reveal the extent to
which the 'severing ties' discourse may have served to discourage such bonds in
the past, or whether it was purely the academics and professionals whose vision
was obscured by the dominant model. However, they do reveal a certain amount
of negotiation between the two discourses with some bereaved people seeking to
justify the fact that they were 'keeping hold' rather than 'letting go'. In some cases
people expressed surprise at discovering the extent to which their deceased loved
ones continued to influence and form part of their ongoing lives.

As with severing ties, continuing bonds have been represented as purely
intrapsychic, in a way which continues to separate the social and psychological
(Klass *et al.*, 1996). As noted by Howarth (2007a: 211), this perspective relies on
the psychological concept of an inner representation of the deceased loved one with
whom the bereaved person interacts. It locates the experience in the mind of the
bereaved person, implying that it is 'imaginary' rather than 'real'. However by
adopting a sociological perspective that emphasises the way people make sense of
and engage with their world, then it is no longer a question of what is 'real', but
how people act in relation to what they take to be 'real' and meaningful for them.
This emphasis is less likely to run the risk of imposing a new orthodoxy that
marginalises those who chose not to or may be were unable to find a place in their
lives for their dead. It can encompass both 'letting go' and 'keeping hold' of the
dead and how people try to manage this paradox (Klass, 2006).

Recent sociological studies have revealed how the dead may retain a social
presence and significance in the lives of the living that may be experienced as
sensory and material (Hallam *et al.,* 1999; Bennett and Bennett, 2000). Hallam *et
al.,* have explored how the dead may continue to live on in a social, as well as
'inner' sense, in terms of exercising agency in the lives of the living (Hallam *et
al.,*1999: 155). They link this to the concept of 'social death' where a person ceases
to be treated 'as an active agent in the ongoing social world of some other party'
(Mulkay, 1993: 33). In contrast a person who is biologically dead may continue to
have an active social presence and influence in the lives of the living. Studies of

elderly widows have revealed the way dead husbands may continue to play an active role in their wives' lives, providing comfort, companionship, support, advice, direction and meaning. Their presence may be experienced not just in the mind but via the senses, such as hearing the sound of a dead husband's footsteps (Hallam *et al.*, 1999: 150). However, for some widows, such presence may not be comfortable or welcome and they may not always wish to maintain their relationships with their dead husbands (1999: 155–156).

Attention has been drawn to the memory-making activities in which bereaved people engage in order to create a space for deceased loved ones that is comfortable to live with. Francis *et al.* (2001; 2005) have drawn attention to visits to the cemetery as one of the key sites within which such memory-making may occur. Kellaher *et al.* (2005; Hockey and Kellaher, 2005) have explored how memories are forged and sustained in relation to cremation and the disposal of ashes. In particular, the practice of removing cremated remains from crematoria has been found to offer bereaved people more scope to create highly personalised spaces for their deceased loved ones. Davies (1996) has highlighted how obituaries in the newspaper are often full of 'conversations with the dead' that demonstrate the variety of ways in which they continue to occupy the lives of the living. Walter (1996) has drawn attention to the way memory-making may take the form of engaging in conversation with others to construct a biographical narrative that locates the dead in the life of the living and restores a sense of meaning and continuity.

Such studies have challenged both individual and cultural determinism to highlight the importance of individual agency and lay practice. In focusing on the meanings people give to their experience, they engage with both the personal and individual as well as the broader cultural and social dimension. In culturally diverse Western societies this focus has drawn attention to the way bereaved people may pick and mix images and ritual forms to craft memory-making activities and spaces that reflect the unique character of deceased loved ones and their relationship with them (Hallam and Hockey 2001). This approach represents a profound shift away from modernist universalism and its model-building to a postmodern celebration of difference (Walter, 1999).

A sociology of bereavement

In order to discover what the experience of death and bereavement means to people in contemporary British society I have drawn upon the crucial anthropological insight that it is the encounter between self and other that is the source of knowledge (Hockey, 1990). It has been argued that we make sense of and respond to our world through an inherited system of culturally specific constructs rather than on the basis of individual 'subjectivities' (Berger and Luckmann, 1967; Lakoff and Johnson, 1980; Hockey, 1990; Bradbury, 1999). This process of meaning-making occurs within the everyday flow of events, speech and behaviour or discursive activity through which we define and structure our social reality. Social discourse then becomes the primary field of study and the research endeavour an interactive, intersubjective process, rather than the researcher being separate from the field of study.

Indeed, such involvement is crucial if one is to appreciate the nature of a particular experience. For 'personal involvement is more than dangerous bias – it is the condition under which people come to know each other and to admit others into their lives' (Oakley, 1981: 58). This means that the researcher is effectively using the 'self as instrument' in the service of his or her research project (Rowling, 1999: 168). Far from being a hindrance, one's 'subjectivity' becomes a vehicle for engaging with and understanding other people's experiences (Howarth, 1998). This includes one's own knowledge, beliefs and experiences and how these inform and shape one's project. Such an approach requires an active, empathic and reflexive engagement with participants, a far cry from the model of scientific detachment promoted by a positivist paradigm.

Thus the findings on which this book is based have emerged from a two-way process in which the human encounter with death and loss not only found expression but actually came into being (Hockey, 1990). What distinguished me from participants was my additional commitment to recording, exploring and explaining what was being constructed between us. This approach requires what has been conceptualised as 'emotional labour' (Hochschild, 1983) in the form of an ongoing self-reflexive engagement with one's project. To this end keeping a research journal proved an invaluable tool for fostering an observer position from which to be able to reflect and comment on the 'realities' in which I was at the same time immersing myself (Valentine, 2007). Alongside the more systematic process of analysing my participants' narratives, recording my initial responses to interviews, recurring thoughts and feelings about them formed an integral stage in coming to appreciate the implications of what people were saying.

In setting out to discover the meanings that bereaved people were giving to their experiences of losing a loved one and illuminate the cultural connections between individual narratives of grief, I was guided by the following questions: how do bereaved individuals make sense of the experience of losing a significant other through available cultural discourses? What do these discourses reveal about the way we treat our dead in contemporary British society? To what extent is bereavement a private or shared experience? Do people separate it from the ordinary business of living? Do they try to forget their dead and move on? Or do they include them in some way and if so how and to what extent? To what extent do people's responses depend on social factors such as age, gender and ethnicity? I wanted to capture something of the way bereavement comes to be lived out in people's day-to-day lives. In focusing on an experience that can profoundly disrupt our personal and social worlds to the extent of threatening our very continuity of being, I hoped to learn more about what it means to be both individual and social beings. For the impact of losing a loved one brings issues of identity and sociality and the relationship between the two into sharp focus.

To this end I interviewed 25 bereaved people, 15 women and 10 men, between December 2003 and May 2005, about their experience of losing a loved one (see appendix). Their ages ranged from 17 to 63, and there was a limited representation of ethnic diversity. Out of 10 male participants, one was Indian, one Spanish, one Irish, one Scottish and the rest were English; out of 15 female participants one was German, one American, 2 Irish with the rest being English. Deceased loved ones included six mothers, seven fathers, two partners, three grandmothers, two grandfathers, two great-grandmothers, one great aunt, one aunt, one godson, and two best friends. There were four sudden and unexpected deaths, one of these being accidental, the other three being illness related. The rest included dying trajectories of varying lengths, three being experienced as prolonged. There were four strokes, two cardiac arrests, one spontaneous brain haemorrhage, 11 deaths from cancer, two from diabetes, three from dementia, one from Parkinson's, one aneurysm and one cot death.

My aim was to focus on bereavement as integral to social life and on those aspects that mattered most to the individuals concerned. So rather than setting out with specific themes chosen in advance, I adopted an open-ended, informal, conversational approach in which I encouraged participants to set the agenda. Riches and Dawson (1996a) have drawn attention to the way that pre-structured interviews only allow participants to pick out isolated items from their own story. This means that they are in effect filling in the pre-existing narrative of the researcher. However, it was my *participants'* version of events that I wanted to hear, *their* world into which I wanted to gain entry, something I could only achieve by putting aside my own agenda. My findings are therefore based on the central concerns conveyed by the responses they gave to my invitation to share their experiences of bereavement.

Interviewing as participation

To claim that an interview-based study can allow entry into local worlds (Geertz, 1983) is controversial in relation to the traditional anthropological approach that promotes the participation of the researcher in a bounded social group (Hockey, 2002). From this perspective interview data is not the real thing, but merely a limited commentary on lived experience. Taking place at a distance from remembered events, interviews represent a snapshot abstracted from the present. Moreover they are restricted to an interaction between two people abstracted from their everyday worlds. Yet, this is to limit the study of socio-cultural categories to spacialised locations, something which is becoming more questionable in our technological society in which social interaction transcends spacial boundaries. It is also to lose sight of how social reality resides in people's thoughts, reflections and communications with each other (Hockey, 2002; Rapport, 2002), the very substance of such interview snapshots.

Indeed it has been argued that the distinction between interview data and 'real life' is questionable in relation to contemporary British society (Hockey, 2002). Rather the research interview is a culturally appropriate form of participation, in keeping with the current nature of everyday patterns of social interaction, which are 'often spacially dislocated, time-bounded and characterised by intimacy at a distance' (Hockey, 2002: 211). As such, the research interview may provide a space for people to engage with and reflect on particular aspects of their lives for which they have little opportunity elsewhere. Such a space can allow the past to be recovered and the future to be contemplated via the present (Giddens, 1991). Such reflections may have an impact on the future, suggesting that the research interview may be transformative. In interviewing people about their experiences of losing a loved one, then the extent to which the interview may change the bereavement experience needs to be considered.

Furthermore, recounting one's experiences to another will inevitably bring into the picture other people who form part of one's life. In the context of a bereavement study, this is likely to include those who have died. Indeed my conversations with bereaved individuals were far from being second-hand commentaries, but rather first-hand experiences in which I was privileged to play an integral part. I was introduced to a host of significant others, both living and dead, the impact of which, as will be conveyed, was a profound sense of having entered a very particular social space. Far from being an issue of how to gain access to 'real life' it was more one of how to negotiate the necessary balance between insider and outsider perspectives. This is especially challenging when studying one's own culture and a social group with which one is identified.

Ethical considerations

Encouraging people to share such intimate and sensitive aspects of their lives demands an ongoing reflexive approach to ethical issues (Rowling, 1999). Such reflexivity has highlighted how the requirements found in most ethical guidelines, such as guaranteeing anonymity and confidentiality, avoidance of harm and gaining free and informed consent are more complex than can be satisfied by, for example, obtaining signed consent forms from participants. Indeed this may do no more than cover one's own back at the expense of addressing the more ongoing everyday ethical concerns (Mason, 2002; Guillemin and Gillam, 2004). These concerns include situations that arise unexpectedly out of the interactive nature of qualitative research and for which there may be no obvious solution. Rather, such situations call for a process of negotiation, compromise and adjustment on the basis of experience. Though standardised ethical guidelines provide a useful starting point and checklist, they can reinforce a tendency to separate ethics from the everyday business of research.

Ethics are integral to the interactive nature of qualitative approaches (Batchelor and Briggs, 1994), requiring the ongoing cultivation of one's own ethical stance in order to achieve an ethical research practice. This has been usefully con-ceptualised as 'microethics', taken from biomedical practice, as differentiated from more general ethical principles, though the two are related (Guillemin and Gillam, 2004). Yet this relationship is not always obvious without a commitment to self-reflexivity, a willingness to acknowledge the ethical dimension when it arises and to take the time to think things through and respond accordingly. A reflexive approach to one's research fosters a recognition and appreciation of our own as well as our participants' subjectivities. This allows us to build a bridge between what we would ideally like to achieve and what is practically possible given the limitations and contingencies of ordinary life. As already indicated, such ongoing reflexivity can be developed through keeping a research journal (Valentine, 2007).

In taking a reflexive approach to one's research, one becomes more aware of how gaining access to the private worlds of others for purposes that may not be primarily for their direct benefit poses a fundamental ethical tension at the heart of the research process (Guillemin and Gillam, 2004). In order to take this into account I adopted the principles of a collaborative paradigm in which participants are viewed as active contributors to the research (Reason, 1988). Though this does not alter the fact that they have not initiated the project and may not want to participate any further than they have to, it does offer a model that is more empowering. Encouraging participants to set the interview agenda and to tell their story emphasised the value of their perspective (Riches and Dawson, 1996a).

However, asking people to share their bereavement experiences includes asking them to recall and recount painful experiences that could generate distress both during and after the interview. Bereavement has been identified as being particularly sensitive due to its emotionally charged nature and the way that interviewing may threaten the bereaved individual through the emotional stress that may be produced (Lee and Renzetti, 1993). This has implications in relation to avoidance of harm and what actually constitutes 'harm'. Is it harmful to encourage someone to talk about their experiences of losing a loved one? It raises the issue of how far drawing attention to possible negative effects should form part of the process of gaining informed consent. It demonstrates how any rigid adherence to standardised ethical guidelines would preclude much research with vulnerable groups whose voices would not then be heard or needs understood (Kellehear, 1989).

My own personal and professional experience, supported by the bereavement literature, suggests that far from being harmful, talking about bereavement can provide relief and reinforcement. The process of 'telling it like it is' has been found to enable people to explore painful experiences whilst retaining a sense of control (Riches and Dawson, 1996a). Using an open-ended narrative approach allowed interviewees to disclose only as much as they could manage. The frustration and sense of exclusion that many bereaved people report as a result of the lack of opportunity to do so has been well documented (Riches and Dawson, 1996b, 2000; Walter, 1996, 2001). It has been argued that such interviews can have a therapeutic function by acting as a cathartic mechanism, which may assist the healing process (Rowling, 1999). Participants have reported how telling their stories helped to ease part of their burden (Handsley, 2001: 15). This was confirmed by the majority, though not all of those I interviewed, both at the time and in correspondence with me afterwards. This included the perception that bereavement was still considered a taboo subject in wider society.

However it is important not to generalise about this, but rather to allow for the individual variation that makes it impossible to predict in advance how someone will react. The ethical implications of intruding into the lives of bereaved people can be both positive and negative. The onus is therefore on the researcher to give special consideration to the possible implications of such intimate and often painful disclosure for bereaved people. Such consideration can be fostered through inviting feedback from participants and being prepared to learn from this. It can be facilitated by enabling interviewees to reconsider their consent away from the heat of the moment and with the benefit of hindsight. In relation to my own study I made interview transcripts available to participants so that they could further reflect upon the implications of their consent. They were advised that if there are any part of the transcript about which they felt unsure, we could discuss this and if necessary exclude it from the study. This also provided an initial validity check by allowing any areas of possible misrepresentation to be addressed.

Interviews lasted between one and two hours with individuals being invited to 'tell me about their bereavement' and encouraged to find their own starting point. Where an individual expressed uncertainty as to where to start or what to say I was prepared to offer some prompting. This took the form of suggesting that they tell me who it was who had died, how, when and where it happened and then gently probing them for more personal details about the impact it had on them. Usually very little prompting was needed to engage the person and explore the meanings of the topics they introduced. The narratives that emerged from this process revealed how, in making sense of experience, people draw upon available cultural scripts, negotiating these according to individual circumstances, purposes and idiosyncrasies. In encouraging participants to tell their stories I was able to capture this process of negotiation to convey the complex, dynamic and reciprocal relationship between individual and social.

Engaging with the data

The process of analysing participants' narratives has raised important questions about what constitutes a legitimate source of 'data'. This is especially relevant to an interactive approach in which exchanges between researcher and participants are likely to occur 'outside' as well as 'inside' the 'field of study' or interview. Moreover, as I was to discover, such 'outside' material, assuming it is recorded and treated as 'data', may have the potential to considerably enhance understanding of one's topic. Thus to what extent should research be limited by the designated field of study? However, if one considers venturing beyond the boundary, then how does one deal with the ethical issues raised by using material that may not strictly be covered by the participant's initial consent? This suggests that the giving of consent should not only be confined to a formal, once-and-for-all procedure but remain open to informal and periodic renegotiation. Where this is not possible, as already discussed, then the researcher must make a sensitive judgement, which takes into account the interests both of the participants and the project.

By approaching the field of study as a discrete entity without recognising its socially constructed nature, one may legitimately limit one's study to 'inside'. Thus the 'real' data can only be found within the confines of the interview and anything occurring outside this should be ignored. One advantage of constructing such a firm boundary is that one may retain a sense of having control of one's study rather than risking exposure to the unexpected nature of 'outside' influences. Yet it is arguably unrealistic to assume that one's fieldwork will have no impact beyond the field, in which case it is better to be aware of the nature of this in order to be able to identify and make choices about such 'outside' influences. Also, such influences are not necessarily tangible but may include the emotional impact of one's engagement in the field, which more often than not will only emerge away from the original encounter.

In relation to the present study the defining nature of the impact of 'outside' experiences could not be ignored. These inevitably consisted of unexpected, unforeseen situations for which I was unprepared. They were therefore less subject to my control. However this made them invaluable as examples of the way bereavement may become integrated into the ordinary business of living. Though I found such experiences uncomfortable, my practice of keeping a research journal enabled me to record, reflect on and process these as data. In so doing, I considerably enhanced my understanding of the implications of my findings.

For example, for one participant, the discovery of a couple of mis-spellings of names and medical terms in the interview transcript proved upsetting for her. My practice of always making a point of checking out the accuracy of the transcript with interviewees had at least enabled her to make this known to me, so that I could make the necessary corrections. I was then struck by just how vitally important this felt to both of us, as though the integrity of the deceased's memory depended upon it. This alerted me to the more everyday, informal ways that the need to honour and respect the dead may manifest themselves (Hallam and Hockey, 2001). Thus very mundane objects may symbolise our link to our dead and come to embody the feelings of care and protectiveness we feel towards them (Hallam and Hockey, 2001; Gibson, 2004). I was further struck by the way the interview experience became incorporated into this participant's grieving process.

Such protectiveness towards the dead was echoed in other interviews. However, it was this 'outside' incident that impressed it upon me with such immediacy, so that I was more likely to recognise its expression elsewhere. For I had been allowed to enter the participant's experience to achieve a 'participatory and holistic knowing' that is 'based upon a participative and dialogical relationship with the world' (Reason, 1988: 10). This incident alerted me to the importance of maintaining a wide, flexible and inclusive frame of reference that does not overlook the deceptively ordinary and insignificant details of daily life (Hallam and Hockey, 2001). It reaffirmed the value of an interactive approach that takes account of the co-constructed nature of the data.

When I came to engage more fully with the data I initially struggled with a resistance towards what I felt would be a violation of the integrity of someone's story, particularly in a context that tends to expose the fragile nature of the self. The profoundly touching quality of stories that emphasised the uniqueness of the person who had been lost evoked feelings of 'reverence' and 'respect'. To engage in 'chopping these around felt like a violation of the integrity of each set of memories and meanings that had been constructed' (Einegal, 2002). I therefore chose to construct personal profiles to allow each account to 'speak for itself' before fully engaging with the analytic process. Such reconstructive activity that served to preserve the integrity and emphasise the uniqueness of each participant's experience seemed to dispel my resistance to the more deconstructive process of cross-sectional analysis. It has also been an invaluable means of both contextualising and familiarising myself with participants' experiences. When I came to identify the cultural connections between these stories, I was able to do so without losing sight of their uniqueness and the role played by individual agency and imagination (Reissman, 1993). In this way, I sought to capture the complexity and diversity of bereavement experiences, for which no simple model could be appropriate.

Structure of the book

There are two main parts to this book, which reflect the way interview narratives were shaped by the chronological ordering of events (Reissman, 1993). For, in each case, my participants would begin their stories by recounting the way loved ones died to convey how ongoing relationships with dead loved ones encompassed bearing witness to that loved one's dying. By means of these 'narratives of dying' they sought to identify and make sense of the events leading up to the death. They would then move on to share their experiences of the impact and aftermath of death to convey how the experience of losing a loved one was intimately linked to rediscovering that person. These closely intertwined 'narratives of loss' and 'narratives of rediscovery' encompassed the events that followed the death.

In the three chapters of Part One, I explore the role of narratives of dying in people's ongoing relationships with dead loved ones and how the meanings people attached to the way loved ones died shaped their bereavement experience. In identifying and exploring the key discourses, concepts and themes that inform these narratives I draw attention to the way my participants negotiated these to convey a central concern with maintaining their deceased loved one's continuing individuality and personhood. The implications of these findings for both understandings of continuing bonds and for sociological theories of identity are considered. Then, in Part Two, Chapters 4 to 7, I focus on narratives of loss and narratives of rediscovery to consider the way people struggled to make sense of the death of a loved one, highlighting how this included carrying on without them whilst at the same time maintaining them as a presence in their everyday worlds. The variety of ways in which they negotiated this fundamental paradox of absence and presence is explored to reveal how social being does not necessarily come to an end with death. The implications of the continuing presence of the dead in the lives of the living for sociological theories of identity and society are considered.

Chapter 1 identifies the key discourses of medicalisation, individualism, relationship, religion and death's timing, revealing how narrators negotiated these potentially competing norms to create meanings that were particular and personal to them. Chapter 2 explores the variety of ways narrators strove to achieve a 'good death' for their loved ones and how such diversity was linked by a common emphasis on the concepts of 'agency', 'social support' and 'awareness'. In exploring these concepts, I illustrate how narrators sought to affirm and sustain the social presence of dying loved ones and maintain their relationships with them in the face of the physical and mental deterioration of the dying experience. In Chapter 3, I discuss the role of deathbed accounts in people's ongoing relationships with their dead. This chapter explores the significance of the dying person's final moments, in a secular, medicalised context, for those who are left behind, to address a current gap in the literature.

In Chapter 4 I focus on 'narratives of loss', and how narrators tried to make sense of a loved one's absence. I highlight how this process was linked to valuing and appreciating who the deceased person was, what he or she meant and would continue to mean to those left behind. In Chapter 5 I draw attention to the importance of material culture in the experience of loss and grief. In addition to public mourning practices I consider the role of more everyday contexts in symbolising and mediating the loss of a loved one in the lives of bereaved people. In Chapter 6 I focus on the restorative dimension of grief, or 'narratives of rediscovery', and what these revealed about the nature and meaning of continuing bonds for survivors, extending existing findings by drawing attention to the way such bonds may encompass caring and reciprocity. In Chapter 7 I explore the variety of ways in which such bonds were located and sustained in people's ongoing lives, illustrating how this process may be carried out inwardly via mental, emotional and imaginative activity and beliefs about life and death, as well as outwardly through social and cultural activity such as conversation, informal and formal rituals and memory-making.

In the final chapter, I draw together the key features that link people's individual stories, highlighting the character and form as well as the content of these narratives. I draw attention to the way narratives are characterised by a central concern to affirm and preserve personhood and relatedness. I consider the complex and highly self-reflexive nature of the way people recounted their experiences, which was subject to an ongoing negotiation and reassessment of competing discourses. This chapter summarises the theoretical contribution of these narratives and draws attention to their practical implications. Suggestions are offered as to how they might inform social policy and practice in relation to living with the experience of death and bereavement.

Part One

Preserving and affirming personhood

I have identified how academic discourses of bereavement have taken a more social turn and how this has highlighted the extent to which the dead may remain an integral part of the lives of the living, thus obscuring the boundary between the living and the dead. This perspective has been reflected in the use of more qualitative, intersubjective approaches to researching death and bereavement. I have drawn attention to the implications of taking a more informal and engaged stance in terms of capturing a fuller picture of bereavement as it interacts with other agendas and priorities in people's lives to form part of their day-to-day social world. Thus the scientific, rationalist model in which the researcher remains separate from the field of study has been replaced with a more 'humanised' approach to researching social life. This approach recognises that the researcher cannot remain separate but rather forms an integral part of the picture. The following three chapters reveal how such shared humanity and intersubjectivity is also reflected in the narrative reconstructions of 25 bereaved individuals of the way their loved ones' died. These dying narratives offer crucial insight into the impact of the circumstances surrounding a loved one's dying on the bereavement experience.

By attending to my own part in the narratives that emerged from these interview conversations, I began to register the way the characters of those who had died seemed to impress themselves on me in a very poignant way. This was conveyed through very intimate, personalised details, which were touching in the way that, far from being idealised, they evoked the deceased person's humanity and therefore mortality. The impact on me was to hold my attention and invite my further inquiry in a way that created a feeling of that person's presence between us. At the end of an interview I was often left with a vivid impression of the deceased person, almost as if he or she had been present with us in the room. Thus the process of constructing a narrative around the death of a loved one served to recreate and perpetuate that person's identity or personhood.

The presence of the dead has been identified in relation to the reported experiences of bereaved people (Bennett and Bennett, 2000) and the bereavement counselling situation (Klass, 1997). My own experience has revealed how such presence may extend to the interview encounter to form part of the relationship between researcher and researched and therefore contribute to the research endeavour and its findings. As such, it represents a further obscuring of the boundary between the living and the dead to reveal how the dead may become integrated in the lives of the living to the extent of finding a place and a voice in the life of a stranger.

This process of 'recovering' and integrating dead loved ones into bereaved peoples' ongoing lives included reconstructing the experience of the way they died. Such reconstruction was characterised by an emphasis on the dying person's unique identity and personhood and the social nature of dying. The dying experience was evaluated in terms of the extent to which it reflected the dying person's characteristic selfhood and continuing agency, as well as affirming the relationship between the dying person and the narrator. Where such continuing personhood and relatedness had to some extent been achieved, this served to redeem what in most cases was a difficult, unpredictable and uncertain process for both parties.

The importance and urgency of preserving and affirming personhood was powerfully conveyed in those cases where the dying process had called this into question. Thus the narrator would still be able to recall how a deceased loved one had taken charge of some aspect of his or her dying and/or the narrator had taken great pains to ensure that any rituals of disposal bore the deceased person's unique stamp. Indeed, making up for a death that had not been sufficiently characteristic of the dying person took precedence over what the bereaved person might have wanted. In some cases, the narrator's sense of having maintained his or her relationship with the deceased person during the dying process provided a further source of consolation.

Chapter 1 draws attention to and examines the key discourses that structured people's 'dying narratives', highlighting how narrators negotiated these to personalise and humanise their loved one's dying by emphasising his or her unique personhood and the relationship between them. By focusing on the relationship between individual and collective resources, it places the narratives in the wider social context of contemporary British society. Chapter 2 explores the significance of personhood and relatedness in relation to the way narrators sought to achieve a good death for their loved ones. It reveals the way that the social presence of dying people could be both sustained and lost in the face of the dying experience, and the implications of this for our understanding of the nature of personhood and agency in contemporary society. It considers the relationship of personhood to the experience of embodiment and to the larger social structure. Chapter 3 introduces and explores the significance of the 'moment of death' in a contemporary medical setting for those left behind. With reference to the historical Ars Moriendi, it examines the deathbed account that formed part of some of my participants' dying narratives. These accounts revealed how a loved one's final moments could be experienced as profound, special and memorable occasions in which the dying person took his or her leave by demonstrating enhanced presence and aliveness.

1 Humanising a loved one's dying

In sharing their experiences of bereavement with me, narrators conveyed how, in trying to reconcile themselves to the death of a loved one, they needed to recall and reconstruct the way he or she died. These narratives of dying entailed a process of evaluating and negotiating such experience in terms of 'how things should be' as they attempted to make sense of their loved one's dying. In relation to an experience, such as bereavement, which has a profound impact on one's taken-for-granted reality or assumptive world (Berger and Luckmann, 1967; Parkes, 1972), including one's sense of identity, this process becomes all the more urgent and poignant. How, and the extent to which, it is achieved depends on the cultural and individual resources by means of which such experience is shaped. In this chapter I identify and examine these resources at a discursive level in relation to the ways in which 25 bereaved individuals talked about and tried to make sense of the experience of witnessing a loved one's dying in contemporary British society.

The role of discourse

Discourse has been identified as both reflective and constitutive of the social order and the interaction of individuals with society (Jaworski and Coupland, 1999: 3). Its language and imagery reflect deep-seated and largely invisible attitudes and ideologies. Discourse therefore has far-reaching implications, for example, discourses about death have an impact on what we do with the dead and how we treat those who suffer bereavement. Thus, if any change is to occur it can only happen at this fundamental level. Yet, as well-demonstrated by the power of modernist rationalist discourses, the promotion of change is far from easy or straightforward. Dominant cultural scripts produce certain versions of reality and inhibit others, producing blindspots or a tendency to become caught up in our socially constructed version of reality (Crossley, 2000). The task of the researcher of social life is to constantly test one's own assumptions against participants' actual utterances to avoid becoming caught up in one's own version of reality. Rather the aim is to discover the strange in the familiar and gain an appreciation of how 'commonsense' experiences are not as self-evident as they may seem, but rather reflect cultural meaning systems.

Foucault (1972) has drawn attention to the way discursive activity may contain hidden repressions and be used to perpetuate existing power relations. Some studies have drawn attention to the blind spots that result from the way dominant discourses produce certain versions of reality and inhibit others, especially in relation to goals that appear laudable and desirable (Crossley, 2000). The hospice movement's ideological goal of enabling patients 'to live until they die' glosses over the non-negotiable effects of the physical degeneration of their bodies on their sense of self (Lawton, 2000). The choices of dying people may be constrained by hospice constructions of the 'good death' in terms of the ideals of dying with dignity, peacefulness, preparedness, awareness, adjustment and acceptance (Hart *et al.*, 1998). The 'open disclosure' and 'shared awareness' of dying promoted by Glaser and Strauss's findings (1965) and by the hospice movement itself, does not take into account the uncertainties of prognoses and that some cultures and individuals value 'shielding' over 'sharing' (McIntosh, 1977; Littlewood, 1993; Seale, 1998: 178; McNamara, 2001; Lock, 2002).

A discursive perspective has revealed the limitations of a positivist paradigm in reflecting the complex and reflexive relationship between subjective experience and social practice and the diversity of bereavement experience within contemporary British society. It has allowed a closer examination of how people experience their bodies, minds and social relationships and create meanings from such experiences that can act as a resource for shaping their world. This approach has drawn attention to the way competing discourses co-exist. For example, when talking about sensing the presence of dead loved ones, Bennett and Bennett (2000) found that bereaved individuals would shift between a rationalist scepticism and a more supernaturalist validation of such experiences. They may modify or even reject predominant discourses, such as those offered by medicine, psychotherapy and religion, which position the individual in a subordinate relationship to the expert. Such discursive activity has produced alternative discourses, such as the 'natural good death', in which individuals may characterise a sudden death as 'good' due to it being both painless and free of medical intervention (Bradbury, 1996, 1999).

Studies of the 'good death' have highlighted the way individuals may weave together normative and individual understandings of the world (Bradbury, 1996; Masson, 2002; Young and Cullen, 1996). These highlight the multifaceted and changing nature of such concepts and the way individuals negotiate these to serve differing needs and purposes. Thus, in bereavement, people have been shown to demonstrate a 'flexible realism' in taking account of the limitations and contingencies of real life (Masson, 2002). Their narratives reveal how they attempt to negotiate the ideal within the context of their lived situation. Though professionals may try to impose a dominant medical discourse on patients and their families, this has been found to be only temporary and bereaved individuals still manage to come to their own conclusions (Bradbury, 1996).

Discursive activity represents a valuable resource for adjusting to the social world and making sense of experience, particularly at vulnerable times, such as during bereavement (Crossley, 2000). Thus, in attempting to deconstruct cultural assumptions, it is important to take into account the way that such scripts may offer people a life-line when their taken for granted reality, including their sense of self-identity feels under threat (2000: 179). In such circumstances people inevitably seek guidelines for managing and affirming their experience. Where there is a mismatch between conventional wisdom and individual experience this may produce guilt for 'not doing it right'. It may also give rise to questioning and negotiating the conventional line to produce alternative discourses.

Indeed, discourse is far from static and has been defined as 'an open, unstable and negotiable conception of how cultural notions influence and can be employed by groups and individuals' (Reimars, 2003: 326). Social norms are neither stable nor consistent, since they emerge from a process of negotiation between cultural resources in the form of available discourses and more personal resources that shape these according to individual circumstances, purposes and idiosyncrasies. Such negotiation includes contested representations of reality, both within as well as between individuals (Hockey, 1996b). This perspective offers a concept of social reality as complex, open-ended and contingent, emerging from the tension between such contested representations.

The narratives of those I interviewed well demonstrated how the discursive process is a complex, open-ended, fluid and contingent one in which discourses interweave, overlap, compete and evolve (Hockey, 1996b; Reimars, 2003: 326). In this chapter the key discourses that informed people's dying narratives are explored in relation to the wider social context in which dying occurs today, as well as the individualised and personalised dimension. This exploration draws attention to the way people shifted between discourses, and negotiated paradox and ambiguity to produce highly individual accounts that are characterised by ambivalence and contingency.

This chapter highlights and illustrates the relationship between individual and cultural perspectives in terms of the individual's reflexive reworking of events in which memories are subject to an ongoing process of interpretative reconstruction (Giddens, 1991). For in the process of reconstructing their loved ones' dying, narrators demonstrated a high degree of reflexivity. Not only were they trying to remember, recapture and convey to me the quality of their experience at the time, but also to reassess it in the light of the present. This involved moving backwards and forwards between the past and the present, as well as attempting to appreciate other people's viewpoints. Though a single interview is limited in conveying such fluctuation and change over time, an in-depth, open-ended, conversational approach to interviewing to some extent allows this to be captured.

In recounting their experiences narrators drew on the broad discursive frameworks of medicalisation, individualism, relationship, religion and death's timing. They negotiated these, in some cases, potentially competing frames of reference, by means of a humanising, person-centred perspective. This perspective provided a unifying thread of meaning in the face of the uncertainties and paradoxes that characterised the experience of witnessing a loved one's dying. Thus the presentation and interweaving of the various discourses was subject to the impact of narrators' concern to both 'humanise' and convey the 'humanness' of their loved ones' dying. For this concern represented not only a celebration of human potential but an acknowledgement of human vulnerability and frailty.

The affirmation and solace that narrators found in their deceased loved ones' uniqueness and continuing social significance reflect both the guiding principles of Cicely Saunders and the hospice movement, as well as that of the humanist and civil funeral celebrants' training in Britain. Such reflection raises the question as to the relationship between lay and professional discourses. Was it the hospice movement that promoted the emphasis on dying people remaining fully themselves or was Cicely Saunders articulating a process that was already familiar to the lay populace? Whatever the answer to this, the narratives of the bereaved people I interviewed would suggest that such emphasis on dying people retaining their characteristic selfhood is important not only at the time of dying but for years to come for those left behind, thus linking palliative and bereavement care.

Constructing a dying trajectory

The concept of the dying trajectory conveys how people perceive 'courses of dying', which take on 'duration' and 'shape', in order to reduce the uncertainty they feel in relation to terminal illness (Strauss, 1971). Dying is thus rendered more meaningful through the concept of status passage or transition (Van Gennep, 1909/1960: Glaser and Strauss, 1965). Indeed, when I initially invited participants to tell me about their bereavement, they would begin their accounts by constructing a dying trajectory. In so doing they sought to make links with the life that had gone before by recounting the continuities and breaks, what cohered and what did not. It was as though the narrator was trying to piece together events to create a dying that 'belonged' to and was characteristic of the individual concerned:

> Of course she'd come from a nursing background and she knew exactly what was happening to her and from September she stopped eating and she stopped eating on purpose because she didn't want to extend her life, so although she was still quite hungry, her mind was quite hungry, there was still a part that she just didn't want to extend her life.
>
> (Pat)[1]

In cases of sudden death there was still an attempt to link the circumstances of the death with what had gone before, but in terms of a violation of this, the death being constructed as an outside agent rather than a process that was, to some extent, integral to the dying person (Prior, 1997: 189):

> It's not often you can say people were robbed . . . I just felt this is wrong. This was a life loved, cherished, determined to be made the best of and someone just went chung, took it off.
>
> (Lorraine)

---

1 Pseudonyms have been used throughout for confidentiality.

Even where the death was more gradual and expected, dying was a process that could gather momentum and become quite relentless and defiant of the normal categories for defining and managing the ordinary business of living. In such cases some comfort could be taken from anticipating a return to normality:

I want a nice quiet year next year now – just a normal year.

(Fiona)

Otherwise, an emphasis on the 'ordinary' and 'familiar' aspects of the experience helped to maintain some semblance of normality. The value placed on individuality, continuity and normality reflected a context in which dying was commonly medicalised and institutionalised. This context placed people in a position of having to negotiate the uncertainties of dying in an unfamiliar and potentially depersonalising environment. In so doing they demonstrated the complex nature of the relationship between the discourses of individualism and medicalisation.

Individualism and medicalisation

Dying in contemporary Britain has been found to be informed by the key discourses of individualism and medicalisation (Seale, 1998; Walter, 1999; Hockey, 2001). The former encompasses both modernist self-sufficiency and self-responsibility and postmodern relativity, diversity and divergence. The latter represents the rationalisation and prescriptiveness of modernity (see Introduction) and forms part of the processes of secularisation, privatisation and professionalisation that have shaped the experience of dying today (Blauner, 1966; Foucault, 1973; Field, 1994).

An emphasis on the authority of the individual to determine his or her own life has produced a movement towards humanising dying, promoted by the hospice movement that recognises both diversity and dignity in dying and aims to support people to die in their own way. This aim includes addressing the emotional and spiritual needs of dying people. It has emerged in reaction to the increasing use of medical technology and institutional practices that have been perceived to dehumanise dying people (Moller, 1990; Ballard, 1996). By reducing dying to a limited number of disease processes, death has been rationalised and deconstructed (Illich, 1975; Elias, 1985), generating the illusion that mortality itself can be cured and controlled (Prior, 1997).

Once the medical perspective of disease as the natural cause of death replaced that of viewing disease and death as acts of God, death became a medical problem rather than a spiritual passage (Richardson, 1987). Doctors, rather than family and priest, took centre stage and became responsible for managing the deathbed (Porter, 1989). As a result the focus of attention has shifted away from the 'inevitable', or the dying person's pending death, and any support they may need to prepare for this practically, emotionally and spiritually. Rather, in the hands of the medical profession, dying has become a condition to be treated and death the result of treatment failure (Prior, 1989). The image of the dying person remaining conscious and interactive has given way to that of the drug-induced patient in a state of unconsciousness.

Indeed, medical science has sought to maintain life and death as rigidly opposed categories. This separation is reflected in the way dying has become institu-tionalised, or located in hospital wards, residential homes and hospices, 'the space in which living takes place' having become 'inappropriate as the space for dying' (Hockey, 1990: 36). The hospice aims to promote a more open encounter with death in which dying can be envisaged as a 'rite of passage' (Froggat, 1997). This approach is having some impact on other institutions (Walter, 1999; Seymour, 2001). However, residential homes have been found to downplay the encounter with death and any experience of transition (Hockey, 1990; Komaromy, 2000). Such an approach has been shown to have the effect of both separating dying people from their own deaths, whilst at the same time marginalising them from the society of the living or treating them as socially dead (Sudnow, 1967; Hockey, 1990).

The narratives of those I interviewed demonstrated how the dichotomous discourses of individualism and medicalisation and the metaphors embedded in these formed a significant feature of this social context. However, they revealed a less clear-cut relationship between the two, one that was characterised by a complex interweaving of individualised and medicalised understandings of dying. Indeed, as others have argued (Elias, 1985: 12; Walter, 1993: 286), critiques of the modern management of dying betray nostalgia for a more natural, pre-modern dying. Yet, my participants' accounts revealed how medicalisation could be both supportive of human value and dignity as well as dehumanising, with shades in between (Seymour, 1999). They adopted a range of positions in relation to the medical profession, from '*they were superb . . . they just did absolutely everything*' to '*I mean generally the sort of standard of care was just absolutely appalling*'.

It has been suggested that the romanticising of pre-technological dying and equating medicalisation with 'bad' death, has tended to inhibit a more detailed examination of the ways in which people incorporate medical technology into their accounts of dying (Timmermans, 1998: 162). Thus in some accounts technology was perceived to have made a positive contribution to an otherwise bad dying by reflecting the willingness of others to do all they could, as reported by Tania, whose mother was dying of ovarian cancer:

So they had to take her back to theatre, and they were superb – they called in more and more senior doctors – they had a senior anaesthetist. 'cos they knew that Mum had not had a good week – to actually help her through . . .

(Tania)

Medical technology could even be perceived to contribute to dying as a social event. For Sandra, whose close friend had died in a car accident, it enabled close others to say goodbye when this would not otherwise have been possible:

... and so he was put on life support machine but it was only so that people could go and say goodbye to him.

(Sandra)

Others, such as Roy, saw medical technology as a double-edged tool that created as many problems as it solved:

... They couldn't do radiotherapy or chemotherapy in any great measure because Dad had Crone's disease. It was compounded by that, so all the doctors could do was book him in for an operation to check the Crone's scarring to see if that was affecting his system, as it were. They found out that it wasn't, but then his body reacted to the anaesthetic, they think, and his whole innards collapsed . . . so they had to attach a stoma to the system. A stoma's what takes the water and all the stuff out and – that affected Dad quite a lot . . .

(Roy)

People's relationship with medicine in contemporary Britain has been found to demonstrate considerable ambivalence, 'a shifting dialectic of trust and doubt, certainty and uncertainty, reverence and disillusionment' (Williams and Calnan, 1996:1613). Trust was demonstrated by the way some of my participants relied on the authority of medical diagnoses and prognoses to try to make sense of an uncertain and unpredictable process:

... She had an ovarian tumour – they did these blood tests and he said if it comes between 0 and – it's up to 20 – then I think it's ok. If it's over 20 to 30 or something then maybe we can do surgery here. But if it's over then she'll go to the Queen Elizabeth, which is a specialist hospital – and then the consultant called me over and he showed me it was 1,170!

(Tania)

Yet it has been found that the omnipotence with which people tend to invest medical practitioners inevitably produces considerable disappointment, resentment and scepticism when things go wrong (Lupton, 1994). Adrian conveyed very poignantly the anger and disillusionment that could be suffered by the perception that a loved one's death should not have occurred:

I did look on the internet to find out what a renal artery aneurysm was and it did say that in 97 per cent of cases it can be managed . . . and, you know, really, don't go into hospital because you're really not going to come out again in certain cases.

(Adrian)

Nonetheless, medicalisation has enabled people to live longer and, in spite of growing disillusionment, is still invested with enormous power (Williams and Calnan, 1996). Indeed, death today tends to be represented as a medical rather than a religious or sacred event: 'she didn't survive the surgery'. This has obscured the relationship between health and wholeness or well-being, which includes the spiritual dimension. Moreover, a preoccupation with health in the narrow sense of fitness of the body has become a survival strategy (Bauman, 1992).

The new public health discourse promotes healthy lifestyles (Richman, 2003). Citizens, as health consumers, have a duty to maintain good health and achieve longevity by adopting appropriate practices. One must work at being healthy, an obligation that is reinforced by media images and slogans such as 'no pain, no gain'. This sense of personal responsibility was reflected in the way some bereaved individuals attempted to make links between the manner of dying and the dying person's lifestyle and habits:

> You know I'm quite fussy about my food and I kind of think I wish my father had had the same views about diet that I do because he might not sort of – 'cos he had a sweet tooth.
>
> (Stephen)

As a result of increased life expectancy and an emphasis on healthy living, death tends to be perceived as a necessary evil that should ideally occur at the end of a long and full life (Ballard, 1996). There has been a shift in focus from the Christian tradition laid down in the Ars Moriendi, which emphasised the importance of one's final moments for preparing oneself for the afterlife, to living well and living until we die (see Chapter 3). This was powerfully demonstrated by Susan, whose great aunt died suddenly whilst still fully engaged in life:

> I just think, well, she had a good life and she was happy and, you know, she was 80. It's a good age to be.
>
> (Susan)

In an individualistic society, quality of life tends to be linked to retaining one's autonomy. Death may be perceived as a welcome release from the prospect of losing one's independence and suffering the indignities associated with the increased vulnerability and helplessness that old age may bring.

> And she was losing her independence and she was such an independent person. So when she lost that it was like losing her life.
>
> (Sandra)

In several accounts this suffering was particularly associated with the 'institutionalised marginality' of residential care (Hockey, 1990: 110). Vivienne revealed the conflict that could arise between preserving quality and quantity of life:

> . . . The night before there'd been kind of arguments in our family – I mean her home was a tip, it really needed kind of renovation and stuff – but she was really

independent and wanted to stay there – and some of the family thought she would be safer moving to a nursing home.

(Vivienne)

For Stephen such conflict was not present. Rather the experience of witnessing his father's dying in a nursing home or, as he put it, 'a waiting-room for death', made him determined not to follow suit:

So my brother and I actually said afterwards that, you know, if either one of us gets into that state then the other one has got – sort of essentially it's a mutual suicide pact, so if we can, then the more compus mentis one will bump the other one off. We take it as a bit of a joke but really it's intensely serious. I do not want to end up like that.

(Stephen)

In spite of any attempt by nursing homes to disguise the fact that residents were approaching their deaths, their loved ones may be only too aware of it:

The problem with old people's homes is that they're full of people waiting to die and you know it just has that atmosphere and just sort of decay and sort of waiting for death really.

(Stephen)

In addition, nursing homes were perceived by some, such as Lynne, to lack the professionalism of hospitals and hospices:

She wasn't getting sufficient care – although the people – they're care workers, they're not nurses.

(Lynne)

Deaths that occurred before the individual had become too dependent on others could be constructed as a *'blessing'*.

Yet, paradoxically, as a result of the increased longevity that medical advances have brought, more and more people today are suffering a protracted, uncomfortable and often painful dying and the loss of capacity and autonomy that may accompany this (Littlewood, 1992; Ballard, 1996). The way this may be fiercely resisted was poignantly portrayed in Roy's account:

You could tell he was fighting the cancer – my dad's one of these people who – he's got to stand up – he's got to do things. He can't sit still for one minute – and it was literally – he'd say, 'do you want a cup of tea?' and he'd be stood there swaying from side to side – you could tell he was sort of trying to keep his balance. And I'd say, 'no no – you sit down' – 'no, I can't sit down – if I sit down – you know'.

(Roy)

Thus it may not be dying itself that carries anxiety but, as expressed by Lynne, the way in which it may occur:

> Oh yes – I don't worry about dying – getting old is different – it's that that is the worry I think . . . No – it's getting old that is the horrible thought – dying's alright.
>
> (Lynne)

Medicalisation and naturalness

Medical intervention in the process of dying has been critiqued as inimical to 'natural death' and synonymous with a bad death (Ariès, 1974; 1981; Illich, 1975; Moller, 1990). Yet narrators did not necessarily construct 'natural' and 'medical' as being opposed or a medical death as bad. A sudden death from a heart attack was experienced by Susan as a natural occurrence that was more aptly described as 'passing on' rather than 'died':

> I think 'passed on' is quite a nice image if anything about death can be nice. It's kind of just like the next stage. So it naturally happens rather than someone 'dies'.
>
> (Susan)

Indeed, dying without medical intervention was represented as unnatural, by Ivan, provoking outrage and anger towards his dying mother and her partner for failing to seek proper treatment:

> I was really angry with her – and I still am and her husband because he just – because she was 73 going on 103 when she died. She was decrepit and she wouldn't have proper medical help.
>
> (Ivan)

For Linda, naturalness referred to the way that a person's dying seemed to conform to its own inherent pattern. It could therefore encompass medicalisation:

> You know when they're dying over a period of time and not suddenly, it's like a kind of musical score that works its way out, you know. Things happen in all sorts of ways and afterwards you realise it couldn't have happened any other way, you know?
>
> (Linda)

However, Janet experienced her friend's medical death as anything but natural. Reporting on the impact on her friend's mother of the way he died, invasive emergency medical treatment was perceived as violating the individual's right to die 'peacefully'. Thus 'naturalness' was equated with 'peacefulness':

Where they'd had to resuscitate him they'd cracked his ribs open to do that – and that was what she was so bitter about. She said, all the pain and everything he'd gone through, he should have gone peacefully and she said it looked like he'd been in a car accident.

(Janet)

Williams and Calnan (1996) have suggested that the increasing lay emphasis on the 'un-natural' aspects of modern medical technology may represent a symbolic struggle for control over the human body. Elisabeth revealed how this struggle reflected the way that the dead body may still be invested with personhood (see Chapter 5, pp. 116–117; Chapter 7, pp. 151–152):

But it was quite hard when they wanted to – I know they've got to do it, but it was hard when they came through and said about being an organ donor – but I remember the youngest who was then 15 saying, 'they're not having my dad's heart – they're not going to disfigure him like that, mummy – they can't have his heart – that's mine – that's ours'

(Elisabeth)

For Fiona, both medicalisation and naturalness were ambiguous:

He just wanted to let nature take its course . . . But I think he was obviously just in such a lot of pain and discomfort and he did change his mind and he did decide he would go for treatment. . .though they had said it wouldn't actually do him any good really. It would just sort of ease the pain.

(Fiona)

Naturalness was also linked to age, reflecting how greater longevity has produced an increased association of death with old age. This has been perceived to make deaths in old age less difficult to come to terms with (Gorer, 1965; Parkes, 1972, 1986). Such a death may be considered natural and therefore less a cause for grief (Komaromy and Hockey, 2001). Indeed, for Susan the death of her great aunt left her with a sense of gratitude:

But then I definitely now just look back and think she had a good life and I was lucky to have known her for the 19 years that I did. So in that sense I don't really feel bereaved as such, I just feel grateful that I had her.

(Susan)

According to Sarah natural deaths that were associated with old age were normative, or simply part of the way things are, rather than an achievement. As such, they were to be accepted:

So it's just one of those things you have to realise is part of the life cycle. Things are born, they age and die

(Sarah)

However, in other accounts a loved one having reached 'old age' in a chrono-logical sense did not necessarily make his or her death more natural or acceptable. Rather the experience of losing a loved one also reflected the value placed on that person and one's relationship with them (see section death's timing, p. 32).

Relationship

In addition to an emphasis on individual and medical details, narrators drew attention to the nature of their relationship with the dying individual. They would position themselves within the dying person's experience, exploring its impact on both parties as well as on the relationship between them. These reflections included experiences of intimacy and mutuality:

> now as I left I remember hugging her and saying 'I love you' and she said 'I love you too' and we both cried.
>
> (Tania)

Such reflections extended to other members of the dying person's immediate family and/or circle and sometimes beyond this to the wider society. Dying was thus constructed as a social, mutual, intimate and shared, as well as a personal and medical event that could impact on a variety of people:

> My son was very, very fond of her and when she stayed with us he would sit and chat to her for hours and say, 'Oh, she's so wonderful, all these things she's talking about'.
>
> (Lynne)

The emphasis on individualism in contemporary British society poses a certain tension between promoting individual rights and responsibilities on the one hand and norms associated with relationship and social support on the other (Laungani, 1996). Accounts conveyed this tension and the different ways that such competing discourses could be negotiated. For example, social support could be directed towards affirming individual choice, as conveyed by Pat who was only prepared to accept a nursing home for her dying relative 'that wouldn't force her to eat'(Pat).

Values associated with relationship and human contact could also compete with the routine of a medicalised system of dying. For Adrian this was experienced as a disregard for the needs of loved ones to spend uninterrupted time with the dying person during their final moments:

> Oh yeah, we didn't go – we stayed until – I mean my mum was more or less kicked off the ward. 'You've been here all day', that was what they said, 'You've been here all day', as if – you know you're on this ward with just this curtain round you and you know your loved one . . . I hate hospitals.
>
> (Adrian)

Yet for Linda a medical setting provided a context that was perceived to promote the social and relational nature of the dying experience:

> But having said that, the hospital were quite good because they did things like put her in a separate room and there was always somebody there. So we would have this rota and there's quite a lot of us, we had six of us to do that and they were very good about things like that and they would always be coming in with cups of tea and sandwiches and you know.
>
> (Linda)

In some cases, social factors would override medical ones as the 'real' cause of death, such as dying of a broken heart, the loss of one's social role and social exclusion:

> My grandmother lived probably about a month after Grandpa died, was diagnosed with all sorts – you know when people have been living together all their lives – basically since they were 16 and for want of a better phrase, she died of a broken heart.
>
> (Sarah)

In a context of individualism and medicalisation, the value placed on relatedness, intimacy and mutuality and norms associated with sociality were in no way diminished. The participation of family and close others in a loved one's dying was perceived as normative:

> So of course I went down to look after Dad while he was at home while Mum was in hospital having the operation.
>
> (Roy)

Thus the adequacy of one's contribution could be questioned:

> So although I was living further away, my brother was an even less frequent visitor to him than I was and certainly in the early stages I did think that my brother could do more.
>
> (Stephen)

Dying as a social event did not always prioritise familial relationships in terms of blood ties, but, as for Lorraine, could include close friendship ties:

> I don't think the fact that you give birth to blood issue, if you like, necessarily assumes any special relationship. It can't, can it, because of how different people are. I mean people are different and so are parents . . . in a sense he was – he was mine, not in that biological sense, but he would have been one of the kids in whose welfare and upbringing I was having a role and I would have a role in the future.
>
> (Lorraine)

In contrast to the more rational, pragmatic perspective associated with medicalised dying, a romanticism was apparent in some accounts of the more social and relational aspects of the experience. Rooted in the Victorian era, romanticism privileges emotionality over rationality, emphasising the value of human affective relationships and emotional expressiveness (Stroebe *et al.*, 1992; Hockey, 2001). As explored in Chapter 3, such values are especially evident in accounts of dying loved ones' final moments, as expressed by Pat (see p. 73):

> I mean it was just absolutely amazing because as I say she died looking straight into my eyes with her hands on my cheek and I knew she knew it was me.
>
> (Pat)

Religion

A person-centred perspective was evident in the way narrators sought to understand the dying experience in terms of religious discourses. In a society that promotes individual autonomy and responsibility and distrusts external authority, religion has become a matter of personal and private choice. In relation to a medicalised, institutionalised system of dying, religious belief provides an 'optional extra' (Walter, 1997a; 1997b). Accounts reflected how its conventional form has given way to a more eclectic, individualistic spirituality:

> I think each member of the family holds their own beliefs. They might occasionally talk to another member of the family about them but it's quite rare that – everybody seems to be valued for their individualism and so they all follow their own set of beliefs and we don't interfere with one another.
>
> (Diane)

In some cases this involved borrowing from various cultural sources, including new age and eastern religious discourses (McNamara, 2001: 8):

> So what I've chosen to believe is that my dad is now part of the living organism of the earth and when we all finally reach a state of higher consciousness then he'll be there. Well he's here now and I can connect with that if I feel I want to.
>
> (Patrick)

Such borrowing extended to a 'pick and mix' approach, with the advantage of allowing people the freedom to personalise their beliefs, as conveyed by Roy:

> I think the nice thing is you can borrow bits of religion and say 'I like a bit of this and a bit of that'.
>
> (Roy)

Most individuals I spoke to did not have clearly defined beliefs and expressed, at the most, some hope and, at the least, ambivalence about an afterlife. Rather, accounts were characterised by an uneasy relationship between the sacred and secular to produce an existential uncertainty:

It's strange 'cos I'm not religious, I don't believe in a god, but I'd like to think that if there's a heaven that she would be there.

(Susan)

Religion could be rejected altogether as '. . .offering no comfort whatsoever'. For Tania, her own capacity to carry the deceased's memory forward into one's life provided the necessary strength to go on living:

My view is you make the most of what you've got now and you know I treasure what I take forward from my mum.

(Tania)

Indeed religion tended to be perceived as a personal attribute, in Lynne's words, as something 'you either have or you don't'. Thus some individuals expressed wishing that they were more 'religious' and able to take comfort from a belief in an afterlife, whilst acknowledging that this could not be contrived:

It would be nice to believe in god and all the rest of it – it would be wonderful and very comforting, wouldn't it – and be able to see people again and all the rest of it, but I can't.

(Lynne)

However, Tania conveyed a sense of relief that she had not experienced any need to turn to religion, whilst for Stephen, the experience of witnessing his father's suffering and dying inclined him away from any belief in a god:

It just isn't part of me – which in some ways I'm quite pleased – I've never shifted 'cos I think that would have really thrown me totally if after my mum had died I'd suddenly started hoping for things which I thought all my life had never been.

(Tania)

If anything for me it made me kind of rather less inclined to go to religion um you know it sort of made me feel if there's a god up there why do you let people suffer like this?

(Stephen)

Religious beliefs held by the dying individual, as an aspect of personhood, were to be respected. Brian expressed anger and concern at the way that others had failed to respect the religious beliefs of his dying grandmother:

I was actually quite annoyed. They had a Muslim chap working in the care home – he'd asked my grandma if he could borrow her Bible and left her his copy of the Koran as a swap – so I thought, 'fair enough', but this went on for a month and a half and I got upset with my family because to me I saw that as a major – they'd taken her book away and they hadn't – a month and a half – if you're a religious person that's a long time without – and no one else seemed as concerned about it as I did.

(Brian)

The two individuals, Andy and Sarah, who did subscribe to specific 'religious' faiths, were able to take comfort in the belief that their loved ones had gone to a better place where they no longer suffered:

It was just like really nice and I thought, yeah, Dad's probably happy now.

(Andy)

However, such comfort was only partial and belief in an afterlife did not always help to justify or make sense of deaths seen as untimely:

I was just like, no this can't be true, and they must have got the wrong person. It was like, no, no, they're not talking about my dad.

(Andy)

It's upsetting to think about untimely deaths – that's not nice.

(Sarah)

Death's timing

Whether a death is constructed as timely or untimely has been shown to have a significant impact on the bereavement experience (Bradbury, 1996, 1999). The concept of normative timetables encompasses social perceptions and expectations regarding the 'right time' and 'right order' for doing things (Finch and Wallis, 1993). It is expected that parents should die before their children (Komaromy and Hockey, 2001). Such norms in relation to both the age and order of dying may be violated by untimely deaths (Finch and Wallis, 1993). This tends to reflect the medical model in being linked to life-stage and the prevention of suffering. Thus, in relation to his father's death at 67, Roy felt that '. . .he had a good innings' and '. . .he's no longer suffering'.

However, when a young person dies, the value we place on leading a full and active life promotes a sense of lost potential and opportunity, of someone having been cut down in their prime. This perception was movingly conveyed by Janet as she reflected on the death of her friend at only 17:

It was just the fact that he'd never reached his eighteenth birthday and it didn't seem fair – there's no justice in the fact that he didn't get to his 18th – and all the things he wasn't going to get to do.

(Janet)

Such untimely or premature deaths tend to evoke disbelief, anger and outrage at what may be put down to either life's unfairness or medical failure or a combination of both. The sudden and unexpected deaths of fit, healthy individuals who were leading full and active lives was particularly shocking and hard to understand:

> For a couple of weeks afterwards it felt like an electric shock each time I remembered it. And it was as though I just couldn't take it in.
>
> (Sandra)

> I went home and smashed a few cups up. It was numbness really. I didn't honestly believe it . . . I didn't realise at the time but I did go off the rails a bit.
>
> (Elizabeth)

Death's untimeliness did not necessarily reflect chronological age, as with Adrian's father. Still full of life and energy at 65, his death did not make sense to Adrian:

> I mean, my dad, if he was anything he was a fighter and the autopsy also revealed that he was in perfect working nick – his heart – they looked at the brain cells, everything.
>
> (Adrian)

Indeed, constructions of death's timing more often reflected the nature of a relationship rather than age (Littlewood, 1992):

> And I can remember as he walked away saying to myself, I know some day he's going to die, but given the nature of the relationship we now have, I hope it's not for a long time in the future.
>
> (Stephen)

This included the meaning of a relationship at a particular point in the significant other's life, as in Stephen's case in which he had been looking forward to a sharing of academic experiences with his father:

> Because particularly at a stage when I was doing something different which was academic and my father was an academic, it would be very nice to actually have someone like that to talk to. And you do feel a little bit sort of cheated.
>
> (Stephen)

The timing of a death could thus have a profound impact on the survivor's life-stage and circumstances. For Andy, losing his father in late adolescence was experienced as particularly overwhelming:

> But I still can't believe it yet. I said to B., my flat mate, it's been such a vast change this year. Like my dad passed away, I had A levels, I went to India, got

my results, came to uni. Like there's been so much happening in one year. I just haven't had time to come to terms with it. I really haven't.

(Andy)

For Tania who was approaching 50, her mother's death was perceived to place severe restrictions on the increased freedom she had envisaged:

I have felt that in the past year or so I've been more restricted than previously, just at the time when I've thought maybe I could do a bit more and my son is grown up and what have you . . . I've put my life on hold for the best part of this past year and I just haven't really got a social life.

(Tania)

It could sometimes be the case that child and parent became closer companions later in life. This meant that even where death occurred at a good age for the dying person, this could still be experienced as untimely for surviving loved ones:

I miss having chats with Dad and knowing that he's there – yeah, I do – I do. I would like him to be sitting in his little bungalow puffing on his pipe – I really would – yeah – yeah, that does make me sad.

(Ivan)

In some cases, the sense of untimeliness was linked to family dynamics. For Tania her mother's death left her with a sense of losing the family member with which she most identified:

and at times I think, 'oh, if only Mum was here' – because Mum – we were the stronger ones. I just feel I've lost, I don't know it's so hard to say – I felt so in tune with my mum – I think that's the best way to put it.

(Tania)

In Diane's case the deaths of her mother, her grandmother and her aunt involved having to adjust to a new role as the most senior member of the extended family, something that left her with the feeling of having no-one to whom she could turn:

On Friday I had a major upset – a major personal upset – and there was kind of nowhere to go with it. I think it's then that it hits home – them not being there – because I know that any one of those three I could nip to the phone and talk to them.

(Diane)

Deaths' timeliness was also linked to the extent of suffering. One impact of medicalisation has been the increase in protracted dying, invasive treatment and therefore the potential for suffering, so that most people's ideal death is one that is relatively pain-free. Thus, a sudden, unexpected death from a heart attack, in which there was perceived to have been no suffering, and which was timely in terms of age-stage, was constructed as a 'nice' way to go:

> But I think that compared to a terminally ill person she didn't suffer, but I think in a sense that it's quite nice that she did pass on so quickly.
>
> (Susan)

Even where the death was untimely, the absence of suffering could provide some consolation:

> I'm glad for him that there was no suffering – 'cos they said he wouldn't have suffered.
>
> (Elisabeth)

In keeping with a person-centred perspective, timeliness reflected not only the 'quantity', but the 'quality' of life. A death occurring in late middle-age could be timely in relation to the nature of the life lived. Thus, Marianne found consolation in the way her mother, though having 'actively neglected her health, actively damaged her health', still managed to avoid a painful dying, as well as enjoy the holiday of a life-time just prior to her terminal diagnosis:

> and they travelled for four weeks round New Zealand and Mum wasn't well but she still really enjoyed the trip . . . So in a sense, you know, in some ways it feels as though she had the journey she really wanted.
>
> (Marianne)

Suffering could include the emotional pain of loss of status and companionship, as with Sarah's grandmother whose death followed closely on the heels of that of her husband:

> But then I can't imagine them being apart. So it's better they went close together. It's upsetting, but in a way she's better off. She's not in pain, she's not going on living until she's 100, 30 years gaga and alone.
>
> (Sarah)

It could include the emotional distress triggered by physical deterioration, as in the case of Michael's aunt whose short-term memory loss was extremely distressing for her:

> Well, it was a blessing really because she was in a state of fairly constant anxiety because she lost her memory
>
> (Michael)

For Patrick, his father's untimely death in terms of age, that provided a release from suffering, was preferable to going on living:

Yeah we were all waiting for it and I mean we were all glad it wasn't years of agony.

(Patrick)

However Linda was left with

The conflict between wanting suffering to end but wanting to retain the loved one's presence.

(Linda)

Indeed, constructions of death's timing tended to convey the ambiguity inherent in the question of 'timely for whom?' Though this could only be answered by the bereaved individual, attempts were often made to imagine oneself in the dying person's shoes. This involved a weighing-up of factors so that timeliness and untimeliness were used in a relative manner and a consideration of the varying perspectives of those involved. Individuals were able to separate their own perspective from that of the deceased and acknowledge that things were not so clear-cut:

I remember thinking at the time, 'For god's sake, please live' and I thought afterwards he would have been so severely damaged that it wouldn't have been a life that he would have liked – or the children to have seen him. He actually used to joke about it. He used to say, 'oh I just want to drop down dead in the garden one day' – and he did.

(Elisabeth)

Negotiating the paradox of dying

As illustrated, the process of reconstructing a loved one's dying was subject to a reflexivity that revealed a capacity to acknowledge and appreciate the double-edged nature of some aspects of experience. This encompassed the changing nature of people's relationship with their experience, or how they see something in a different light at different times. Though Andy bemoaned the untimely nature of his father's death in relation its impact on his own life, he was also able to view the situation from his father's perspective:

He was in a lot of pain. Like sometimes I think maybe when my dad passed away – maybe that was good, because he was going through pain. It's made me grow up.

(Andy)

No dying was represented as wholly good or wholly bad. Rather experiences were full of ambiguity, so that almost as soon as a positive feature was recalled, its more negative side would become apparent and vice versa. For example, supporting and tending the needs of the dying individual could evoke a painful awareness of the extent of his or her helplessness and loss of agency:

But you know you sort of think this isn't – it's sort of almost degrading really. But he's lying there, having all these people having to do things for him and he's always done everything for himself and you sort of think this isn't what we want for Dad, this isn't what he would want so . . .

(Fiona)

Ambiguity was reflected in the way that the same themes could be identified as conveying both what was good and what was bad about the dying. For example, awareness could be both a burden and a resource (see Chapter 2, p. 65).

Summary

With reference to the concept of the dying trajectory, this chapter has focused on the way narrators tried to piece events together to create a dying that 'belonged' to and was characteristic of the individual concerned. In so doing, it has sought to convey the extent of ambivalence and paradox that may characterise the dying process and how people negotiated the pain, disruption and uncertainties associated with this.

The tension inherent in predominant discourses of individualism and medicalisation was often apparent. These two discourses could also be mutually reinforcing. A more social discourse in which dying was represented as a shared as well as a medical and individual event contributed a further, important dimension. Individualism did not diminish the value placed on relationship and sociality. Individual and social factors, such as loss of agency or status, being excluded or marginalised, sometimes overrode medical ones as the cause of death. Narratives demonstrated how individual and social factors were not necessarily compromised by medicalisation. Indeed, in some cases a medical setting served to enhance the dying person's unique character and selfhood. A romantic discourse conveyed the nature of the relationship between narrators and dying loved ones, particularly in relation to dying moments. These affirmed both the dying person's unique individuality and the intimate bond between him or her and the bereaved person.

A person-centred perspective was evident in the way people negotiated beliefs about life and death. Some accounts reflected an eclectic, individualistic spirituality, in which beliefs were personalised by borrowing from different religions. Most people conveyed ambivalence and uncertainty. Religious belief tended to be represented as a personal attribute that could not be contrived, some people wishing they were able to take comfort from religion and others having no desire to do so. As an aspect of the dying individual's personhood it was to be respected. Death as a transition to a better life offered some comfort to those who did subscribe to a particular faith. However, such belief did not necessarily help to make sense of 'untimely' deaths.

The timing of a death, both in relation to the deceased and to the bereaved person's life stage provided another source of meaning. Though premature deaths were considered an outrage, perceptions of the deceased person's energy for life and the value attached to the relationship tended to outweigh considerations of age.

Such value included having experiences in common, having someone with whom to identify or turn to in times of difficulty. Some individuals found the timing of a loved one's death especially difficult in relation to the stage of life they had reached. As a result they were left feeling either overburdened, or else unable to reap the benefits associated with the particular life-stage. However considerations of death's timing were also subject to putting oneself in the dying person's shoes. Some narrators were able to appreciate the relative nature of death's timeliness or untimeliness.

The process of dying in a more general sense was considered bad by all participants due to the potential for loss of independence, agency and personal relationships and the impact of this on one's engagement in and therefore quality of life. Yet at a more personal level the experience was somewhat ambiguous. Narrators were able to identify and salvage redeeming features. Recounting the 'ordinary' human details of their experience generated positive as well as negative feelings: tears of sadness, anger, cynicism and defeat would give way to humour, optimism, hope and gratitude. This was the case even in relation to deaths that were considered to be untimely.

Indeed, narrators constructed rich and nuanced pictures, in which some aspects of dying were salvaged, some remained ambivalent and others unredeemed. These were characterised by a reflexivity in which nothing was set in stone, but rather represented one's relationship with one's experience at a particular point in time. The way specific details were recalled and conveyed was not clear-cut, but rather involved a weighing-up of good and bad factors or a process of negotiation in the face of what was full of complexity, uncertainty, ambivalence and paradox. The medicalisation of dying did not necessarily serve to depersonalise or routinise it. As indicated, it could provide a framework in which bereaved people made sense of an uncertain process and the dying person was perceived to demonstrate his or her own particular and unique version of dying. No two cancer deaths were the same, since the responses of dying individuals were represented as deviating from the norm.

Accounts revealed people's capacity to salvage redeeming features of what was essentially a painful, distressing and uncertain experience. However, this did not come across as an attempt to force the issue or convince oneself. As the next chapter will demonstrate, there were plenty of examples of people acknowledging what felt bad and could not be redeemed, or given meaning. Rather, such salvaging seemed to reflect a recognition and appreciation of those aspects of the experience that provided evidence of the dying person's continuing personhood and the acknowledgement of this by others. It was as though these aspects offered reassuring reminders of the resilience of the human spirit and personal relationships. Indeed, the pleasure and pride which narrators took in conveying to me the uniqueness and value of their dying loved ones, represented an affirmation and preservation of personhood, from which some consolation, hope and support could be drawn.

The threat that death posed to the social bond (Durkheim, 1915; Huntington and Metcalf, 1979; Bloch and Parry, 1982) was thus foreshadowed in the dying experience. Anthropologists have argued that this requires the reaffirmation of society's core values (Hertz, 1907/1960; Huntington and Metcalf, 1979). In a context in which dying and death have become institutionalised and routinised, accounts reflected the increasing concern with humanising the dying experience, something which included the personal and the social. Rather than a preparation for the afterlife and meeting one's maker, dying has become a person-centred affair in which it is personhood rather than the soul that is at stake. This raises important questions for sociological theory in relation to what it means to 'be a person' in contemporary society. These will be taken up in the following chapter as part of an exploration of what makes death 'good' for bereaved people in contemporary British Society.

2　Constructing a good death

The good death, as an ideal of how one should die, has been found to structure not only the care of dying people but also the experiences of bereaved people (Bradbury, 1999). This chapter examines some contemporary constructions of what made death both good and not so good for the 25 bereaved individuals I interviewed. If, as the last chapter has demonstrated, it is the dying individual's unique selfhood that is at stake, then achieving a good death depends on remaining socially present, or retaining personhood. This emphasis on continuing personhood in part reflects the secularism and humanism that has been identified as forming a significant feature of contemporary British society (Walter, 1997a). However, in relation to the bodily incapacities of dying, it raises questions about the relationship between social identity and embodiment, suggesting that this may be more complex than sociological theory has assumed (Hallam *et al.*, 1999; Lawton, 2000). The value placed on continuing personhood and the extent of awareness this implies, also poses a dilemma in relation to the value that is placed on the achievement of a painless and peaceful death.

The concept of personhood refers to an individual's social significance, something which implies that he or she possesses certain culturally dictated attributes (Lawton, 2000: 4). As such, it is subject to variation across cultures. In the contemporary West the notion of personhood reflects the influence of psychology, which has promoted a model of containment. According to this model the body is taken to be the locus of individuality, the exercise of agency depending on the possession of a functioning body that acts with rational intentionality. A person is perceived to be 'coherent, bounded, individualized, intentional, the locus of thought, action and belief, the origin of its own actions, the beneficiary of a unique biography' (Rose, 1996: 3). Lawton (2000: 7) has drawn attention to the way sociological accounts have emphasised the 'performative' aspects of embodiment, or 'the bodily ability to act as the agent of one's embodied actions and intentions' (see e.g. Goffman, 1959; Butler, 1990, 1993; Featherstone, 1995). The relationship between self and body is thus represented as a straightforward one, in which the body is taken to be a fixed, material entity.

However this model of a unified, bounded, performative body that acts with rational intentionality has been powerfully critiqued for failing to appreciate the limits of individuality and rational intentionality. It does not adequately account for our sociality and interdependency and how our actions may be dictated by more emotional and intersubjective considerations (Battersby, 1993, 1998; Rose, 1996; Hallam *et al.*, 1999; Lawton, 2000). As discussed in Chapter 1, it fails to reflect the complexities of the experience of being in a body that is vulnerable to illness and ageing and must eventually die. For it only recognises the performative body and neglects the 'multiplicity' of embodied experience (Lawton, 2000: 105). By taking the body as a fixed entity rather than as process, it fails to capture the complexities and subtleties of social being.

This model has produced various forms of social exclusion. An ailing body may produce a diminishment of self through the loss of bodily ability to act as an agent of one's embodied actions and intentions (Brody, 1987: 27). Such an intentional, embodied social identity comes under serious threat through the processes of ageing and dying (Lawton, 2000). Indeed, by making selfhood dependent on bodily capacity, those who are ageing or dying may be considered already dead prior to their biological death (Mulkay, 1993; Hallam *et al.*, 1999).

Yet the narratives of those I interviewed revealed how bereaved individuals negotiated the precarious nature of personhood in ways that challenged any straightforward relationship between personhood and embodiment. Though for some individuals the impact of the dying process made it hard to hold onto dying loved ones' continuing social presence, others were able to sustain meaningful contact and recognise other ways of being, acting and engaging in social life. Indeed remaining one's characteristic self in the face of bodily deterioration could be perceived as an enhancement of personhood. Exercising agency and having an impact on one's social environment was not necessarily linked to rational inten-tionality or a performative, bounded body.

Personhood is also dependent on interpersonal relationships and the evaluations of others. The extreme vulnerability and bodily dependence of dying people has been found to expose them to depersonalising treatment or being treated as objects (Field, 1989; Seymour, 2001). My participants' narratives conveyed how the attitudes and responses of others may affirm or undermine the dying individual's personhood. Thus accounts sometimes placed the narrator in the role of affirming the dying person's continuing social presence in the face of others, family members as well as professionals, who were failing to appreciate this. They betrayed the narrator's own ambivalence in this and his or her consequent struggle to hold onto a loved one's personhood in the face of the impact of his or her failing physical and mental capacities.

This chapter highlights the extent to which bereaved individuals were preoccupied with trying to preserve and affirm the personhood of dying loved ones in order to achieve a good death. This preoccupation suggests that the experience of bereavement may provide the impetus to reconstruct a loved one's personhood in relation to the way that he or she died. As will be demonstrated, such reconstruction revealed an alternative discourse in which personhood was more subtle, fluid and intersubjective than that dependent on rational intentionality and bodily integrity. Personhood can, in fact, be manifested through signals, gestures and facial expres-sions as well as interaction between people. Its maintenance was found to depend on the nature and extent of both the dying person's and the narrator's agency and awareness in relation to the dying process, as well as the social and socially supportive nature of the experience. Thus personhood was preserved and affirmed through a complex linking of individuality and sociality, revealing an emphasis on the themes of 'agency', 'social support' and 'awareness'. These three themes are used to structure the following discussion of my participants' dying narratives.

Agency

At least she lived out how she wanted to live.

(Vivienne)

As already discussed, sociological theory has linked the capacity for agency to intentional embodied action. This has prioritised the fully functioning body, to neglect the realities of both ageing and deteriorating bodies as well as the experience of illness and disability (Hallam *et al.*, 1999; Lawton, 2000). It has also obscured the more emotional and relational aspects of personhood. Though the capacity to act and have an impact on one's surroundings implies autonomy, self-determination, choice and responsibility, since we are social beings, this depends on such action being recognised and received by others. Our sense of agency therefore includes feeling valued, affirmed and taken seriously by others. Where such recognition is absent, our capacity for agency may be considerably undermined.

Thus any understanding of agency needs to include an appreciation of our vulnerability and susceptibility to each other (Barnes, 2000). This is especially the case in relation to experiences, such as dying and bereavement, which interrupt the ordinary, taken-for-granted business of living and can severely threaten and disrupt our sense of autonomy and personhood. Life in the face of death takes on an existential uncertainty by reminding us of our shared fragility (McNamara, 2001: 1). The bodily and cognitive impairment that commonly accompany terminal illness may severely reduce the individual's capacity to choose and to act for him- or herself. In such cases the extent to which we are able to die 'in our own way' is likely to be very dependent upon the responses of others.

My participants' narratives conveyed how agency has both a relational or intersubjective as well as an individual dimension (Battersby, 1998; Barnes, 2000). These two dimensions have been identified as 'taking ownership' and 'empower-ment', the latter depending more on the sense of social recognition and validation. Narrators were particularly concerned to recognise, emphasise and affirm the ways in which dying individuals were perceived to have demonstrated their continuing autonomy by taking some degree of ownership or 'doing it their way', in spite of a deteriorating body. Such representations of agency cannot be encompassed by a model of intentional embodied action. Narratives also revealed the limits of such capacity for agency in the face of failing physical capacity and how the experience of dying could increase one's sense of vulnerability and susceptibility to others and forces beyond one's control, to produce a loss of ownership and a sense of disempowerment.

Taking ownership

Dying individuals were perceived to take ownership of their dying through 'negotiating "the system"', 'showing character' and 'taking charge' of some aspect of their dying.

Negotiating 'the system'

Recent theoretical perspectives suggest a critical and dynamic relationship between medicine and the lay populace (Giddens, 1991; Lupton, 1994; Williams and Calnan, 1996). Interview narratives reflected this relationship in the way medical norms provided the context in which dying could be experienced as 'typical' or 'not so typical'. A typical dying scenario potentially placed the individual at the mercy of a medicalised system which included the following two aspects: the physical, emotional and mental pains and indignities of progressive bodily degeneration and the accompanying reduction in scope and quality of life; medical supervision and treatment of which could tend to depersonalise and objectify the dying person (Field, 1989; Seymour, 2001). However, my participants' narratives demonstrated how the impersonality and indignities of the 'dying system' could be negotiated, manipulated and even defeated by the dying individual's 'personhood'. It was therefore, to some extent, possible to 'beat the system' rather than being beaten by it. Where the system was perceived to have taken over, this was represented as an outrage to a dying loved one's personhood. Such narratives conveyed the complex nature of the relationship between individual agency and social and institutional structures.

Some of my participants represented their loved one's dying as quicker and therefore easier than the norm, that is, less painful and with less opportunity for invasive, medical intervention. This meant that in spite of the sudden, unexpected and shocking nature of the onset of her mother's illness, Tania was able to take some comfort from the way it did not follow the usual pattern:

I think – knowing what ovarian cancer normally does – those seven weeks and then to pass away, I think was an absolute blessing.

(Tania)

So, too, was Marianne, in relation to the untypical nature of her mother's cancer:

I always think of it as not a typical cancer experience, where you have a test and then you're hoping you have treatment and hoping and waiting . . . She went into hospital for ten days and then they found the lung cancer and then she died very soon after that . . . So, in some ways, for her to die quickly and relatively painlessly to me seems, under the circumstances, maybe not a good thing, but better than the alternative.

(Marianne)

In contrast, extended dying could involve losing the capacity to take pleasure in the things that one once enjoyed. This was experienced as defeating for the dying person, diminishing his or her quality of life, as for Roy's father and Lynne's mother:

> And Dad had – the sad thing is that Dad liked wine and cheese – he loved wine and cheese. But in the last six months his taste buds changed or something happened – I brought some cheese up for him – 'No, no I can't eat that' . . . But, no, that's the sad thing, his favourite foods in the last six months he couldn't eat them.
>
> (Roy)

> It was very difficult for her because she was always a great reader and she couldn't read anymore, she'd read the same page over and over and over again because she couldn't, you know.
>
> (Lynne)

Yet for some, their dying loved one's continuing mental capacity in spite of bodily incapacity was perceived to defy the system, representing a competing discourse in which personhood resided in the mind rather than the body. For Pat's aunt to suffer a massive stroke that was physically debilitating yet 'left her mind completely intact', was something 'the doctors were unable to explain'.

> Her mind was all intact – a very, very lively mind, I mean a razor, razor sharp mind and very contemporary as well, even though she clearly was not – I mean by that point, towards the end anyway, she was 90-plus years old.
>
> (Pat)

Some individuals, such as Vivienne's grandmother, were able to beat the system and retain their autonomy by resisting entry into a medicalised space and remaining in their own homes:

> She never had to go into a residential home – that's a good thing – she lived her life as she wanted to – that's a good thing.
>
> (Vivienne)

Where medical treatment was deemed necessary, as in the case of Fiona's father, a compromise could be reached:

> No, he was at home and he would just travel in — I think it was once a week and he would just take a journey down to the hospital and have his chemotherapy and then go home. So it wasn't a case of staying in hospital.
>
> (Fiona)

However, the system might still eventually catch up and in fact be perceived as the only option in terms of offering the dying person some relief since

Dad was just in so much pain. He was on the bed and I don't think he was really aware of who was there because he was in so much pain.

(Fiona)

But, once in hospital, the extent and value of such relief was questionable:

Obviously they'd given him lots of morphine and things, but his breathing was very laboured – sort of glassy eyed, didn't really know who was there. So that was quite upsetting.

(Fiona)

For Adrian, medical intervention was perceived to take control and claim ownership of his father's dying by preventing his fight for life:

It was only when they gave him that injection that he – I mean he'd been resuscitated twice and he was still there – he was still there and I mean it does make you feel, it does make my mum feel that there was no choice there.

(Adrian)

Several accounts drew attention to the way the system could assert its ownership through its 'spaces of dying' (Hockey, 1990). Stephen described the depressing impact of the nursing home environment on his father:

In the last year while he was in the home he was terribly depressed by it and just being surrounded by old people who from time to time disappeared and never came back themselves.

(Stephen)

Lynne conveyed her distress at the way such an environment had reduced her mother to tears, a person who did not normally show vulnerability:

I hated going and seeing her in that home ... because she hated it so much and you'd see tears in her eyes – because my mother never cried, you see, until she went there – she never showed any weakness – and you saw how desperately unhappy she was.

(Lynne)

However, she also conveyed how such depression and unhappiness could be considered an understandable and inevitable consequence of ageing (Matthews, 1979):

and she was obviously depressed, as well, but I think that's obviously fairly common with elderly people once they realise their faculties are going and they can't do – they can't get out.

(Lynne)

Showing character

Dying loved ones could demonstrate their ownership by the extent to which their style of dying reflected their character. Tania's mother continued to show characteristic consideration for others by presenting a brave face, in spite of being in considerable pain. This was a source of pride for Tania, turning a 'bad dying' into a 'good death':

> My mum was a strong person . . . and I think she showed tremendous dignity . . . and when one doctor asked her, 'How's the pain? How are you doing?', she said, 'Not so bad.' But it must have been awful. She never, ever cried – she's got such amazing courage, you know . . . I just feel the way she handled herself especially the news that she had cancer and everything, there's not one minute that she didn't put us before herself – there's not one minute that she didn't try and make it easier for us.
>
> (Tania)

Lynne experienced her mother's attitude of defiance or non-acceptance of death as evidence of her continuing aliveness and spirit:

> She was one of these people who would never, ever – however ill she was, want to be put out of it – she would never want euthanasia – she clung hold of life very, very hard . . . But, no, she really fought. No matter how poor the quality of her life was she didn't want to go.
>
> (Lynne)

However, for Adrian, the way his father put up a fight was a poignant reminder that he did not feel ready to die:

> He was perfectly conscious and he was still fighting – he was still going – I mean my dad, if he was anything, he was a fighter.
>
> (Adrian)

Such fighting was not always considered in a positive light. The popularisation of Elizabeth Kübler-Ross's (1970) five stages of adjustment made by dying patients in hospital has emphasised her final stage of 'acceptance' as the desired outcome for all dying individuals. This has had a profound and lasting impact on service provision, with 'acceptance' being promoted by professionals in institutional settings as a means of avoiding upset (Field, 1994).

Thus, for Jason, the way his partner did battle with her dying, though demonstrating character, was self-defeating, 'acceptance' being perceived to offer an easier dying:

> I mean she really fought it. She – it was like she took on board the fact that she was going to fight cancer until she won and actually the cancer was stronger

than that. It killed her. And I kept thinking it was the wrong way to do it. That was my sort of attitude you know. Why don't you just enjoy what time you've got left and accept things as they are and just not fight it so much?

(Jason)

However, acceptance was not necessarily an easy option. As de Beauvoir (1966: 106) has observed: 'for every man his death is an accident and, even if he knows it and consents to it, an unjustifiable violation'. As the last chapter illustrated, the pain suffered by Fiona's father forced him to relinquish his desire 'to let nature take its course' and accept treatment.

In some cases demonstration of character was perceived to have contributed to the person's premature dying. Adrian's father's 'fighting spirit' was double-edged, giving rise to competing discourses. On the one hand living life to the full was considered positive and courageous, but on the other hand it could mean a lifestyle of overdoing things and neglecting to take sufficient care of oneself:

You know he burnt the candle at both ends as well.

(Adrian)

For Patrick, in keeping with the public health discourse, his father's lifestyle and habits were considered to have been directly responsible for his premature dying:

I'd always kind of figured my dad was going to die of lung cancer at quite a young age. I assumed that – like when I was eight or nine I realised the effects of smoking and thought, 'Right. Dad's a goner'.

(Patrick)

For Ivan, his mother's refusal to take responsibility for herself was put down to her characteristic selfishness:

She was decrepit and she wouldn't have proper medical help and she wouldn't have homecare and she wasn't poor – I mean they were comfortably off. But she was just a very, very selfish woman and I was quite angry in the way she died.

(Ivan)

In some cases the impact of terminal illness was considered to produce a loss or change of character. Jason conveyed his shock at the change in his partner's physical appearance:

In the state she was in she looked like she'd shrunken and got very old. She'd always been a very vibrant woman with rich chestnut dark hair and a very strong figure and she'd kind of shrunk and got very thin and it was a shock to see her.

(Jason)

Stephen reported how his father's change of character had a produced a reversal of roles that they both found extremely uncomfortable and hard to tolerate:

> And basically you'd have to do pretty well everything for him, and you could see that I hated doing it because I felt the roles were beginning to reverse, and you could see that my father hated me having to do it because, you know, I was doing what he used to do for me, and when that started to happen then the sooner it stopped the better.
>
> (Stephen)

Yet, for Lynne, her mother's response to the physical symptoms she was suffering served to demonstrate her character:

> Also her mouth was so sore and she had – the growth had actually grown up to fill the roof of her mouth and it was all sort of coming over her nose and it was all erupting, so she had bandages all round. She was always a very proud woman about how she looked and everything . . . but she really was upset about the fact that she had this thing and she had this great bandage over her face.
>
> (Lynne)

Taking charge

Attention was drawn to the initiative and foresight shown by dying loved ones in relation to some aspects of their dying, for example, ensuring that their funeral requirements were documented and made available to others whilst they still had the capacity to take charge of their own affairs. Such initiative was experienced as demonstrating his or her consideration and support for those who were to be left behind, as represented by Pat:

> She'd left very very clear instructions about what she wanted, exactly what sort of burial she wanted – she wanted a cremation – who she wanted to do it, you know, and how she wanted it to proceed – very very clear instructions which, thank god, you know, that's one thing I take from her – write a list, . . . it made life very easy 'cos so many of those decisions I just didn't have to make.
>
> (Pat)

For Jason, the way his dying partner had taken charge of her own affairs whilst she was still able to do so was experienced as having taken everything out of his hands:

> And she'd made all the arrangements about the funeral and everything beforehand, before she went into the hospice. She'd sold her house, put the money in trust for our son and arranged with the solicitor to release money

as it was needed. So she took over virtually everything and really I had nothing to do with the funeral or the burial, or whatever happened to the money.

(Jason)

These examples revealed how the dying person's agency may operate after his or her death, in contrast to the social death that may be attributed to someone while they are still alive. As such they pose a challenge to sociological theories that link agency with embodiment. Rather, they convey a more far-reaching and encompassing view of social being that extends beyond the body and material dimension.

In some cases the capacity to show initiative and act independently was regardless of bodily capacity. Thus the dying person was perceived to take charge of his or her dying by waiting until a particular loved one was present:

But I mean in some ways I sometimes wonder whether – 'cos I was the last one of the close family who she hadn't seen – and, in a sense, whether she'd waited for me to come; because it was two days after I was gone that she passed away.

(Marianne)

He lasted far longer than we ever thought he would . . . so I saw Mum and Dad back together again. Dad looked a lot better because he'd seen his wife again.

(Roy)

As illustrated and explored more fully in the following chapter, some dying loved ones were perceived to recover their aliveness and presence to take charge of their final moments by means of a gesture of 'leave-taking'.

However, for others it was the professionals who took charge of the dying individual's final moments. The loss of ownership this could produce for both the dying person and their family was powerfully conveyed by Adrian. Thus he reported how he and his family had felt manipulated by the consultant into consenting to discontinue his father's treatment for a condition that was not normally life-threatening:

But having been told there was nothing they could do for him I kind of went along with it . . . and so there was no choice there you know – a consultant had made the decision for everyone, they'd made the decision for him, they'd made the decision for the family.

(Adrian)

Indeed, my participants' narratives illustrated how the extent of their own capacity for agency in their loved one's dying structured their experience. They conveyed how they negotiated their own role in a loved one's dying and sought to 'take ownership' through 'being constructive' and 'giving voice' to their loved one's needs.

Being constructive

Playing a constructive role in the dying person's treatment and care allowed the narrator to stay in touch with and retain some control over the messiness of dying (McNamara, 2001). It also represented an expression, continuation and reinforcement of their relationship and therefore an affirmation of the dying individual's personhood.

For some, such as Roy, being constructive included being able to rely on one's own experience:

> Given that I work in care anyway it wasn't such a roller coaster as for my brother – I mean, I felt for my brother the day I turned up and I literally took over.
>
> (Roy)

For Pat it included attempts to engage her dying aunt on the basis of her knowledge of those things that might give her pleasure:

> And you know I'd take things into the home, like she loved her sherry, Harvey's Bristol Cream and she'd always have sherry out of these beautiful cut crystal glasses . . . so I took her glasses in and a little tray and a bottle of sherry and things like this to try and engage her somehow with something that would give her some type of pleasure – or I'd bring in some books that she liked.
>
> (Pat)

For Stephen it involved giving his dying father a break from the monotony of life in an institutional setting:

> But for that first year that my father was in the home I tried to make an effort to put him in the car and drive him off somewhere.
>
> (Stephen)

In Diane's case it meant taking the opportunity to ensure that her mother was able to meet and spend time with a family member she had not yet seen:

> And she became very poorly and we thought she was going and then she kind of recovered a little bit and one of my children lived in Belgium at the time and she had a little girl and she'd never seen the little girl, so we took her to Belgium so she could spend some time with her.
>
> (Diane)

However one's efforts might not be appreciated or bear fruit, preventing one from taking ownership of the situation. For Pat it became increasingly difficult to find a way of engaging her aunt and providing her with some source of pleasure:

And as time progressed and we got to about the November, she'd stop even having her sherry, 'cos even though she wasn't eating she'd have her sherry. But she stopped having her sherry, she stopped listening to the radio, so she was slowly, very slowly disengaging.

(Pat)

Some narrators felt that they had already lost their loved ones as persons. The impact of the diminished quality and scope of their lives, especially in an institutional setting had effectively rendered them 'socially dead'. As indicated, this implies that they had ceased to exist as active agents in other people's lives. As a result of her great grandmother's institutionalisation, Jane felt at a loss as to how to engage with someone who had once played a key role in her life:

And I went to see her in the home a few times and that was hard because what do you say? Because she was starting to lose it, and a few days before she died I went to see her and I looked at her. I was quite religious at this time, still have my beliefs but I'm having a bit of a crisis with that, and all I could see in my mind was that she'd already died, in a sense, and all there was was this frail shell of a person – breathing but not there.

(Jane)

Such experiences reflected the importance and value that could be attached to verbal communication in the maintenance of relationship and personhood. Indeed, the dying individual's failing capacity for speech could leave the loved one feeling at a loss and already bereft. In Stephen's case this produced a sense of waiting for his father to die:

You could just sometimes sit there with him just watching television and not really have any kind of obvious communication with him and so about the last year it was really a feeling of just waiting for him to go.

(Stephen)

Yet he also conveyed his appreciation of how other family members found a way to continue to communicate and maintain their relationship with his father:

By the end he would hardly say anything, and then he might say one word, and particularly my mother and my stepmother, when they went up to visit him, they kind of got into this art form where they would talk to him all the time, and it was like having a conversation but with only one person speaking, and unfortunately my brother and I just weren't as good at doing that.

(Stephen)

'Lingering' deaths in which the dying person remained in a state of unconsciousness produced an uncertain situation. For Ivan this left him feeling that all he could do was to put his life on hold and wait for his father to die:

And then it was just a matter of weeks and weeks and weeks of hanging on and hanging on and actually, towards the end, hoping he would die because there was no way back and he was just fading away.

(Ivan)

Imminent deaths could be experienced as no less uncertain and threatening to one's sense of ownership:

Linda and my dad stayed with Mum through the night – we actually got back in time – I really started to panic on the way back thinking, 'has she died? Has she died?', – I just couldn't have stood it if she'd died and I hadn't got back.

(Tania)

Giving voice

Where the dying individual was in the hands of professionals, by taking the role of his or her advocate, loved ones were able to help shape the situation. This included using one's knowledge, understanding and experience of the needs of dying loved ones, as well as establishing a rapport with professionals.

For Stephen, whose father became unable to speak for himself, this included giving voice to what he felt his father wanted and trying to ensure that this was carried out:

And it got to the point when basically they wanted the bed ... and my stepmother phoned me up and said to me did I have any views about him being helped on his way ... And my father was actually quite profoundly religious and he basically would have taken the view that he would go when his maker had decided it was for him. So I immediately said on the phone, 'No, tell them just to leave him as he is ...'

(Stephen)

For Tania and Linda, their own medical experience enabled them to negotiate with professionals on behalf of their dying mothers:

I would just answer back and do it all for my mum with a huge front of, 'ok, let's see what are the options ...' Mum would always rely on the fact that I would pick up and say, 'You know, I checked absolutely everything at that hospital' – and she would have enormous confidence in the fact that I would be there.

(Tania)

I called the nurse in and I said, 'Look, she's really – she might be pain-free, but she's really very uncomfortable, and could you move her?', and ... I got the nurse to make her comfortable and then she gave her another painkiller injection.

(Linda)

For Linda such negotiation involved the use of patience and tact with professionals to try and ensure that her mother received sufficient care. This depended on networking to obtain sufficient information to be able to negotiate with nursing staff to ensure that her mother's needs were fully met:

> I found myself . . . trying to make sure Mammy was alright and that she was going to get some kind of pain relief. And because I have a lot of contacts in palliative care, I would be on the phone saying, 'What do you think she should be having? How do you think I could suggest that?' But having said that, the hospital were quite good because they did things like put her in a separate room and there was always somebody there . . . And finally they gave her morphine . . .
>
> (Linda)

Empowerment

The value placed on retaining 'agency' was further conveyed through the behaviour and responses of others that contributed to dying individuals having some control over their situation or empowerment in relation to their dying. As discussed, this encompasses the more relational dimension of agency, or the need for social recognition, as well as a more fluid and intersubjective understanding of agency and personhood. It depended upon 'respecting' and 'protecting' the dying person's wishes and 'subjectivity' in the face of treatment that could 'objectify' and 'depersonalise' him or her.

Respecting the dying person's wishes

Discourses of 'individualism' as well as 'relationship' provided a structure in which significant others could make decisions about how to respond to dying loved ones and, if necessary, act on their behalf. Thus 'getting it right' for the dying person was considered especially important.

For Diane, getting it right included ensuring that her mother was able to die at home as she wished:

> We got it right for her – she never, ever wanted to die anywhere than at home – so she was very, very worried about going into care – so we managed to do what she wanted. So I think in lots of ways – while we were upset at the loss of her, we felt that we had managed to engineer the circumstances for her to go in the way that she wanted to go.
>
> (Diane)

Getting it right could involve negotiating competing discourses in which the demands of individualism ran into those of social support. Thus Pat was prepared to respect those wishes of her aunt that went against what might be considered to be in her best interests:

So she stopped eating and we were looking for a home that wouldn't force her to eat.

(Pat)

For Vivienne, this meant that her dying grandmother's insistence on staying at home took precedence over the possibility of extending her life in a nursing home:

So in the end she got – she kind of – she got what she wanted and she ended up staying all her life in her home – but then it kind of did show to us that she couldn't look after herself and had she been living in a residential home she might still be alive now – but then that's not actually what she'd want anyway.

(Vivienne)

For Fiona this meant accepting her father's intention to refuse treatment:

It was quite upsetting, but at the same time you sort of learn to accept it because you think, 'Well you know, he's at that age and that's his decision' and you just learn to accept it.

(Fiona)

However in the face of the demands of practical reality, respecting the dying person's wishes could not always be achieved. In Pat's case, the need for nursing care took precedence over her aunt's wish to remain in her own home:

So we put her into this home. She didn't like that – she was very angry with me over that – she didn't understand why she couldn't go to her own home.

(Pat)

Protecting the dying person's subjectivity

Narrators were at pains to ensure that increased vulnerability did not obscure their loved ones' continuing social presence and value. This involved a determination to subjectify rather than objectify them, when they were no longer able to act for themselves (Seymour, 2001). This was reflected by the emphasis that was placed on valuing and affirming the verbal and non-verbal gestures that were perceived to demonstrate the ways in which dying individuals remained uniquely and characteristically themselves. Thus, Linda endeavoured to affirm her dying mother's powers of communication and comprehension in the face of others who failed to recognise these, including family members as well as professionals:

Like some wouldn't have understood that she could still communicate you know . . . and I'd say, 'Mum, it's me' and she would squeeze like that and then the tears would come down her face, so you knew that she knew, you know.

(Linda)

Humanistic values that upheld human autonomy and dignity provided a context in which loved ones were able to make decisions about the dying individual's care needs:

> She's got to have some dignity and some control over what's happening . . . they were quite happy to leave her to kind of set the pace, if you like . . . and of course we were letting her set the pace as well – 'cos, gosh, she was such an alive woman that I didn't want to remove all kind of power and dignity from her.
>
> (Pat)

Indeed, Pat was concerned to ensure that her dying aunt had the opportunity for freedom of movement even though she was unable to exercise this:

> And they said fine, they had a room for her but it had three steps – it had an ensuite area but it had three steps out of the room so she'd probably never leave the room, you know. And I just thought, 'No, that is not on', you know, she's got to have the opportunity to leave, even if you know it's in all likelihood she won't.
>
> (Pat)

Such humanistic values provided a context in which loved ones could evaluate the dying person's treatment by professionals. The ethnographies of Glaser and Strauss (1965) and Sudnow (1967) have shown that considerations of social status and worth may operate in relation to hospital care and treatment of dying people. By means of the concept of 'social death' they drew attention to the lack of social value given to dying people whose experience was institutionally shaped. A focus on treatment has been found to neglect the patient as a person, who instead becomes a passive recipient at the hands of the expert (Field, 1989: 147).

Linda expressed outrage at the way professionals refused to adapt the system to the needs of her mother and failed to treat her as a person:

> I do really think that Mammy had about 36 hours of extreme distress that she didn't need to have . . . and they wouldn't administer any of the drugs because they had this kind of practice that you could only give those drugs once, which isn't actually the way.
>
> (Linda)

> She kept being dressed in other people's clothes and I was cross about this . . . but the registrar was dreadful, she was just old school, you know, and she was saying, 'I don't really think they should have their own clothes, I think they should all have ponchos'.
>
> (Linda)

Adrian considered such depersonalising treatment to be dictated by ageism:

> I mean there is that feeling at the back of your head that if he'd been younger would they have pursued the aneurysm, 'cos aneurysms can be managed, I think ... But talking to the consultant, there really was this idea that – all he could say was, 'Don't vote for the government at the next election', which is just pathetic, and if this is all about finances and 65 is over the hill.
>
> (Adrian)

Depersonalising treatment was not confined to hospital settings, but was also associated with some nursing home regimes.

> You know a lot of the homes were just vile, they were just vile and they weren't Edith and they weren't what we wanted for Edith.
>
> (Pat)

For Brian, such treatment left him with the painful image of his grandmother having suffered an undeserved bad death:

> I was appalled at the way they were keeping my granny – it was a sad end to such a dignified life.
>
> (Brian)

Objectifying and depersonalising treatment could occur through professionals unwittingly making negative assumptions about the dying person's powers of comprehension and neglecting to keep them informed of their situation. For Stephen, the social death that resulted from such mistaken assumptions had a negative impact on his father's capacity to maintain sufficient hope to go on living. Such treatment was thus felt to have caused him to deteriorate more rapidly than he might otherwise have done:

> I was phoned up and told he's going to be taken into hospital for a few days just for the consultant to have a look at him, but I have this horrible feeling that they probably didn't say it to him and so, as I say, he was unaware of what was happening and that probably made him even more depressed.
>
> (Stephen)

Narrators conveyed how they negotiated their own sense of social value and empowerment through 'feeling needed' and 'having done all one could'.

Feeling needed

Feeling that one had something to offer in the situation depended upon the value of one's presence for the dying individual, other family members and for professionals. Tania illustrated how she provided a reliable, supportive, reassuring presence for her mother, which in turn was reassuring for her father and sister:

She kind of grabbed my hand and said, 'come in' . . . and she turned to me and said, 'What do you think?' – and kind of relied on what I was saying. . . and she would have enormous confidence in the fact that I would be there . . . and that put my dad and my sister's minds at rest.

(Tania)

Roy conveyed how his own carework experience enabled him to step in to support his parents by taking time off work to care for his dying father when his mother needed to go into hospital:

So I went down to look after Dad while he was at home while Mum was in hospital having the operation.

(Roy)

In contrast, Lynne conveyed the disempowering nature of her experience of trying to get her mother to eat, especially as the professionals refused to back her up in this:

. . . but they wouldn't – if she wouldn't eat anything they wouldn't make her. So basically I had to try and help her eat and in the end she just didn't – and of course they won't do anything – they won't do anything to help, so it was – I found that very difficult because she was so thin by that time anyway – and I just thought – oh, you know I wish at least – 'cos they explain to you that they're not going to get her better – she's not going to get better – that's it – but on the other hand you've just got this thing that you ought to feed her.

(Lynne)

In attempting to make sense of this experience she revealed how a discourse of individualism could be hard to reconcile with norms of social support and family relatedness.

Lynne suffered a further sense of disempowerment by becoming a target for her dying mother's anger and resentment at her situation:

So I just went every day and sat with her – and she got very cross – 'Oh, you're useless', 'What are you doing here?', 'You're just waiting for me to die' – and that was actually another thing, I just thought, 'This is what I'm doing, I'm sitting here waiting for her to die', and I felt terrible.

(Lynne)

Feeling needed could also depend on being heard and taken seriously by professionals:

The doctors came and explained things again . . . and my advice was letting Mum go, and, you know, they gave us a couple of things they could do – lighten the anaesthetic so that she might open her eyes – but I said, 'absolutely not, no',

> because she wouldn't know us, she could be frightened and there's no risk we'd
> ever take that she'd be frightened at any point . . .
>
> (Tania)

For Lorraine a sense of inclusion formed a memorable feature of her friend's dying due to the willingness of staff to provide an 'open awareness context' (Glaser and Strauss, 1965):

> So we'd known there were all the symptoms, then there were the tests, and
> then there was the confirmation, and then there was the fact that one could
> go and visit and talk reasonably openly about things and talk to the staff who
> would tell you what was going on, you know . . . fantastic – absolutely fantastic
> people. So I think there was an openness about it.
>
> (Lorraine)

Having done all one could

The sense of having acted in a way that felt beyond reproach and unhampered by feelings of regret or guilt provided a further source of empowerment for narrators. It encompassed a sense of validation and completion through having demonstrated to themselves as well as others that there was nothing more they could have done in the situation. It was conveyed by means of reflexive comments on those aspects of the experience to which they felt reconciled at this point in time, leaving them with positive feelings.

For both Sandra and Adrian, the sense of having achieved positive relationships with their dying loved ones, Sandra's grandmother and Adrian's father, provided a source of self-validation that eased their grief:

> But for me it was ok 'cos I knew I had been nice to her. So it was easier 'cos
> I didn't regret anything I'd said or done.
>
> (Sandra)

> That's made this easier for me because I think I've done – I had a really good
> relationship with him and I don't think – there's no regrets, I couldn't have done
> more to see him or be in touch.
>
> (Adrian)

For others a sense of validation and completion was achieved through having managed to be there at the end with other family members to share the dying person's final moments:

> I managed to get home when he died and we were all there, which I was really
> pleased about, and we got a call at, like, 7 in the morning saying we should come
> round as it's going to be soon. So it was, like, 11 o'clock that day or something

and all six of us were there, so it was really nice . . . I have two brothers and a sister and there's my mum, and my sister's boyfriend was there as well.

(Patrick)

I just couldn't have stood it if she'd died and I hadn't got back – but I did and I'm so pleased about that. And I have to say the wonderful thing was that there was my sister, her husband and my dad and all of us round the bed and we all stood and we talked to her.

(Tania)

In contrast, for Andy and Stephen, the feeling that they could have done more for their dying fathers was a source of continuing regret, guilt and self-doubt:

The thing I really regret most is I didn't visit him enough . . .

(Andy)

I did feel guilty for quite a while . . . and it did kind of – sometimes you could feel to yourself that this is actually quite convenient 'cos there's no way that you could be expected to participate very much in what was happening 'cos you're several hundred miles away on another lump of rock.

(Stephen)

This was the case for Lynne even though she did not know what more she could have done:

I feel guilty about all sorts of things so that sort of thing and the guilt of that, you know, when she was dying, if I could have done more – though I don't know what I could have done – so, yeah, I still get guilty feelings about her, really.

(Lynne)

For Lorraine, the realisation that for a second time she had not been able to 'hear' or engage with the dying person's awareness of impending death was a source of regret. Her own need to remain as positive and optimistic as possible, reinforced by the optimism of the professionals, took precedence over the needs and awareness of the dying person. Lorraine was thus resolved to do things differently next time:

I think also because of the last visit that I'd had with him he tried to tell me – and this is the second time this has happened and I'm never fucking doing this again. If somebody tells me they're dying, I'm going to fucking listen. You can't get over that because people know – I've done that twice. I deeply regret that. It's not a way to listen to people who are dying.

(Lorraine)

Social Support

that was nice for the whole family to be there with him.

(Patrick)

Achieving a good death was also linked to the extent to which it was a participatory experience that reaffirmed the social bond. Narrators conveyed how important it was that their loved one's dying was a social event that provided care, comfort and reassurance to those involved and supported their loved one's value as a person. Social and individual considerations did not necessarily conflict and were often mutually reinforcing. As indicated, the experience of death both threatens and therefore reinforces our sense of social solidarity. This was reflected in the concern shown by narrators to promote the dying person's continuing social inclusion in a way that promoted his or her unique contribution.

Accounts sometimes reflected the uneasy relationship between the social or relational and the medical, or the tension between the ideals of caring and the realities of clinical practice. This tension raises the issue of how to strike a balance between intervention and quality of life. It reflects a tension between 'doing' and 'being' or 'responding' in which the modernist, scientific focus on problems as having solutions rather then being part of the natural order of things tends to prioritise 'doing' (Hockey, 1990: 182–183). From a medical point of view dying becomes a problem to be solved or controlled rather then a state of being that, if embraced, can perhaps be given some meaning.

However, in spite of the cultural emphasis on 'doing', narratives revealed an alternative discourse in which simply 'being there' for another and responding according to the needs of the moment had validity. Though an inability to 'do' anything was often a source of distress and disempowerment, the value of care rather than control, or 'being there' as a loving presence was also acknowledged. Indeed this was something that was perceived to provide some continuity and normality in an otherwise exceptional situation. It also helped to preserve the dying person's social presence and individuality. Social support for the dying individual thus depended on the 'presence of close others' and the way this might serve to 'normalise' the situation.

The presence of close others

For Pat, simply 'being there' as a familiar presence could provide a safeguard against her dying aunt becoming depressed:

There wasn't a day that I wasn't in the home with her for one or two hours minimum, but more like three or four hours with her, and a lot of the time I'd just be sat there doing some work, you know, but I'd be with her 'cos I couldn't bear leaving her alone 'cos I could see her slipping into a depression.

(Pat)

For Fiona and Patrick 'being there' included making physical contact in the form of spontaneous gestures of care and affection such as 'stroking' and 'holding':

> . . . and I was just sat on the bed next to him holding his hand and stroking his hand.
>
> (Fiona)

> . . . we were just all sitting there watching him, holding him, whatever.
>
> (Patrick)

Diane and Fiona conveyed how being available to receive the dying individual's signals and gestures of contact represented a means of enabling him or her to become more comfortable:

> And I think if people are comfortable – it was the same with my husband's grandmother – she was very very agitated when I arrived and she spoke to me and as soon as she spoke to me and held my hand she just laid back on the pillow and got comfortable.
>
> (Diane)

> Every now and again his hand would go up as if he wanted something, but he wasn't able to tell you and my niece, she's the one that works in a care home and obviously used to working with people, was saying, 'Are you thirsty?' And I think he gave some sort of reaction or motion as if to say yes. So she went off and got, like, swabs, they're like sponges on sticks and she was dipping that in water and wiping his lips and things, trying to make him feel a bit more comfortable.
>
> (Fiona)

However, 'being there' could also be very distressing in terms of the helpless witnessing of the dying person's suffering:

> Oh, it was just awful being there . . . just those last ten minutes or so of his life – just tossing and turning and trying to – struggling.
>
> (Adrian)

Normalisation

Studies have demonstrated how we may react to the threat posed by death by invoking and adhering to the norms of everyday reality (Glaser and Strauss, 1965, 1967, 1971; Sudnow, 1967). Maintaining connections with familiar and valued aspects of our lives may also offer some security and comfort in what can be an extremely uncertain, disruptive and frightening process. It could be argued that this is especially important in the context of the way dying is 'sequestered', occurring in the institutional settings of hospitals, residential homes and hospices (Hockey,

1990). For this requires the dying individual to give up the familiarity of his or her own home and adapt to an unfamiliar environment. In this context the availability of close others could provide dying loved ones with a vital link to 'normal' life. Narratives revealed how this enabled them to remain in touch with those aspects of life that affirmed their uniqueness.

Such normalisation could involve recreating treasured moments from the past, such as the 'quiet time' that Linda used to enjoy and share with her mother at home, in which they would listen to the radio together:

> Yeah, well it was great because it just so happened that I got the kind of late afternoon slot and I ran into the town because I'd been trying to get this piece of music that I knew she would have liked. It was a compilation of a radio programme – I'd been looking for it for ages and just before I went into, you know, to have my time with her I ran out to the music store and it was there and it was like kind of pulsing at me on the shelf, do you know what I mean? So I bought it and I went in and we had that and we were really quiet and it was lovely and she was very peaceful.
>
> (Linda)

Sometimes humour served as a means of retaining some normality. Tania and Roy conveyed how this could provide a sensitive way of responding to the dying person's dependency without compromising his or her dignity:

> Oh, we used to joke. When I said I was staying up for longer she said, 'Oh, there's loads of sheets in the airing cupboard – when I've popped my clogs you know you'll never be short of sheets', – and you know it's always been that kind of thing.
>
> (Tania)

> It was like an emotional roller coaster 'cos your father's in so much pain and unable to help himself, and literally to pick him up out of the chair you'd sort of hands on your shoulder and you'd lift him up and, 'Shall we dance, Dad?' and, you know, try and make a joke of it, but you were dancing across to try and get him to the loo or to get him to the kitchen – just get him across the room for whatever reason he wanted.
>
> (Roy)

For Fiona, normality was maintained by responding receptively and sympathetically to her dying father's brave attempts to carry on as normal, as well as engaging in 'normal' conversation with other family members in a way that she felt that her father would have wanted:

> But he was sort of saying strange things, like he would say to me, 'Oh, we need some butter' and I was like, 'OK, I'll make sure we get the butter.' But obviously he's thinking practically like, you know, Fiona needs some tea, so we need to

get some butter in. So he's still thinking things like that . . . It made me smile. I was stroking his hand and he was talking about getting some butter in so . . .

(Fiona)

We were just trying to be as normal as possible really. We were talking to him and hoping he could hear us and saying who was there – I don't know, we were just trying to sort of be like the normal mad family that we are and just talk about everyday things and . . . I think it helped because it was just us trying to be normal rather than – and Dad had always said right from the beginning – and I know that people can't always do this – but he always said he doesn't want people crying . . .

(Fiona)

For Stephen the residential home setting was perceived as offering no possibility of maintaining a link with normal life:

'cos whilst it was a very nice old people's home where he ended up, the problem with old people's homes is that they're full of people waiting to die and, you know, it just has that atmosphere and just sort of decay and sort of waiting for death, really.

(Stephen)

Narrators conveyed that, within a framework of medicalised dying, their own need for support depended on 'having faith in the professionals'.

Having faith in the professionals

In spite of the privileging of individualism and personal authority, some narrators conveyed how they were only too ready to take support and reassurance from the presence of more expert authority. This reflects a valuing of professionalism in relation to an experience that is no longer common-place, but rather sequestered and privatised (Giddens, 1991; Mellor, 1993). People may thus feel less equipped to deal with death, so that the burden of one's own authority may be too great. In several accounts the presence of trusted professionals provided both the reassurance of knowing that their dying loved one was in good hands, as well as that of being able to share the burden of responsibility.

For Lynne, simply knowing that her mother was in the hands of nursing professionals as distinct from care-workers was reassuring:

I felt in some ways relieved because a) she hated where she was, b) she wasn't getting sufficient care – although the people – they're care workers they're not nurses – you know – and I thought perhaps she'd be more comfortable – she would actually have some proper medication to help relieve the pain.

(Lynne)

Furthermore, the care and understanding of professionals served to mitigate the distress of bearing the brunt of her mother's anger:

> So she would get very angry with me and I used to sort of go into the next room and bellow me eyes out – but they were very good – there were social workers who would come and talk to you and things – and the people there were wonderful.
>
> (Lynne)

Even though Tania knew that 'the writing was on the wall', having confidence that her mother was receiving the best possible treatment provided some consolation:

> So they had to take her back to theatre, and they were superb – they called in more and more senior doctors – they had a senior anaesthetist – 'cos they knew that Mum had not had a good week.
>
> (Tania)

However, for Adrian his father's treatment at the hands of the medical professionals left him with many unanswered questions, especially as the autopsy found his father to be '. . . in perfect working nick':

> There are lots of questions to be asked about his death . . . I mean there is that feeling at the back of your head that if he'd been younger would they have pursued the aneurysm, 'cos aneurysms can be managed, I think.
>
> (Adrian)

Awareness

> I think somebody should know when they've only got maybe a couple of months, because that's no time at all.
>
> (Fiona)

As a result of what has been termed the death awareness movement (see Glaser and Strauss, 1965; Kübler-Ross, 1970) contemporary Western, especially Anglophone, society now tends to construct open communication and awareness of death as desirable. This constitutes the reversal of a trend of non-disclosure in the 1950s and 1960s to which Glaser and Strauss were the first to draw attention, identifying a 'conspiracy of silence' and 'ritual drama of mutual pretence' in relation to the process of how patients come to realise the terminal nature of their condition. In exploring the dying trajectories of terminally ill cancer patients, they found that the experience of those who were dying was largely shaped by the need to resolve uncertainties. They found the nature of communication between professionals, patients and their families to be crucial to this, an 'open awareness context' being perceived to empower the dying and their loved ones to prepare for and make end-of-life decisions. Glaser and Strauss thus concluded that most patients and their families were looking for information and wanted to be aware of their dying condition. Such awareness has also been perceived to allow and facilitate 'anticipatory grief', thereby helping the dying person to prepare for his or her impending death, and bereaved people for bereavement (Fulton *et al.*, 1996).

However, other studies have drawn attention to the complexity of the issues surrounding awareness and disclosure. These include the uncertainties of terminal prognoses (Seymour, 2001; McNamara, 2001: 54–67) and the fact that giving information does not necessarily result in open awareness (Williams, 1989; McIntosh, 1977; Timmermans, 1994). Professionals are likely to face difficulties in managing the process of information-giving in the face of the emotional distress of patients and their families. Such communication may be further exacerbated by having only partial knowledge of the patient's wider history and social context (Seymour, 2001), as well as the need to take account of cultural diversity. Indeed the concept is insufficiently nuanced to encompass the emotional impact of disclosure and the extent to which someone is able to grasp the situation on the basis of information alone. Nor does it address the shifting and fluctuating nature of awareness (Timmermans, 1994; Young *et al.*, 1999).

It has been argued that the prioritising of openness reflects individualistic values and is less compatible with a context where the emphasis is on social support and protecting people from distress and upset, preserving relationships and keeping hope alive (Gordon and Paci, 1997; Mitchell, 1998). Thus there is a need to take account of and respect differing cultural norms and expectations, as well as styles of relating within the more informal, domestic sphere, rather than the institutional setting. Findings in relation to anticipatory grief are inconsistent and the present study would suggest that an awareness of impending death does not necessarily make dying or bereavement any easier. Rather, it tends to support the observation that such concepts can become prescriptive in that some bereaved individuals end up feeling that they ought to have been more prepared and managed their grief better. Indeed such a reified approach obscures individual agency and creativity in relation to the way that awareness may be negotiated to preserve relationships and identities. As a process rather than a fixed state, awareness may include both acknowledgement and denial of death as a fluctuating dimension of people's relationships and sense of identity.

The present study demonstrates how the concept of open awareness may be perceived as a mixed blessing, and not straightforward (McNamara, 2001: 80–91). This included the way the uncertainties of prognosis could render inappropriate any explicit talk of dying. Also, in practice, it could impose a burden as much as it could empower, since, it depended on the dying person staying conscious and coping with the physical, mental and emotional pain of his or her situation. Some accounts placed the emphasis on the positive aspects and others emphasised the burden of awareness. Yet, in either case, awareness was valued for the evidence it provided of the dying person's continuing 'presence' and 'availability' to them, so that the relationship could continue.

Dying narratives revealed how such awareness by the dying individual encompassed his or her 'continued mental capacity' in the face of the physical deterioration associated with dying, and an 'intuitive knowing' that in some cases was given more authority than any professional understanding.

Continued mental capacity

For Fiona, her dying father's continuing awareness enabled him to respond positively to his terminal prognosis and continue to live and round off his life in his own way:

> So he thought, 'Oh great, I've got two months', and so to him that seemed quite a long time – so obviously he could do what he wanted to do, you know, see people . . .

> (Fiona)

In Pat's case her dying aunt's continuing mental capacity alongside her physical disability allowed their relationship to continue and take on a more intimate quality:

> . . . and you know they were kind of gentle and sweet, very intimate moments in this time period.

> (Pat)

However Pat also drew attention to the paradox of remaining mentally alive whilst physically deteriorating and the suffering that this entailed:

> . . . and of course then her body was beginning to deteriorate more and more and she was getting bed sores and just shrinking in front of our eyes, you know physically, even though this mind was still as much as it was there five years, ten years previously, you know, a really contradictory state.

> (Pat)

Brian reflected on the suffering he felt that his dying grandmother endured by being aware of her loss of capacity and dependency and the impact this had on her quality of life:

> You could tell that she was getting frustrated with her body, you know, and that must be difficult as well, not being able to do things, and you could tell in her eyes, she's almost cursing in her eyes because she's getting angry because she can't do things – it must have been difficult for her and I don't think – a woman of such independence – I don't think she enjoyed being in the home anyway you know.

> (Brian)

For Stephen's father another source of suffering was other people failing to appreciate his continued awareness by making the assumption that his loss of speech meant the loss of his mental powers. Stephen's experience illustrates Glaser and Strauss's findings that non-disclosure can be isolating for the dying person:

> But I think he was more aware than he was able to let on and I think that's why he declined very suddenly when they took him to hospital, 'cos maybe they thought he wasn't as conscious as he was, so they probably just took him to hospital and didn't really explain anything to him. Whereas I think he must have realised, 'God, I must be really bad for them to take me to hospital', and, as I said, he just deteriorated really, really quickly.
>
> (Stephen)

Indeed, in cases where the dying person became mentally absent and unavailable to loved ones, this was experienced as highly distressing and disorientating, as reported by Pat:

> I mean she wasn't really there . . . you know, there'd be moments when she'd look at you and you'd suddenly see the look of recognition and then it would just be gone and then she'd be back in this just hellish place where she was literally screaming . . . and we couldn't, you know, comfort her at all – and it was just way too painful to watch what was going on.
>
> (Pat)

Such mental absence could be drug-induced, posing a dilemma for narrators who did not want their loved ones to suffer, whilst at the same time wanting them to stay present and available:

> Gradually as time went on she spent more time out of it basically . . . because she was on drugs which were obviously soporific anyway – morphine and things to relieve the pain . . . But I'd rather think of her prior to that, when she was shouting and ranting.
>
> (Lynne)

Intuitive knowing

Even where dying individuals had not been informed of the prognosis, they could still be invested with an awareness of what was going on. Such 'suspicion awareness' (Glaser and Strauss, 1965) was not necessarily perceived as negative but, as conveyed by Tania, provided evidence of the dying person's self-knowledge and continuing powers of comprehension:

> She knew – I'm convinced she knew all along . . . she – when she had to go back to theatre she said to me she knew things hadn't gone right.
>
> (Tania)

As promoted by Elizabeth Kübler-Ross, such awareness or 'right to be heard' (1975: 7) was to be respected and taken seriously as representing the true picture of the situation, regardless of what others, including the professionals, as conveyed by Lorraine in relation to her friend:

> She wanted to talk about her impending death, although in fairness I think there had been a lot of surgical optimism about her treatment . . . But at the same time if the shadow of death crosses somebody's heart we have to be open to it, 'cos people know.
>
> (Lorraine)

In several cases the dying person was perceived to demonstrate and communicate an intuitive knowing that his or her 'moment of death' was imminent, as conveyed by Diane in relation to her mother:

> . . . and then she suddenly looked across at me, I said something and she smiled – and with that it was almost as if she'd gone at that point . . .
>
> (Diane)

Fiona revealed how her father's intuitive knowing provided some consolation in relation to her mother's decision not to disclose the terminal nature of his illness:

> At that time she decided not to tell Dad, which whether that was the right decision or not I don't know. I probably think it's the wrong decision because I think somebody should know when they've only got maybe a couple of months because that's no time at all. But that's her decision and it's her husband, so you have to go with that – and at the same time I think, well, Dad's not stupid. He knows what's going on and he probably realises that there isn't much time anyway, so . . .
>
> (Fiona)

This example demonstrates how attitudes towards disclosure may differ within families. It also revealed how such differences could be resolved through norms about who had the final say.

Stephen conveyed how intuitive knowing could also be perceived as a burden, something that his father's failing capacities prevented him from articulating and sharing:

> I personally think that he was more aware of what was going on but he was unable to communicate but was very aware towards the end that my mother and stepmother were just running around all over the place for him, and I think that he himself would have preferred them just to get on with their lives.
>
> (Stephen)

Narrators conveyed how their own awareness played an important role in helping them to negotiate the disorderly and random movements of the dying process.

This depended on 'knowledge and information' and 'reading the signs' in relation to the dying person's prognosis.

Knowledge and information

Open communication and the 'sharing of knowledge' (Kübler-Ross, 1975: 32) between all involved, including professionals, was experienced by Lorraine as bringing people together and enhancing the quality of the experience. This formed a memorable feature of her friend's dying due to the willingness of staff to provide an open awareness context (Glaser and Strauss, 1965):

> I think because of the way that Anne and her partner were open about what was happening . . . when you bring people into a problem as opposed to trying to separate it, that makes it a different kind of quality of experience. So we'd known there were all the symptoms, then there were the tests, and then there was the confirmation, and then there was the fact that one could go and visit and talk reasonably openly about things and talk to the staff who would tell you what was going on, you know.
>
> (Lorraine)

In contrast, where significant others were not sufficiently put in the picture by professionals, this was experienced as disempowering. As already discussed, studies have drawn attention to the negative impact of non-disclosure and a 'closed awareness' context. Rather, 'the right to know' has been promoted as a means of allowing people to take ownership of their dying (Glaser and Strauss, 1965; McIntosh, 1977; Field, 1989). Thus, for Adrian, poor communication was experienced as having a negative impact on the family's decision-making and capacity to respond adequately to the situation. This extended to a sense of having been misled in relation to his father's prognosis:

> I was told he was poorly, but there was no indication whatsoever that he was going to die. Apparently that's the language they use in hospital speak and apparently everybody knows that in quotes, but I didn't and I'm sure a hell of a lot of other people don't. If I had known – if they'd said your dad's dying, then my other sister, who lives close by, could have been there.
>
> (Adrian)

For Tania, the awareness that resulted from knowing that her mother was unlikely to recover enabled her to make a point of spending time alone with her in order to say goodbye:

> I actually went to see Mum in intensive care and said all that I wanted to say. I asked for a bit of time on my own and I actually felt that I had said what I wanted to say that was important while I was there.
>
> (Tania)

For Pat, information was felt to be a means of gaining some control of an uncertain situation, especially in the case where this was her first direct experience of the death of a close relative:

> I kept pushing the nurses, the doctors, is she going to live longer – how long can she live because her body was just shrinking and you know to me it was like surely to god she's going to die soon? I just became obsessed with knowing, just trying to get some certainty over this very uncertain process.
>
> (Pat)

Where the individual had pre-existing medical knowledge, this was experienced as burdening as well as empowering. For Tania, whilst it allowed her to play a constructive role, it also faced her with the harsh reality of her mother's situation:

> . . . so the doctors would actually say an awful lot to me which I found incredibly hard to take.
>
> (Tania)

Reading the signs

The capacity to read the situation was dependent on the narrator's intimacy with the dying person and in some cases enabled them to be prepared for and respond positively to the person's final moments. This was movingly conveyed by Lynne in relation to her mother's enhanced presence at the point of death:

> I dunno, I think I realised that this was it, so I said 'I love you, Mum', and then she closed her eyes and her breathing slowed.
>
> (Lynne)

Reading the situation allowed Diane to ensure that her father was given the opportunity to say goodbye to his dying wife:

> But I felt from that moment when she was sat in the chair that was her saying, 'I'm on my way out' . . . So it was about kind of like making the situation as big as we could possibly make it for my dad – it was about making sure he had time to say goodbye to her.
>
> (Diane)

In Marianne's case, being at a distance and reliant on information from others, trusting her own reading of the situation, based on her knowledge of her mother, ensured that she acted on her own initiative:

> I was in London. And I think Dad didn't want to tell us how serious it was and I kept saying, 'Shall I come home?' – 'No, no, the doctors don't know what's

going on.' And eventually I said 'No, I wanna come home. I don't care what you say'.

(Marianne)

However, this could be double-edged, as in Fiona's case in which being able to read the signs brought home the critical nature of her father's condition:

So we went into see Dad because he wasn't well enough to travel, and he just didn't look very well at all and I think it was at that particular point I could – it really hit me – that he didn't have good colour in his face and he was very tired and didn't have any strength and rapidly losing weight and I think that was when I thought, 'OK, you know, he really is poorly now and it's not looking good'.

(Fiona)

For Linda, whilst her reading of the situation ensured that she was with her mother during her dying moments, it left her with a sense of regret that she had simply 'let her mother go', thus conveying an intersubjective experience of agency:

. . . and at the time it felt right, you know . . . but I have this really, really deep regret that I let her go, do you know what I mean?

(Linda)

Summary

This chapter has explored participants' narratives of dying to reveal the variety of ways in which they struggled to preserve and affirm their dying loved ones' personhood and their relationship with them in order to try to achieve a good death. This process was articulated through the themes of 'agency', 'social support' and 'awareness', producing a complex linking of the concepts of individuality and relationship. Agency extended beyond embodied action and could be experienced via, as well as through, one's relationship with another. Social support was directed towards preserving, reinforcing and respecting the dying individual's personhood. Awareness was not only dependent on the availability of information and communication, but had a more subtle, intuitive and relational dimension. It transcended bodily integrity and the capacity for speech. It was ambiguous in that it could entail increased suffering. Yet, on the whole, it was valued for providing evidence of the dying person's continuing social presence.

In conveying their experiences, narrators came up with humanised versions of the medical discourse, by means of which they personalised and socialised a medicalised dying. In some cases the dying person was represented as retaining ownership and social presence, something which served to redeem the experience for their loved ones. For others medicalisation was perceived to have separated dying individuals from their own deaths, neglecting both their personhood and social needs, so that ownership could not be recovered. Both the narrator and his or her dying loved one were then left with a sense of outrage and impotence. The narrator's sense of having maintained his or her relationship with the dying person to some extent mitigated the dehumanising impact of any loss of agency and ownership that had been suffered.

The emphasis on individuality and personhood meant that a good death could take many different forms. In some cases peacefulness was an essential feature, whereas in other cases the dying person's fighting spirit was celebrated. Character could assume greater significance than bodily integrity, which was not necessarily a prerequisite for personhood. Indeed the way dying individuals coped mentally and emotionally with the frustrations imposed by the loss of bodily functioning could serve to demonstrate courage, powers of resilience and therefore an enhancement of their personhood. Retaining mental clarity could be perceived as providing greater evidence of personhood than a functioning body. Continuing awareness and therefore personhood could be attributed where both verbal as well as physical functioning had deteriorated. Rather personhood was located in signals, gestures and facial expressions. However, under such circumstances this was experienced as only being apparent to narrators and lost on those who did not know the dying person.

Trying to achieve a good death was a joint project in which the role of narrators could be crucial in the face of others who did not know the dying person sufficiently. This placed them in the role of challenging the social exclusion that some dying individuals suffered. To this end their reassuring presence and understanding of their loved one's needs provided the person with a vital link to normality and those aspects of life that affirmed his or her personhood. In some cases it was the dying person who redeemed the situation by unexpectedly laying claim to his or her final moments and demonstrating personhood when all seemed lost. These cases revealed the unpredictable nature of the dying process, with unexpected twists and turns that could be for the better or for the worse.

Indeed, narratives of dying revealed how trying to achieve a good death entailed a complex negotiation of paradox and ambiguity which conveyed a more subtle, fluid and relational understanding of personhood than that based on embodied, performative agency. Such negotiation revealed the complex inter-relationship between individual agency and the social structure. As introduced in the previous chapter, it conveyed the hope and comfort which bereaved people may find in deceased loved ones' individuality and personhood to suggest a link between bereavement and palliative care. Such importance that my bereaved participants attached to their dying loved ones remaining fully present and fully themselves is further developed in the following chapter, which explores the significance of final moments for bereaved people's continuing relationships with their dead loved ones.

3 Dying moments

This chapter focuses on the way my participants conveyed their understandings and experiences of a loved one's dying moments. In so doing, it considers the sociological significance of an experience that has been largely overlooked in relation to the way that contemporary British society approaches death and bereavement. It illustrates how, in a medicalised context, which emphasises the biological nature of dying, for some of my participants their loved ones' dying moments represented gestures of leave-taking, in which elements lost to the medical discourse, but vital to making sense of mortality, were recovered. These elements include the spiritual, humanistic, social and emotional aspects of the dying experience. The way in which these moments were recalled emphasised the dying individual's continuing or recovered agency and personhood, in some cases to include an 'enhanced aliveness' at the point of death and the sacred, intimate, emotional and social nature of the occasion. Such emphasis points to a resurgence and reformulation of the 'sacred good death' and a contemporary Ars Moriendi, as Pat's words so poignantly represented:

> But she was lying there in bed, you know and her eyes were open, big smile on her face and she kind of gestured for me to come over and I sat down next to her and – I was weeping and she put her hand on my cheek and she just looked at me, wiped a tear away and died – like that – with her hand on my cheek you know.

> (Pat)

First, I place the concept of the 'moment of death' in its historical and theoretical context to highlight the impact of changing cultural scripts on people's individual experiences and understandings of death and bereavement. In tracing these changing cultural scripts I draw attention to a current gap in the sociological literature in relation to the social significance of deathbed moments as distinct from the dying trajectory as a whole (Glaser and Strauss, 1965; Strauss, 1971: 5–13). Then I explore the way the moment of death is represented in my participants' dying narratives. In this exploration I highlight both the exceptional nature of those cases in which a loved one's dying moments provided an opportunity for leave-taking, as well as the socially significant nature of dying moments more generally. Indeed, the importance of such moments is implicit in accounts of those who were not present or able to say goodbye. Extracts from participants' narratives illustrate how they sought to manage the gap between their hopes and expectations of the deathbed scene and the nature of what they actually experienced.

Building on the traditional Ars Moriendi and insights from a study of contemporary farewells by the dying (Kellehear and Lewin, 1988–1989), I explore the sociological significance of these contemporary deathbed accounts for their authors in making sense of bereavement. Highlighting the discourses that inform them, this exploration identifies their main features, and draws attention to their role in bereaved people's ongoing relationships with dead loved. It considers the relationship of a person's dying moments to his or her dying trajectory as a whole and what they reveal about current values, beliefs, hopes and fears about the transition from life to death. The implications of these values for contemporary understandings of what constitutes a good death are also considered.

Finally, I explore the implications of these 'moment of death' narratives for sociological theories of identity. This exploration addresses and contributes to the current debate on what it means to be a person or have 'personhood' in contemporary Western society, something which centres on the meaning of and relationship between 'self', 'agency' and 'embodiment'. To this end, it provides further evidence for a discourse that does not assume any straightforward definition of and relationship between these concepts (Hallam *et al.*, 1999). Rather, illustrations from my participant's narratives demonstrate the complex and diverse ways in which dying moments are understood. These understandings call into question approaches that fail to take account of the experience of mortality and theorise personhood and agency as not only dependent on embodiment, but on a narrow definition of embodied experience.

Background

Historical studies of the Middle Ages have revealed how a person's dying moments played a key role in turning the dying experience into a shared social event (Ariès, 1981; Hallam, 1996; Cressy, 1997; Houlbrooke, 1989; Bell, 2005). Traditionally the moment of death was considered a crucial preparation for the afterlife and invested with profound personal, social and religious significance. Thus life and death were inextricably linked, and most crucially by means of a person's dying moments. Indeed, dying was constructed as such a key transition in a person's life that a craft of dying was developed and enshrined in a body of Christian literature, the Ars Moriendi. This literature was based on eleven woodcuts depicting death as a series of deathbed temptations, with the dying person resisting these to take control of their own death and therefore destiny (Lock, 2002). In the fourteenth and fifteenth centuries texts were widely disseminated to provide detailed instructions for the benefit of both the dying and their helpers on the best way to prepare oneself for what was perceived as the moment of destiny when the soul would be released to its fate (Houlbrooke, 1989; O'Connor, 1966; Taylor, 1651, cited in Bell, 2005).

The popularity of these texts reflected a time of great political instability in Europe and an emerging concern about the fate of the individual soul in the light of people's increased sense of the fragility of life (Duclow, 2003).

By the eighteenth century a variety of patterns of deathbed behaviour had developed to reflect distinctive religious denominational emphases. Thus the Quakers emphasised a state of 'holy quietude and composure', whilst Methodists promoted 'joyful dying' (Houlbrooke, 1989). A more narrative rather than instructional style of deathbed literature emerged in the form of John Wesley's inclusion of exemplary deathbed scenes in the *Arminian* magazine. These represented an adaptation of the traditional Ars Moriendi as a means of constructing and promoting the Methodist doctrine of universal redemption for all repentants (Bell, 2005). Along with other organised religious groups, Wesley took advantage of the deregulation of publication laws following the collapse of the Licensing Act in 1695 to disseminate the Methodist vision of the good death through printed periodicals. Selected and edited narrative reconstructions of deathbed scenes provided a growing national readership not only with examples of how to die in exemplary fashion, but also reassurance in the form of tangible proof of the redemptive power of such 'holy deaths'. These accounts therefore downplayed the physical and biological aspects of dying in order to emphasise and focus the reader's attention on the spiritual significance of the event and the mental preparations being made by the dying person. Modelled on the death of Christ, alone and suffering on the cross, dying was a process that held the potential for regeneration through overcoming one's fear of the flesh (Lock, 2002).

The Ars Moriendi, whether in its original form or adapted to suit a particular religious denomination, instructed the dying person to make the following preparations: examine one's life, seek God's forgiveness, forgive others, confirm one's faith, place oneself into God's hands and ensure that one's family was provided for both materially and spiritually. Attended by family, friends, neighbours and ministers, the individual's dying moments formed an important social as well as individual occasion. A ritual drama, in the spirit of the original woodcuts was enacted at the site of the deathbed in which the living kept vigil and administered the last rites and the dying person engaged in battle between the forces of good and evil. The occasion was characterised by highly charged moments in which every word, deed, expression and gesture assumed meaning (Hallam, 1996; Cressy, 1997: 309; Bell, 2005). In such an atmosphere of heightened spirituality and emotionality, the experience could have a profound and memorable impact on survivors, as revealed in surviving accounts of deathbed experiences (Kastenbaum, 1989; Houlbrooke, 1989; Hallam *et al.*, 1999; Bell, 2005). As indicated, the accounts themselves served to reassure and inspire their readers.

In modern, Western societies, as Kastenbaum (1999) has observed, this once dominant concept has become destabilised by medical and technological advances and consequent changes in clinical practices. These have made it much more difficult to assume any actual definable moment of transition. Alongside this the dominant religious, philosophical and scientific beliefs that informed and supported traditional death-bed conduct have been increasingly questioned and marginalised. Today, aside from changing belief systems, the family's presence at the deathbed may not always be practical or possible. Even where death is expected, dying trajectories are uncertain, hospitals schedules may have to be negotiated and people may live at a distance.

Social science studies of contemporary death have tended to focus on the wider concept of dying trajectory rather than the narrow concept of moment of death, which only represents a small part of a very complex process (Bradbury, 1999; Masson, 2002; Lawton, 2000; Seymour, 2001). In a medicalised and individualised context dying has become the culmination or last stage of life rather than a transition to the next. One perspective that has gained prominence is that of Elisabeth Kübler-Ross, who has represented dying as the 'final stage of growth' (Kübler-Ross, 1975) in an attempt to challenge what has been perceived as the medicalised bad death. An individual's dying moments thus form the end point of either the medical bad death experience or what ought to be our final flowering (Kübler-Ross, 1975).

Thus, there would seem to be a significant gap in the academic literature in relation to the sociological significance of people's dying moments as distinct from the dying process as a whole. Yet, there is evidence to suggest that people do still attach significance to dying moments. Two studies, one by Kellehear and Lewin (1988–1989) and the other by Kastenbaum (1990) have explored people's hopes and expectations in relation to their deaths, both those who were terminally ill and those who were not, to discover the extent to which dying moments formed the focus of these. These studies have highlighted how people's hopes and expectations tend to be associated with the deathbed scene and the wish to be with and have the opportunity to say goodbye to loved ones. The study by Kellehear and Lewin, focuses on the sociological significance of dying people's farewells, highlighting the absence of research in this area (1988–1989).

More recently Donnelly *et al.* (2005) have drawn attention to the continuing importance of dying moments for family carers in relation to a study of the home deaths of patients who had been referred to a palliative care service in the mid-west of Ireland. The findings from this study reflect a palliative care setting and cultural context in which traditional and religious beliefs and practices still play significant roles. The express aim of the study was to bring clinical and conceptual attention to a practice that still held an important place in the local community. In contrast, as demonstrated in the following section, the narratives of dying moments that have been supplied by my participants have emerged from the interviews I conducted with a diverse sample of bereaved people whose loved ones died in a variety of ways and settings, in a more secular, fragmented, medicalised context. They were not interviewed specifically about the moment of death, but rather volunteered the information as part of the process of recounting and making sense of their experiences of losing a loved one.

For some of my participants, their dying loved one's final moments did not feature or made little impression, for a variety of reasons. In some cases the bereaved person was not present, in others there was no obviously definable 'moment', and in others certain medical decisions, such as whether or not to resuscitate them, took precedence. Some of my participants were not concerned, some even relieved that they had not been present during their loved one's dying moments, especially in cases where it was felt that their loved one had already died to them. Indeed it can no longer be assumed, as was once the case, that the final moments formed a central feature of the dying experience.

Yet, the significance of dying moments was clearly apparent in the way that my participants struggled to make sense of such moments in their absence, such as expressing disappointment and guilt at not having been present, and providing some form of justification. Thus Fiona struggled to reconcile herself with having taken a break from being at her father's hospital bedside. Yet she was able to take some consolation from being told by others that dying people may sometimes wait until close loved ones are not present:

> At the time I felt quite upset that I'd gone off for a stupid cup of tea and I should have been there with Dad . . . but people keep saying to me but maybe, 'cos you don't know how people are feeling when they're in this state and maybe he was more aware of who was around and maybe he didn't want to let go while I was there.
>
> (Fiona)

Fiona also found some reassurance in the fact that her father did not die alone but that other close family members were with him, thus reflecting the value attached to the social nature of dying moments:

> But he wasn't on his own, my brother-in-law was there with his niece and they were with him, holding his hand.
>
> (Fiona)

Marianne made sense of the way her mother died alone in a hospital bed through a discourse of individualism. This took the form of the perception that dying people may choose to slip away when loved ones are not present:

> Nobody was with her . . . But having said that, you hear so often that people die when they're by themselves, that some people really want to slip away.
>
> (Marianne)

Narrators who had not been present would sometimes reflect on the dying persons' final moments in the light of how they 'ought' to occur, for example, peacefully:

> Yeah — me and my wife saw him – he was in bed . . . in the bed next to the window so he could look out across the bay he so loved – his eyes were open when we got there – but he seemed very peaceful. And then he stopped breathing and I just watched his pulse disappear. I think Mum was quite . . . she

was really upset, but she was quite pleased that he died peacefully. His favourite Glenn Miller was playing at the time.

(Roy)

The significance attached to dying moments was also apparent in the way people imagined them, as conveyed by Michael:

So one imagines this sort of ideal deathbed scene, you know, it's time now, or whatever, and wanting to say something to each other.

(Michael)

However, such moments could also disappoint, even when people had taken pains to try to create an 'ideal' setting, as reported by Roy, whose father died at home with his family, his deathbed positioned so that he could look out to sea:

It was a body that was functioning – you know – breathing – that was the weirdest thing – watching the pulse just disappear – I thought 'God it's not like the films because he didn't have any last' – 'ooh, Roy, I want you to –', or anything like that.

(Roy)

Thus narrators tried to make sense of the discrepancy between the hopes and expectations attached to their loved ones' dying moments and the nature of their actual experience. However, for six people, dying moments stood out as highly memorable and treasured experiences. These moments were characterised by an intense recovery of aliveness and presence in which the dying person initiated contact with the narrator. This took the form of a gesture of intimacy and 'relatedness' that signalled their loved one's imminent leave-taking.

The final leave-taking

Kellehear and Lewin's study (1988–1989) provides a useful framework for considering the sociological significance of leave-taking. Though based on farewells that were contemplated or planned by dying people, findings from their study are relevant in emphasising three main sociological functions of farewell behaviour: *reaffirming social bonds, making dying a socially real and shared experience, and helping people to disengage.* The narratives of those I interviewed confirm, elaborate and extend these from the perspective of those left behind.

In relation to *reaffirming social bonds*, Kellehear and Lewin point out how farewells demonstrate how those involved value each other in a way that provides a lasting source of bonding and attachment for survivors. Farewells thus reaffirm past and present relationships and help ensure a place for dying people among the personal and social worlds of survivors. In relation to the six cases in question dying moments represented an important link between past and present, playing a key role in affirming and preserving the continuing bond between the living and the dead, as conveyed by Pat in relation to her aunt and Diane her mother:

I mean even now about five years later, thinking about it it's just an amazing moment of connection.

(Pat)

Yes I suppose it's kind of like all those little truisms and things that she'd said, they're still very very present after all this time.

(Diane)

In contrast to the medicalised accounts of loved ones' dying trajectories, these constructions conveyed a very different quality of experience, regardless of the setting in which dying occurred (Four were in hospital, one in a hospice and one at home). A romantic discourse evoked the intimate, social nature of the occasion and celebrated the profound and enduring power of the social bond, as expressed by Pat:

Yeah, I think it's that and it's just the power of that connection – and you can make – such a connection with someone and be literally with them as they die.

(Pat)

With regard to *making dying socially real* rather than remaining an individual, private, subjective experience, the act of leave-taking is a reciprocal one and thus a shared social experience. Also, in the process of recounting the experience to another, as in the interview situation, its social reality and significance are reaffirmed, reinforced and reassessed. Indeed, narratives revealed how dying moments took on a life of their own as distinct from other aspects of dying and as such were invested with special meaning, as expressed by Lynne:

And suddenly she woke up – and she had these very bright blue eyes and she sort of looked at me – 'cos I was sitting by her bed at that time and my sister was in the chair – and I said, 'Hello, Mum, you've woken up, you know, you're looking really good', you know the things that you say – and my sister joined in and, you know, just sort of said things like.

(Lynne)

Dying moments also *facilitated disengagement* for bereaved individuals. Kellehear and Lewin note how people prefer to be forewarned of sudden departure, especially in relation to dying. Indeed, accounts revealed how people found it difficult to cope with the uncertainty of dying, so that dying moments could actually provide relief from such uncertainty. In the words of Vivienne:

It was the not knowing what was going on that really upset me . . . almost more than the death itself.

(Vivienne).

Accounts conveyed the paradoxical nature of such disengagement in view of the enhanced connection experienced by narrators with their loved ones at the very point at which leave-taking occurred. Thus recounting these moments was bittersweet, evoking both pleasure and sadness as they negotiated their loved one's simultaneous presence and absence. For these constructions, in emphasising the dying person's enhanced presence at the same time underlined his or her absence, as reported by Adrian in relation to his father:

> And he was clearly in a lot of pain and disorientated but he was conscious enough to lean over and give me a hug, which was an amazing thing . . . I just kept touching him and he just kept getting colder and I didn't want him to go . . .
>
> (Adrian)

A contemporary 'Ars Moriendi'

As indicated, in contrast to the medicalised language narrators used to convey their loved ones' dying trajectories, these narratives conveyed a very different quality of experience, regardless of the setting in which dying occurred. A discourse of romanticism evoked the dramatic, highly charged, intimate and memorable nature of the occasion, which bore witness to the enduring nature of personhood and the social bond, as Pat so vividly recalled:

> That was just an amazing moment – I mean, it was just absolutely amazing because, as I say, she died looking straight into my eyes with her hands on my cheek and I knew she knew it was me and I knew it was just that moment of recognition – of connection, absolutely non-verbal you know incredible . . . and so you know we kind of said our goodbyes at that point.
>
> (Pat)

In so doing they also celebrated the power of the 'individual' to *overcome a medicalised social order* for which death represents a failure. For these examples of individualised dying or dying in one's own characteristic way were far from medical failures but rather served to affirm and preserve the dying individual's personhood, agency and social presence.

A sacred or 'set apart' quality was in evidence, though one that was defined by the spontaneous and unexpected nature of these moments rather than adherence to a prescribed form. They were not subject to the planning and preparation that characterised the historical Ars Moriendi. They nonetheless represented examples of 'dying well', the dying person taking their final leave whilst conscious and interactive, with a calm acceptance of death. The significance of the dying person's demeanour now lay in its demonstration of personhood and relatedness rather than the capacity to perform the necessary preparations for the soul's impending journey. Thus these contemporary moments of death represented affirmations of *this* life rather than preparations for the *next*, celebrations of the life that had been lived and would continue to live on for those left behind.

The role of loved ones was not that of ensuring that the dying individual was sufficiently prepared to meet his or her maker, but rather to support the individual to die as far as possible in his or her own way. This was a role that involved negotiating the disintegrative aspects of the dying process and was fraught with setbacks. For, in all cases dying was experienced as full of twists and turns, encompassing much pain, disruption and uncertainty. Indeed, these final moments all arose out of dying trajectories that were experienced as bad, that is, as lingering, painful, unpredictable and defeating for both parties, as in the case of Linda's dying mother:

> She was in a lot of distress, physical distress, really bad physical distress . . .
>
> (Linda)

These contemporary deathbed scenes were not represented as occasions of preparation but rather of waiting, with those in attendance often feeling helpless, though sometimes discovering unexpected resources on which to draw. There was no script but rather people often felt they were being faced with an unknown quantity:

> She was very distressed and we couldn't, you know, comfort her at all, and the only thing – 'cos I was getting emotionally desperate, I didn't want to stay, didn't want to go . . . and the only thing I could think – she loved the Miss Read books . . . so I grabbed one of them off the shelf and started reading to her.
>
> (Pat)

Indeed, the dying person's unconsciousness or confusion could render the other feeling that their loved one was already lost to them. Such gestures of intense presence and contact during dying moments were therefore experienced as a gift, leaving people with a sense of having recovered their loved ones. This was something that remained with them as a source of validation and reassurance. They could therefore be perceived as restorative, in a context in which personhood and sociality were under threat:

> Had to go out for a cigarette . . . went back in and she was still, absolutely still and sitting there kind of looking at me with a big smile on her face . . .
>
> (Pat)

> . . . but then my gran seemed to make a big recovery . . . and was chatting away and I sent her a postcard from when I'd been in Ghana so she was asking about that so she obviously remembered who I was.
>
> (Vivienne)

In some cases the nature of this recovery was perceived as being characteristic of the life that had been lived (Masson, 2002; Sandman, 2005). Pat's aunt recovered her characteristic mental alertness and Adrian's father displayed his characteristic fighting spirit. For others there was a sense of the dying person becoming 'more of themselves' or demonstrating an extended self-hood. Thus Vivienne's grandmother assumed an uncharacteristic clarity, and Lynne's mother, an uncharacteristic acceptance, following an angry and defiant dying. In both cases these represented qualities that the bereaved individual had noticed before but were less in keeping with more dominant characteristics.

Within this context of an affirmation of personhood and sociality, which could include demonstrating qualities that were previously lacking or less apparent, individuals constructed a variety of meanings from the experience. These included a profound and enduring sense of connection with the deceased, coming to know the person more fully, being shown that death was not to be feared, confirmation that one had got it right for the dying individual, feeling recognised and acknowledged, feeling privileged to have witnessed a loved one's final moments, and having been able to say goodbye:

> Well I know the moment he died, you know I was there and it was 12.30 . . . Yes I feel very privileged to have been there.
>
> (Adrian)

Such meanings did not negate or obscure but rather were juxtaposed with the more distressing, demoralising aspects of the dying experience to produce highly ambivalent constructions. They revealed the limitations of linear stage-model approaches to conceptualising the dying trajectory by demonstrating a more paradoxical and contingent view of the way people die:

> Although the final moment was easy and beautiful, it wasn't an easy death.
>
> (Pat)

Yet an appreciation of the 'ease' and 'beauty' of these deaths was as much a function of their defeating as their redeeming aspects. By reflecting the vulnerability and frailty of the human condition they also affirmed the transcendental value placed on the unique individual life and the intimate relationships between individuals. Together with the unanticipated and restorative nature of their occurrence, these final moments represented the triumph of the human spirit over routine, impersonal medical settings in which dying mainly took place. Their paradoxical nature suggests a more complex relationship between individual agency and society's structures (Hallam *et al.*, 1999) than that represented by theories that prioritise either the one or the other. They call into question theories of identity that are predicated on a fully functioning body.

Social identity and embodiment

In considering the sociological significance of dying moments as gestures of leave-taking, I have noted how this was a function of the relationship between the dying person and his or her loved one. What transformed dying moments into significant personal and social events was their reciprocal and shared nature (Kellehear and Lewin, 1988–1989). As such they represented an intersubjective expression of personhood and agency that was mutually reinforcing and empowering. Final moments reflected the dying person's continuing social presence in survivors' ongoing lives to provide further evidence of the way that personhood and agency does not necessarily depend on embodiment.

In recounting their loved ones dying moments, narrators conveyed a recovery of their agency that not only shaped these moments, but had a profound and continuing impact on their experience after loved ones had died. They conveyed how dying persons took charge of their own dying and leave-taking in a way that took narrators by surprise, yet the impact of which was dependent upon their mutual responsiveness. Also, the dying person was perceived to recover his or her characteristic selfhood after suffering considerable bodily deterioration, in some cases becoming more than themselves, to assume an enhanced aliveness, presence and relatedness to loved ones. Thus, the dying person's social presence and exercise of agency could neither be linked to a performative body nor separated from the responses of loved ones. Rather these dying moments were co-constructed between the two parties, to represent an expression of selfhood that was based on 'inter-personal engagement' (Csordas, 1994: 9, cited in Hallam *et al.,* 1999: 7).

Dying moments thus brought into sharp focus how the self was constructed through social interaction and intimately linked to the selves of others. They represented a more fluid, relational and intersubjective expression of agency and personhood than can be encompassed by the concept of a unitary, bounded, embodied, performative selfhood (Battersby, 1993; Rose, 1996; Hallam *et al.,* 1999; Lawton, 2000). They revealed how the experience of mortality demands a more complex and nuanced conception of being in a body that goes beyond performance to encompass the multiplicity of embodied experience (Lawton, 2000). These narratives also conveyed how personhood and agency may transcend the body itself to encompass the continuing social presence of those who have died in the lives of those they leave behind (see Part Two).

Summary

This chapter has revealed the complexity of the way my participants articulated their experiences of their loved ones' dying moments, which included the following range of features: occasions for leave-taking, unanticipated 'recovery' and changed status to enhanced aliveness, reclaiming one's dying from medicalisation, celebrating and preserving personhood and affirming continuing bonds. However, these positive features in no way obscured the more painful and distressing aspects of the dying process. The ambivalent and nuanced picture these narratives have revealed of the way people may die today and the impact their dying may have on the loved ones they leave behind poses a challenge to psychological stage theories of dying and grieving.

These narratives revealed the limitations of the medical model, in which the emphasis on treatment and cure inevitably represents death as failure. In contrast to the impersonal and distancing language that participants sometimes used to convey the medical management of the dying process, when recounting their loved ones' final moments, they represented these as sacred, memorable, dramatic, emotional and social events. Such representations, far from conveying death as failure, revealed profound and treasured experiences in which dying people demonstrated their freedom from the medicalised social order.

Whilst these vivid, special and memorable moments represented a variety of individual meanings and resources for their narrators, in all cases they provided solace and reassurance that deceased loved ones would remain part of their ongoing lives. Recollecting and sharing them with me thus formed part of the process by which my participants forged continuing bonds with their deceased loved ones. They revealed how these bonds affirmed the 'transcendental' value placed on the unique individual life and the intimate relationships between individuals. They conveyed how being uniquely oneself encompassed both the strength and vulnerability of the human condition.

These moment of death narratives pose a challenge to sociological theories of identity that, by failing to take account of the experience of mortality, are based on an oversimplified linking of personhood and agency with a performative body (Hallam *et al.*, 1999). By taking the body's agency as a starting point, such an approach neglects the experiences of dying and bereaved people. The way my participants conveyed their loved ones' dying moments both confirm and extend findings from recent studies, which demonstrate how people's relationships with their bodies, with others and with the wider social world are considerably more complex than sociological theory has tended to convey (Hallam *et al.*, 1999; Lawton, 2000).

Part Two

Absence and presence

After recounting their experiences of the way loved ones died, my participants would turn their attention to the impact of the death itself. In attempting to make sense of this, they conveyed how death was neither final nor incontrovertible to produce the closely intertwined 'narratives of loss' and 'narratives of rediscovery'. As already discussed, the dominant paradigm of grief in academic and professional discourse has seen a shift from one that emphasised relinquishing ties to one that promotes 'continuing bonds' with dead loved ones. The narratives of those I interviewed revealed how such bonds formed a central aspect of grieving, representing not only an 'inner', 'psychological' dynamic, but a profoundly social experience. In other words, they may serve not only the health and well-being of the living, but also reflect the strength and enduring power of the social bond that continues beyond the life–death boundary. In so doing, they challenge the modernist separation between the living and the dead and definitions of society in which its dead members are excluded (Hallam *et al.*, 1999; Howarth, 2000, 2007b).

In this second part of the book I draw attention to the way continuing bonds are not grounded in traditional religious or cultural structures but tend to be constructed in individualised ways. Indeed, narrators sometimes conveyed embarrassment about, or sought to justify, the continuing significance of dead loved ones in their lives, wondering if they ought to have 'moved on' or 'got over it' by now, according to conventional psychological wisdom. Some were surprised by the strength of their feelings of attachment to dead loved ones that emerged whilst being interviewed:

It's quite weird to realise you're more upset than you thought.

(Vivienne)

Indeed my own appreciation of the key role played by the deceased's continuing presence in the experience of bereavement also took the form of a surprise discovery. I have already described how, as interviewing progressed and accounts were scrutinised, I became struck by the way the characters of those who had died seemed to impress themselves upon me in a very poignant way (see introduction to Part One). This often included the use of the present tense so that the dead were represented as still around, whilst at the same time being sadly missed. Thus a sense of the deceased person's presence was mixed with an equally powerful sense of his or her loss:

> I suppose it's contemplating the love you had for that person and the fact that you can't physically access them again. So there's the sadness there, but there's the joy, if you like, of being able to remember all these other things – so it's like two emotions, isn't it? I think it's also thinking about how much worse off you'd be if you hadn't known them. I don't think you can have it any other way – you can't think about the good things without remembering that they've gone. But that's not a reason for not thinking about the good things. It's joy and sadness mixed together
>
> (Diane)

It was as though the interview had created a space for the deceased person, which was characterised by a dichotomy of presence and absence (Francis *et al.*, 2001; Moss and Moss, 2001). The more I listened to what participants were saying the more I realised the extent to which they were introducing me to that person, putting particular emphasis on his or her idiosyncrasies. As already described, the impact on me was to really hold my attention in a way that created a feeling of his or her presence between us. Yet it occurred so naturally that at first I took it for granted. However, such an experience of presence could only have emerged out of an approach that allowed me to enter my participants' worlds through encouraging them to tell their stories (see Introduction). For the process of constructing a narrative around the death of a loved one inevitably served to recreate and perpetuate that person's identity (Walter, 1996, 1999).

Walter has drawn attention to the value of 'conversational remembering', especially with others who knew the deceased person, as a means of constructing a memory of him or her with which it is comfortable to live (1996). My interview conversations with bereaved participants also pointed to the advantages of talking to someone who did not know the person. Indeed it could be argued that where knowledge is shared people are more likely to gloss over details, make assumptions and take certain aspects for granted. If the other person 'knows' then we may simply take comfort in a sense of shared understanding. However, sharing one's memories with another who did not know the person required a detailed recollection.

One of my participants made this very point, that the interview encouraged her to recall details that she would normally have omitted as being 'common knowledge'. Also I was struck by the way participants often seemed concerned with accuracy and would question and revise what they said in the light of further reflection. Where I responded with an assumption or reflection of my own, they were quick to correct me where this did not accurately reflect their experience. It was as though my lack of knowledge acted as a stimulus to their 'remembering', and that such remembering involved a search for the 'right words' to convey their understanding.

For some people the interview process was experienced as a rediscovery of the deceased, or even a recovery of something that the dying process in some cases seemed to have severely destabilised. Such rediscovery included a realisation that the deceased person still continued to influence and exercise agency in their lives:

I've covered more than I thought I would – it's probably helped me even more than – I mean the fact that I didn't even think of how dignified she was – that struck me more than anything.

(Brian)

This was the case even where the survivor had so far made no other attempt to actively sustain the deceased person's continuing presence and was regardless of age, gender, ethnicity, length of bereavement, the nature of the relationship or manner of death. Such rediscovery was reflected not only in the interview experience but in the narrative details which conveyed the variety of ways in which the dead continued to occupy spaces in the lives of the living. Yet such rediscovery was also a poignant reminder of absence and was inextricably linked to this sad fact.

Such observations eventually brought me to realise that all my participants were engaged in trying to construct a space in their lives for dead loved ones that allowed those left behind to go on living in the everyday world. This process of construction included negotiating the painful paradox of presence and absence, such negotiation being characterised by a need to honour the deceased's memory or 'to care about what happens to them as if they were not dead', and 'as if we had been given a second chance' (Kellehear, 2000: 169–173). As illustrated in Chapter 6, the way participants conveyed their continuing bonds revealed a discourse of care and protectiveness, as reflected in the concern shown to respect and cherish a loved one's memory:

It was so important to me to be able to talk about Mum and commemorate her life. To get people who hadn't known her to understand what she was like, what was good about her.

(Marianne)

It was further reflected in my own concern to protect and respect my participants' narratives.

Such continuing engagement with dead loved ones was represented and conveyed in an extraordinary range of ways. Some participants were more comfortable than others with the challenge this posed to dominant medical and psychological models, something that may reflect social factors such as age and gender. However, the way that it formed a central feature of all accounts suggests that the experience of bereavement may cut across and, indeed, demonstrate the socially constructed nature of such categories. By taking us into the world we share with the dead rather than the living, bereavement creates a liminal state of being 'betwixt and between', which, as Turner has identified (1969: 94), is characterised by a loosening of the

usual conventions and categories to render the social order more fluid and transformative.

The continuing bonds discourse has been taken to represent an inner relationship
in a way that separates the social and psychological (see e.g. Field, 2006; Schut *et
al.*, 2006). Yet the concepts of 'intrapsychic' and 'internal world' are metaphors
that form part of the psychological discourse of bereavement (Árnason, 2000;
Anderson, 2001). So although 'links to the dead can even be confined to the
privatised imaginations and memories of the bereaved' (Hallam and Hockey, 2001:
93) these internally located spaces are still inherently social (Hockey, 2002).
Indeed, as illustrated in Chapter 6, my conversations with bereaved individuals
demonstrated the way they negotiated competing discourses, one which 'psycho-
logised' the experience and the other that allowed it to be 'real' (Bennett and
Bennett, 2000).

These conversations demonstrated how the process of articulating and sharing
one's experience with others could affirm, reinforce and allow one to reassess its
social reality and significance (Walter, 1996). Talking to me about deceased loved
ones would trigger moments of realisation for narrators, who often exclaimed 'I'd
never thought of that before'. Some reported how the decision to be interviewed
had prompted them to talk about the person to someone prior to the interview. In
one case the interview clearly served as a means of reconnecting with the deceased
person, the transcript serving as a memento to ensure preservation of the person's
memory. In other words the bereaved individuals from this particular sample were
clearly relying on an interpersonal or interactive process to reconstruct their
relationships with dead loved ones. Also, such reconstructions were largely social
in nature. Even where this involved dreaming about the deceased, recounting it to
another served to legitimise and increase its significance.

In addition to locating the experience of continuing bonds in the internal world
of the bereaved person there has been a tendency to take a prescriptive approach
in which such bonds are treated as the means by which he or she may achieve a
healthy resolution of grief. As noted by Klass (2006), such an emphasis reflects how
the continuing bonds paradigm arose out of the discovery that what had been
pathologised could actually form part of healthy adjustment. However, it runs the
risk of simply replacing one norm of 'letting go' with another norm of 'keeping
hold', rather than focusing on the way people make sense of their worlds through
negotiating competing discourses according to their own personal agendas.

By taking a sociological perspective that is grounded in people's own understandings of their experience, then it becomes possible to ask questions such as
'how do people treat their dead?' and 'what role do the dead play in the lives of
the living?' This approach has drawn attention to the complex and social nature of
grief, the extent to which the dead may remain part of the lives of the living and
the variety of meanings people may give to such experience. In relation to my own
study, participants' narratives have contributed fresh insight into how such
continuing presence can be experienced as mutually beneficial, the survivors
having a sense of caring for deceased loved ones in various ways, such as: placing
objects in the coffin to ensure the person does not become lonely; visiting the

grave to provide comfort and companionship to him or her; conducting a continuing dialogue with the deceased person to try and resolve difference; pursuing an activity associated with the deceased person with a sense that he or she would feel validated by this; standing in for the deceased in their absence; keeping the deceased person's memory alive in a way that resonates with what they would have wanted; creating a funeral in the person's image; tending the grave site; talking to others about the person to ensure that he or she has not been misconstrued.

The following four chapters explore how my participants experienced, negotiated and made sense of the impact of a loved one's death on their personal and social worlds through constructing narratives of loss and rediscovery. These closely intertwined narratives reveal how people were engaged in locating and sustaining deceased loved ones in their ongoing lives, something which included carrying on without them whilst at the same time maintaining them as a presence in their everyday worlds. How they negotiated this fundamental paradox of absence and presence is identified by means of the following themes: defining the loss; materialising loss; rediscovering presence; locating and sustaining presence. Chapter 4 draws attention to the way participants sought to define just what it was they felt they had lost, and how this process revealed the inherently social nature of loss. Chapter 5 explores how participants materialised their loss through both public and private, formal and informal objects and activities that resonated with their dead loved ones' memories, and how such materialised absence evoked presence. Chapter 6 focuses on the more restorative dimension of grief to explore the nature and meaning of continuing bonds for those left behind. Chapter 7 considers the variety of ways in which narrators sought to locate and sustain the presence of dead loved ones in their ongoing lives.

4 Defining the loss

In the chapters comprising Part One of this book I have explored how bereaved people negotiated the precarious nature of personhood in the face of the physical and mental deterioration of the dying process. This chapter demonstrates how such negotiation characterised people's experiences of the immediate aftermath of death. Thus my participants constructed narratives of loss that revealed a preoccupation with defining just what it was they felt they had lost. Drawing upon a variety of metaphors and images, they demonstrated how memory, emotion and imagination combine to structure and shape experience (Hallam and Hockey, 2001: 3). I had expected people to talk in terms of private and individual grief reactions and symptoms, yet their accounts conveyed the inherently social nature of grief. As with their dying narratives, they focused on their day-to-day experiences of loss, in which their own responses were intimately linked to their encounters with the people, places, objects and activities that this encompassed. Furthermore, they placed the deceased at centre stage, as conveyed by Vivienne:

> But your reactions are probably more complex than just crying, 'cos you – I dunno, you think more about – you think about their lives or whatever . . .
>
> (Vivienne)

Psychological models of grief have emphasised the importance of acknow-ledging and facing the loss as a prerequisite for letting go, leaving the deceased behind and moving on in life to form new attachments (Freud, 1917; Bowlby, 1980; Raphael, 1984). This approach constructs grief as a task, or work that serves the health of the grieving individual and reflects a discourse of self-control and self-responsibility. However, the narratives of those I interviewed conveyed how 'You do not work through bereavement. It works through you' (Ironside, 1996: xvii). Acknowledging and defining their loss enabled people to give shape and meaning to the experience. Such meaning was linked to identifying and appreciating just who the deceased person was and what he or she meant, and would continue to mean to them. It formed part of a process of affirming and preserving the personhood of dead loved ones, thus demonstrating how social being does not necessarily come to an end with death. The way people negotiated competing discourses, such as 'letting go' and 'keeping hold', demonstrated the complex and reflexive relationship between individual and social representations of grief. It revealed the complexity of human attachment and how letting go and keeping hold were not necessarily mutually exclusive.

This chapter examines these narratives of loss and how my participants tried to make sense of the experience of losing someone who once formed an integral part of their lives. This process of meaning-making revealed how they grappled with the shocking and disturbing absence of what had been so reassuringly present to produce definitions of loss that were both highly individualised and had features in common. Such defining activity formed part of a dynamic, ongoing process of reflection in which the deceased was remembered, recovered and rediscovered. Indeed, it was the experience of loss that provided the impetus to such remembering (Hallam and Hockey, 2001). Thus absence was intimately linked to presence rather than representing part of a progressive coming to terms with bereavement, as promoted by stage theories. Moreover, whilst the experience of loss was reported to have been felt most keenly in the immediate aftermath of death, it could also be evoked in all its intensity after a considerable period of time.

Experiencing loss has been distinguished from 'expressing' loss by means of the concepts of grief and mourning, the former being identified as an internal, individual state or process and the latter as external, socially prescribed practices (Katz, 2001: 6). This has produced a conceptual and disciplinary split in which grief, or the private, internal, emotional state, has become the province of psychology, and mourning, or outer observable behaviour, that of anthropology. However, attention has been drawn to the way such a division into what people 'feel' and what people 'do' obscures the socially constructed nature of what we think and feel as much as how we behave (Lofland, 1985; Bradbury, 1999; Hockey, 2001).

My conversations with bereaved individuals revealed how such a distinction between 'feeling' and 'doing' did not reflect the way people talked about the experience of bereavement. Rather, their narratives of loss encompassed thoughts, feelings, actions, interactions and events to form vividly descriptive and moving stories. The terms 'grief' and 'mourning' were rarely used and when they were they were used interchangeably. In a couple of cases in which individuals did make reference to the 'grief process', this was as a technical term that appeared to mean little to them. Also these conversations were as much expressions of loss as any socially prescribed practice, demonstrating the active, constructive nature of discursive activity. I have already described (see Introduction) how their impact on me was a profound sense of having entered a very particular social domain. This domain was characterised by diverse, contradictory and contingent constructions of experience, not by fixed, consistent or logical models, as expressed by Diane:

All the images you get – like on the TV – are about absolute sadness, and yes, there's sadness but there's also reflection and other things like that. It's definitely more complicated than just tears.

(Diane)

These conversations conveyed how the experience of loss is intimately linked to the extent to which we are interactive, social beings. They revealed how our sense of self is dependent on our relationships with others, so that when a loved one dies, our sense of who we are as a person is under threat. As Bradbury has discussed (1999), we lose not only someone we care about, but also that part of ourselves that was constructed through our relationship with that person. The social nature of grief thus lies as much in the impact on our sense of selfhood as it does in public and private mourning practices (Bradbury, 1999: 176). Indeed, narrators represented their experience of loss through both these dimensions. They talked about losing specific aspects of the self as well as the deceased person. They talked about the impact of loss on their relationship with others, both those who knew their deceased loved ones and those who did not. They referred to certain beliefs and values that helped them to make sense of their loss. They materialised their loss through objects and practices or 'material culture', to include more formalised ritual as well as the ordinary, everyday business of living.

These themes are explored in a way which aims to capture the complexity, diversity and contingency of the way people negotiated their loss as well as shared features. This chapter focuses on the way bereaved individuals experienced and defined their loss with reference to the deceased person, the self, others and beliefs and values, whilst the following chapter examines the way people materialised their loss.

The deceased person

Though narrators used expressions of 'missing' the deceased person and experiencing a 'gap' in their lives, they would not stop there but go on to define and, indeed, evoke such 'absence'. Some of my participants drew attention to the 'quality' of their loved one's absence, something which Linda, in referring to her mother, conveyed as being tangible:

> ... but you know I really feel her absence – a real silence you know ...
>
> (Linda)

Others emphasised the 'extent' of their loved one's absence, Adrian drawing attention to the way the experience of losing his father reflected the impressive nature of his presence:

> He was one of those characters, sort of very charismatic and very ... yeah, I mean just quite an extraordinary person. So I mean it's a great loss really 'cos these big characters when they disappear it just – it leaves – any death leaves a gap but he was quite a character.
>
> (Adrian)

For Andy, the extent of his father's absence was conveyed with reference to the multiple roles he played in his son's life:

It's like I've lost so many roles. I've lost the role of a father, the role of a friend. And my dad was like a brother, so I've lost the role of a brother. I feel like I've lost so many different roles – like I feel as though I've lost about six different people all in one person.

(Andy)

Narrators took pains to try to capture specific characteristics of their deceased loved ones that they felt they had lost, something which drew attention to the uniqueness and value of his or her life and its irreplaceable nature. Andy conveyed how much he missed his father's easygoing, jovial nature:

Like, my dad used to make me laugh – I still have a laugh with my mum but not as much as I used to with my dad . . . Like, as much as I love my mum I just want him back. My dad used to do things differently to how my mum does. My dad was a lot calmer person and Mum tends to get worked up really easily with things.

(Andy)

For Adrian it was his father's physical presence that was sorely missed:

Occasionally I get these awful sort of realisations that in this whole vast universe, this wide vast expanse of – I will never be able to physically give my dad a hug again and that really brings it home – just the enormity of the cosmos and everything and yet the one thing that I would really like to do is not available to me . . . and that hurts.

(Adrian)

Sandra and Ivan conveyed how such characteristics reflected the nature of their relationships with their loved ones, such as shared jokes and chats:

Sometimes when I remember all our jokes I'll feel really upset because I'll want that back and I can't have it . . . There were a lot of long running jokes between us and I can't do those jokes anymore – and they meant a lot to me.

(Sandra)

I miss having chats with Dad and knowing that he's there – yeah, I do – I do. I would like him to be sitting in his little bungalow puffing on his pipe – I really would – yeah, – yeah that does make me sad.

(Ivan)

For some, the disorientating impact of losing a loved one was reflected in the way they felt they had lost a major reference point that provided a source of validation and support in their lives. For Tania, such loss reflected the closeness that she and her mother had shared:

She's the person closest to me that's gone and the others, as much as I like my sister and my dad, it's not the same understanding and it won't be.

(Tania)

For Linda, the loss of her mother left her feeling adrift in her life, whilst for Michael losing his aunt represented a loss of connection with a valued aspect of his roots:

I have this last year felt completely anchorless, you know. Just like I have to find my bearings all over again. I have to you know find where I'm ok all over again.

(Linda)

Well my aunt represented something to me which was I suppose, a part of the family, which was a small rural community and in a sense when she went that was kind of an end of an era for me, the end of that connection.

(Michael)

In Sandra's case, her dead friend represented an irreplaceable source of validation:

He was one of the people who made me feel really good about myself – and that was really important. He made me feel special. I don't think anyone else has made me feel so special.

(Sandra)

Fiona conveyed how her father represented a constant and reliable source of support and guidance to which she could no longer turn:

And when I'm unsure of things it would always be a case of 'I'll phone Dad' or 'I'll ask Dad what that is' or 'Dad will know the answer to that' and of course I can't do that now.

(Fiona)

In some cases the reinforcing nature of a loved one's presence became apparent in certain situations. For Marianne, it was during times of upheaval that she became aware of how much she missed her mother's non-judgemental ear:

When things happen . . . Mum was very good at just listening and maybe giving her view, but never sort of, 'Oh you should do this or why don't you do that?' That's when I miss her most.

(Marianne)

For Elisabeth, the loss of her husband's practical ability was evoked when things needed fixing:

And it's the silly things you know – the fence falls down and, 'Oh god, if Andy were here he'd put it up just like that' you know and I'm struggling to do it . . . and I can't do it as good as him because I'm not skilled in that way.

(Elisabeth)

Stephen particularly missed his father in relation to his academic studies in that this was a part of his life that he had hoped to be able to share with him:

I would like him to be around now so that when I do go through the occasional bits of sort of depression or frustration about it you know he'd actually be able to sit down with me and say, 'Don't worry, it'll be over in two year's time'.

(Stephen)

Some people defined their sense of loss in terms of the lost potential of a valued relationship, especially in relation to deaths that were perceived as untimely. As indicated in Chapter 1, such untimeliness more often reflected the nature of the relationship rather than the age of the deceased person. Both Stephen and Patrick reflected on the lost potential of their relationships with their fathers. Stephen expressed regret that the 'equal' relationship he had begun to establish with his father before he died could not be fulfilled. Patrick wished that he and his father had known each other better and wondered if his father would have felt the same way:

I sort of thought . . . well I know he's going to die before me and now we've achieved this quite nice equal relationship, adult to adult rather than father to son, I want to keep this going on as long as I can.

(Stephen)

So I'd have liked to have known more about him and I don't know if he'd have liked to have known more about my life as well – maybe – maybe not.

(Patrick)

Some of my participants demonstrated a capacity to identify with dead loved ones and appreciate the opportunities which they had lost, as conveyed by Janet and Sandra, in relation to the premature deaths of their friends, both only 17 years old. For Janet such lost opportunity evoked a sense of unfairness, whilst for Sandra it was a source of guilt:

Like, he's never going to get to see any of the opportunities. Yeah, he went to school and then to college – but then you think in that last year he went to college – there's so much more he could have done and maybe he wouldn't have chosen to go to college, but done something else.

(Janet)

Sometimes I think about the fact that he's not around and then I feel guilty. When I see what some of us are doing I think he could be doing that. I can picture him and how he'd be having a nice time at university, but he never got that chance. But he deserved it because he worked so hard. So I do feel bad that he hasn't got that chance.

(Sandra)

The sense of lost opportunity was not only linked to the deaths of young people. Both Adrian and Fiona felt that their fathers had missed out by dying at 65 and 67:

Well he'd just turned 65 on the 27th. So he was also looking forward to his pension.

(Adrian)

He was only 67 and he was always very active and very, sort of, young at heart, and you know, out with the grandchildren, playing with the grandchildren.

(Fiona)

The self

The way people shared their experiences of loss revealed the extent to which those who had died formed an integral and crucial part of narrators' sense of identity, as conveyed by Adrian in relation to his father:

He's absolutely central to who I am.

(Adrian)

In so doing, they conveyed the social nature of the self and how the impact of losing a loved one produced a diminishment and disruption of selfhood. The process of defining their loss thus represented an attempt to negotiate this experience. It revealed the complexity of their relationships, which were defined less by specific roles, and more by intimacy, as in Tania's attempt to define the loss of her mother:

Another thing I do feel is I've lost my other half – a part of me . . . and at times I think, 'Oh, if only Mum was here' – because Mum – we were the stronger ones. I just feel I've lost, I don't know it's so hard to say – I felt so in tune with my mum – I think that's the best way to put it.

(Tania)

In Andy's case, the death of his father was experienced as having taken away his carefree spirit and capacity for joy, leaving him feeling depressed and disempowered:

Before, I used to be chirpy chirpy like, bubbly, like always outgoing. It's brought me down – it really has . . . Because I can get moody so easily at times . . . like

I'm just not that bubbly, keeping on top of things, like things going straight over my head.

(Andy)

My participants' narratives conveyed how the impact of losing a loved one on the sense of self could be experienced as a loss of control, which could manifest in a variety of ways, such as Elisabeth's response to the sudden death of her husband:

I was angry – I went home and smashed a few cups up.

(Elisabeth)

For Stephen, such loss of control was linked to an inability to concentrate, something which affected both his work and his relationships:

So sometimes, you know, you could be having a conversation with somebody and they would say something and suddenly it would remind you of something about your father and . . . so the main problem was being sort of distracted both in your work or a little bit socially with people in a way in which you couldn't really kind of control.

(Stephen)

Some participants conveyed just how distressing and disruptive the experience of losing one's powers of self-control could be. Adrian reported an increased tendency to lose his temper since his father died, something he experienced as uncharacteristic and a source of shame:

I just snapped over some stupid, stupid thing at dinner-time and, I mean, that – I mean, it's awful and it makes me feel horrible afterwards, 'cos I'm not usually like that and to, you know, lose my temper over some ridiculous thing at the meal-time, that's awful.

(Adrian)

Tania's uncharacteristic and uncontrollable behaviour was experienced as shocking to her family and a threat to her integrity and capacity to support herself:

. . . but what absolutely shocked them rigid, and me, was that I started to cry and didn't stop for hours and they'd never seen this because I'd never broke down in front of them, really – I was absolutely at my end . . . plus I'm self-employed and there were problems at work and I was basically letting the business slip and it's my livelihood.

(Tania)

Sometimes losing control was experienced as numbing, as identified by Bowlby (1961; 1980) and Parkes (1972, 1986) as forming the initial phase of grieving. Thus Pat described her initial reaction to the death of her aunt:

And I think I was probably just bloody numb do you know what I mean? There weren't tears, there weren't tantrums – I just remember sitting in this house . . . that didn't have central heating, it had an open fireplace, sitting there wrapped up in a blanket shivering.

(Pat)

Fiona reported a sense of being unable to take anything in when she first returned to work after her father's death:

I just couldn't speak to anybody . . . And I just remember being sat at my desk looking at my computer not soaking any information up and just feeling really suffocated.

(Fiona)

Losing control was also represented in terms of a loss of agency and self-determination or a sense of being prevented from taking full charge of one's life. Tania reported that her mother's death prevented her from getting on with her life in the way that she had anticipated, whilst Elisabeth conveyed how she felt that her inability to stop loving her deceased husband prevented her from forming another relationship:

I have felt that in the past year or so I've been more restricted than previously, just at the time when I've thought maybe I could do a bit more and my son is grown up and what have you. Also I feel I've lost a bit of my life as well because I'm never here – I haven't even got a social life.

(Tania)

I think it's because I suppose I still love my husband so until I can get over that hurdle it's going to be hard to have another relationship.

(Elisabeth)

As a result of her mother's death, Lynne felt she had been put in a position of having to act towards her sister in a way that went against her normal inclinations and that it had cost her a real effort to do so:

I've felt that I've had to support my sister ever since . . . we've never been particularly close and I've felt I've had to really make an effort to change myself and change the way I feel about her in order to provide some sort of support.

(Lynne)

These narratives revealed the tension inherent in a discourse of individualism in which one must behave with both authenticity and self responsibility (Beck and Beck-Gerhshiem, 1995, 2002). They revealed the limits of an individualistic understanding of agency, which fails to take into account our sociability and the extent to which we are affected by others (as discussed in Chapter 2).

Some people compared their sense of loss of integrity to losing parts of the body. Such linking of the self with the physical nature of the body captured both the extreme nature of the pain of loss as well as the extent of the loss itself, as conveyed by Andy and Adrian in relation to their fathers:

> It kind of feels like a part of me's gone. It's hard to explain. It's like someone's chopped half my leg off and just taken it ... Like I said it's like someone's chopped half my leg off and taken it away because it's taken away so much from my life.
>
> (Andy)

> It's as though I have to live without my arms or something like that – without something, but I can't put a finger on it because it's not visible ... I have to try and learn to live without this vital you know like my sight or something, because that's how integral my dad was.
>
> (Adrian)

For some this was achieved through metaphors of wounding, such as 'heart-break', 'surgical' or 'stab wound', as expressed by Linda, Adrian and Elisabeth:

> ... and I have found myself incredibly sad about Mam, really, really heartbroken sometimes.
>
> (Linda)

> Something I've kept in mind is that I really feel like I've had an amputation and I can't see which limb has gone and that it's not a visible limb, but it most certainly is an amputation – there's no other way I can describe it.
>
> (Adrian)

> When I missed him I really missed him, you know, you get such pain, like a knife in your chest or something
>
> (Elisabeth)

For Lynne, the loss of her mother was experienced as a wound that would never fully heal. However this incurable wound was also experienced as a part of herself that would always remember her mother, thus linking the pain of loss with the impetus to remember:

> Yes it's still quite raw ... but there's certain bits of you which they never actually quite heal over and obviously a lot of that is not going to heal over ... I think in a way I'd rather feel that than not – at least it's sort of paying tribute to her in a way, you know, I'm not going to forget about her.
>
> (Lynne)

For several people the pain of loss was felt to be permanent, something which, in Elisabeth's case, involved negotiating competing discourses of letting go and holding on. Thus, in relation to the loss of her husband, the almost defiant tone in which she conveyed the permanent nature of this reflected a context in which others were urging her to get over her grief and move on:

> I mean I'll always miss him and that's all there is to it
>
> (Elisabeth)

In Janet's case, following the untimely death of her friend at 17, she felt that she had reached a point where her grief, though considerably more bearable, would simply remain with her:

> I mean I don't think it's ever completely going to go away, but I think this is it now – I don't think I've got any more – I don't think it will get any worse, but I don't think I'm going to get any better.
>
> (Janet)

The experience of loss could be registered and reinforced by comparing oneself to others who were perceived still to be in possession of what one had lost. For Stephen such comparison made him feel prematurely deprived of a father:

> But there is the sort of feeling that you have . . . that you lost about a decade of having a father and that does rankle sometimes in the sense that I know people the same age as me who've got both their parents around and you know, I'd never say anything, but sometimes you do feel a bit jealous.
>
> (Stephen)

Andy felt deprived of his father as a reassuring, validating figure at a time when he felt that, in comparison to his sister and brother, his own life had hardly begun:

> He saw so much of my sister and brother and, like, he saw nothing of my life. I feel I've just lost out – like, I've lost out so much.
>
> (Andy)

For Linda, her sense of loss was linked to being unable to sense her mother's continuing presence, something which was exacerbated by the fact that her sister could:

> . . . but sometimes when I talk to one of my older sisters . . . and she'd say, 'Oh I really feel Mum around now', or, you know, and I'm thinking, 'Well, she's not round me', and – I'm jealous, do you know what I mean? I'm really jealous, 'cos I don't feel her around.
>
> (Linda)

Others

The experience of grief following the death of a loved one is an interactive, intersubjective one, encompassing relationships with others who are also grieving as well as those who are not. Narratives of loss reflected the complex, diverse and negotiated nature of such an experience that disrupts and challenges the normal, established patterns of social functioning. They promoted and reflected a discourse of individuality in relation to people's right to grieve in their own way, as conveyed by Vivienne in terms of being authentic:

> There's nothing wrong with the way you react and you can't force yourself to feel something you don't feel 'cos that's worse and – you react how you react.
>
> (Vivienne)

However, she also gave voice to the way that an acceptance of diversity, whilst promoting tolerance, may leave people feeling insecure as to whether their grief is appropriate (Walter, 1999):

> . . . 'cos it's like you don't know how you should react really.
>
> (Vivienne)

For Diane, such diversity could create an atmosphere of acceptance that was constructed as helpful:

> . . . but in this funeral we had about four generations of people all handling it in a totally different way and therefore it was – if you kinda like suddenly started crying a bit nobody – you know, you wouldn't say, 'Oh god, they're crying' and all the rest of it. People just kind of like coped with it in their own way and I think that's often helpful.
>
> (Diane)

In Sarah's case, which, on the basis of this particular group of bereaved people, would seem to be less representative, grieving was felt to be a more private affair. Thus she shared with me her preference for keeping her grief to herself:

> I'd prefer to keep it to myself. I don't think there's a need to share things all the time . . . your grieving's inside.
>
> (Sarah)

It has been noted how grief is being expressed more openly and the boundaries between private and public expressions becoming blurred (Small, 1998). The more restrained style of grieving that characterised the mid to late twentieth century reflected norms about ensuring that a person's grief does not impinge too much on others and that others should not intrude on a person's private grief (Gorer, 1965; Walter, 1999). However the turn of the century has witnessed an increasing emotionality, which privileges the open and shared expression of grief (Walter,

1996, 1999). This approach reflects the therapeutic value invested in emotional release and how expressing one's feelings has become associated with self-authenticity (Lupton, 1998; Hockey, 2001).

Thus Sarah sought to justify emotional restraint in the face of the competing discourse of emotionality that she witnessed in others:

> I think I might be unusual perhaps – V thinks I'm cold. But I just think there's no need to be openly emotional to be well-adjusted. It's not like I'm cutting myself off inside just because I'm not screaming every time something reminds me of one of my grandparents. But other people do.
>
> (Sarah)

However, privatised grief and emotionality were not necessarily mutually exclusive. Tania's need to remain strong and to cope in the face of her father's and sister's emotionality prompted her to find private spaces and outlets, such as her car, in which to give vent to her feelings of grief:

> It became a bit of a thing to get in the car and I'd sob and sob.
>
> (Tania)

Grieving in private could therefore reflect family dynamics and the adoption of different roles rather than any privileging of emotional self-restraint.

Participants also defined their own loss with reference to the impact of the grief of others. Some people emphasised the unexpected and surprising nature of the impact of other people's grief on their own grief experience, as in Diane's case in relation to the deaths of her mother and grandmother:

> I think I wasn't quite prepared for how upset my children would be.
>
> (Diane)

Tania, in relation to the death of her mother, felt unprepared for the distressing impact of her father's grief:

> The part that I have found – I don't think you could call it surprising, but what I was unprepared for was the impact that my dad's grief has had on me – he just cried all the time – you know I'd go up to Newcastle and we'd go in and he'd be crying and little things would tip him. He was devastated and that just absolutely tore me in two to see the grief of my dad.
>
> (Tania)

For Julian, in relation to the death of his grandfather, the surprising nature of the grief of his father and uncle was linked to cultural norms related to gender and emotionality (Thompson, 1997). Though it is becoming more socially acceptable for British men to express their grief outwardly, this was not the norm in Julian's family:

The day before we went to see his body . . . There was me and my father and my uncle . . . and my father and Uncle Alan are both blokey blokes – quite macho and strong and they said, 'hello' to the guy at the funeral parlour and when the guy closed the door my dad and uncle Alan burst into tears which I'd never seen them do ever before – I'd never seen my dad cry – and then we all held hands and then put our arms round each other.

(Julian)

Adrian's sense of the loss of his father was experienced as both separate from and part of that of his family. This meant that he was able to appreciate and identify with the pain experienced by his mother and sisters, something he found particularly upsetting to witness:

I come from a very tight-knit family – like my sisters and my mum and we're – they're going through a lot of pain. I'm not going through the same pain that they're going through. I'm really not, so it's awful to watch . . . But their grief is my grief and my grief is their grief – I mean it's so interconnected.

(Adrian)

The ways in which the impact of the grief of others was understood and talked about sometimes reflected cultural norms in relation to grieving rights and who was perceived to be the 'primary griever'. An appreciation of and sensitivity towards the grief of those who were more closely related to the deceased person could take precedence over one's own grief, as for Janet in relation to the death of her friend:

My feelings are mostly with his mum more than anything and his family.

(Janet)

Indeed the grief of the identified primary griever could overshadow and be experienced as more distressing than one's own sense of loss, as conveyed by Vivienne in relation to her grandmother's death:

I was more upset for my parents than for me.

(Vivienne)

For Sarah, her own expression of loss was defined by the needs of the primary griever and the importance of protecting and respecting his or her sensitivities:

You do whatever the grieving person wants . . . If I'm upset around G. then I'm going to upset him and he's the one with the primary loss.

(Sarah)

Though studies have highlighted the importance of talking to others and sharing one's grief, the impact of another's grief could also inhibit such sharing for fear of upsetting the other, as in the above example. Vivienne too, revealed how her sensitivity towards her parents' grief and concern to protect their feelings inhibited her need to talk about her grandmother's death:

> So perhaps I didn't realise I needed to talk about it, but I didn't want to be the one to bring it up because I didn't want to upset them because then my concern was still more with them . . . and I still don't know what I'd say to my dad.
>
> (Vivienne)

Similarly, her father's sensitivity to and protectiveness of his daughter's feelings meant that he, too, tended to avoid the subject:

> I think my dad just wanted to make sure I felt better and all I was really worried about was him more than what I was feeling at the time about my gran dying – it was more like you don't have a mum or dad now.
>
> (Vivienne)

In contrast, Andy challenged such norms as failing to reflect the mutuality of the loss of a family member and the shared nature of grief:

> It's not an individual thing. It happened to all of us – and how Mum makes it out at times is that she's lost the person. Like it's had no significance on our lives at all and she's lost the person, so her life's hard – and that p's me off. It's like you should be there to support me as well when I'm giving you that support. And that does make me feel alone.
>
> (Andy)

In some cases, as a result of the impact of the grief of close others, narrators felt obliged to take the role of supporting them. This reflects how within the same family people may respond very differently to the death of a member, since each family member loses a different aspect of their identity (Riches and Dawson, 2000:20). As a result of her father's death, Fiona took on the role of supporting her mother who now felt unable to manage the practical business of living:

> We've been helping her out with all the paperwork and sort of practical side of things 'cos Dad did everything. Dad paid all the bills, he drove the car. And now she's left and she just doesn't know anything . . . It's been very tiring because there's phone-calls nearly every night, 'cos Mum's received something else in the post that she doesn't understand and she doesn't know how to fill out this form and what are they asking for and so it's dealing with things over the phone every night and visiting most weekends.
>
> (Fiona)

For Andy, the demands made on him by his mother's grief as a result of his father's death were a source of both guilt and anger. This can be seen, in part, to reflect the way particular social roles are accompanied by wider cultural expectations, as well as how such roles may need to be renegotiated after a death. As the eldest son, Andy felt torn between the expectations of his mother and his need to pursue the educational opportunities that were available to him:

> But the thing that annoys me about my mother – like, she'll ring me. I ring her every night to give her the support she needs. But she'll ring me and still start sobbing over the phone or she'll blurt out, 'My life's a mess la la la'. She makes me feel so shit about being down here at uni.
>
> (Andy)

Tania felt the need to distance herself from her father's grief and assert her own style of grieving in order to begin to pick up the pieces of her own life:

> . . . and I said to my dad I won't have – I don't want deaths mentioned and I do not want seven weeks every year of my life this is when this happened this is when that happened – I can't do that – it's not the way I want to deal with it at all.
>
> (Tania)

Some people focused on the impact on others of their own grief, highlighting their experiences of family and friendship networks and the extent to which these provided support. Relationships with family and friends in terms of social support have been identified as a crucial factor in coping with bereavement, especially in relation to providing a safe, accepting place for the expression of difficult feelings (Riches and Dawson, 2000). Julian conveyed how some friends of his were able to empathise, share and support him in his grief for his grandfather:

> . . . because they were my friends I talked to them and said, 'Oh my granddad's died' and straight away they were sympathetic because it permitted them to think about people they'd lost and they'd listen to me and say, 'Oh that's how I felt when I lost so and so'.
>
> (Julian)

Yet, just as family relationships may demonstrate a hierarchy of grieving rights, Sandra revealed how this could extend to friendship networks. Thus, for Sandra, such sharing with and support from friends was not forthcoming. Rather her experience of the loss of her friend was compounded by being excluded by those whose grief was considered to take priority:

> . . . but you know the thing I found difficult was that his best friends didn't acknowledge me as much as they could have – like they didn't involve me in any way in their grieving process.
>
> (Sandra)

With regard to family networks, it has been noted how family members may sometimes feel threatened by the way another member's grief and preoccupation with the deceased person may cause them to feel shut out (Riches and Dawson, 2000). The response of Elisabeth's children to their mother's continuing distress and preoccupation with her husband's death was to invoke the competing discourse of 'letting go':

> Like, I just can't let him go completely. But the kids sort of say, 'Oh, Mum, come on he's been dead for a long time, you've got to put it behind you and get on with it.' But it's hard it really is.
>
> (Elisabeth)

Elisabeth's experience reflected how the responses of family members to each other's grief reflected roles and status within the family and the expectations and obligations associated with this. Having lost their father, Elisabeth's children did not want to lose their mother too but, as acknowledged by Elisabeth, needed even more of her. Thus they inevitably wanted her to be 'over it'.

Narrators' perceptions of the impact of their grief on non-grieving others reflected the extent to which they found them to be supportive or unsupportive. However, they also demonstrated a reflexivity that was willing to make allowances for others. For Andy, social support was a mixed experience through which he defined his sense of loss as both socially cohesive and socially isolating. Though he felt very supported and affirmed in his loss by certain close friends, he felt unsupported and neglected by others. However in retrospect he acknowledged that this was not deliberate:

> And all my friends were so brilliant at college. They were just there to support me . . . And B., I always feel like I can just go and knock on her door and talk to her and cry on her shoulder. And it's just so comforting.
>
> (Andy)

> And I think that first day I went back to college was the hardest thing. Like, I saw people – and, like, people who usually talk to me they just didn't know what to say – and they just looked at me and put their head down. And I felt really shit – really shit. At the time I thought 'Don't they give a fuck?' Though now I realise they didn't mean it.
>
> (Andy)

Sandra experienced her mother as both someone with whom she could share her sense of loss as well as someone who failed to support her:

> In a way one of the hardest things was when my mum came to pick me up afterwards and she noticed how the streets were lined with young people dressed in black 'cos all of his friends came to his funeral – and pretty much the whole school was there . . . And that especially struck my mum and she cried because she just saw these young people walking round in black.
>
> (Sandra)

> But my parents weren't that good at giving me time to grieve. They were more interested in making sure I was revising and I felt like, 'Well, I've just found out today that my friend's died and I've been given a day off and I've got to get over it by tomorrow'.
>
> (Sandra)

Yet, with hindsight, she reflected that if her parents had allowed her to drift away from her studies she may not have attained her place at university. Her experience highlights the cultural imperative attached to gaining qualifications and the pressures this may place on young people today. Indeed, the response of her school to the death of one of its pupils was to encourage his friends to stay focused on their forthcoming 'A' level exams. Such an emphasis on 'getting on in life' could not accommodate the need to grieve.

Lack of support from others could also have the impact of throwing people back on their own resources, as conveyed by Diane:

> I think people have avoided talking to me about it – and that goes for people at work as well as at home . . . whether they thought I would cope anyway or whether they were scared that I couldn't cope – I don't know . . . I suppose I've just used other mechanisms. I think the whole business of planning the funeral and what I was going to put into it on a personal level – that was my way of coping with lack of support.
>
> (Diane)

Beliefs and values

Bereavement research has highlighted how the experience of loss may challenge people's taken-for-granted or assumptive worlds (Parkes, 1972; Goldsworthy and Coyle, 1999). For some, existing understandings and beliefs about life may be able to assimilate new realities, thus preserving a sense of continuity. For others, existing interpretations of reality may not be able to accommodate the new experience. However, it is more likely that people will experience a mixture of the two possibilities, especially in a social context in which there is a tendency to rely less on the certainties offered by religion or conventional wisdom and more on a self-reflexive and contingent approach to understanding and interpreting life.

Indeed, the narratives from this study demonstrated a complex and creative interplay between individual and cultural resources, reflecting the diversity of people's lifestyles and circumstances (Bradbury, 1996; Handsley, 2001; Masson, 2002). The way people acknowledged and defined their sense of loss was variously shaped by their understandings and beliefs about life and death, both spiritual and secular. Such beliefs could also be challenged and reshaped by experience.

In some cases narrators took support from the ongoing demands of living, reflecting a discourse that promoted 'getting on with life' as a means of coping, as conveyed by Adrian:

Particularly having young children you have to sort of get on with the day-to-day things of life and that helps.

(Adrian)

In Vivienne's case this approach was expressed in terms of 'not giving up' her decision to stay in Ghana to complete her gap year:

I am glad I stayed there 'cos otherwise I would just think back on Ghana as, 'Oh the time I had doing a couple of months volunteering and then my gran died so I had to come home' – you kind of leave with a negative . . . so it might be my family – like not giving up – you know I'd gone out for the four months so I should stay for the four months.

(Vivienne)

Some people, such as Lynne, drew on a discourse of 'nature', in which death formed part of the natural order of things:

About three months after Mum died my little grandson was born and I think that's helped – a new life and a new role . . . being a grandmother – I mean it shows – it's a cycle and someone's born and people die and we're all part of that cycle and we're all going to snuff it and we're all going to get older and die and we'll be replaced and that's part of – it's like in nature – trees and birds and animals and things – you see it – it's all part of the same process.

(Lynne)

In Diane's case, this was a discourse that she associated with a family member who had died and that had come to make sense to her as a result of her mother's death:

. . . the continuity of life. My husband's grandmother used to say it put things into perspective for her. She was very upset when she lost people but always there was a new person that she didn't know and it was about getting to know that person and watching that person grow and develop – and it kind of puts you somewhere in the whole sequence of things and you saw a point to life . . . and I can see now what she meant.

(Diane)

For some, a religious or spiritual perspective could provide a source of comfort. Adrian's belief in an afterlife enabled him to experience his father's absence as only temporary:

But I do tend to think that I just won't see them for a while – that this is you know very much one material aspect of our essence.

(Adrian)

However, religious belief was not always comforting but could produce a sense of confusion by seeming to contradict one's actual experience. Andy found it hard to reconcile the death of his father with his belief in a righteous god:

> You know in our family religion plays a really big part and I just believed if there's a god up there obviously he will save my dad. He's such a good person to other people – and obviously they don't take good people away from you.
>
> (Andy)

Others positively rejected religious explanations. For both Tania in relation to her mother and Janet, her friend, the deaths of their loved ones were experienced as irrevocable losses:

> It may sound very harsh and hard to say I actually don't believe in an afterlife – I don't believe that I will ever see my mum again . . . so I only went back to the crem once because my dad had to do something. And I said never again – I never will go back again – that's no place for me – I don't like it – the ashes.
>
> (Tania)

> It's like I don't believe in life after death. I don't believe he's up there now and he's living another life and I don't think he's looking down on any of us.
>
> (Janet)

Others were more ambivalent. Though Lynne expressed scepticism of religion, she still expressed hope for something beyond the mundane to provide a sense of meaning:

> But I still don't believe there is a place – I don't think my mother's sitting up there on a cloud, but I don't know you always think that or part of you hopes there is something outside of all this 'cos otherwise what's the point?
>
> (Lynne)

Stephen was able to take comfort in keeping an open mind, reflecting that, in the absence of an afterlife, death provided at least an end to suffering. However if there was indeed an afterlife then, as a good person, his father would end up in a better place:

> I think my brother and I, who are both non-religious, our view was, well, when he dies and if there's nothing there afterwards, well then, there's nothing there and he's gone and at least he's not trapped or suffering. But if there is something there, then we reckon that he was a good man he'll end up in heaven rather than hell therefore if there is an afterlife then for us that was fine and he's gone somewhere better.
>
> (Stephen)

The experience of loss could have an impact on the beliefs and values that people already held, promoting revised or new understandings and perspectives. In Sarah's case the loss of her grandparents was experienced as a rude awakening:

> It forces a realisation that people you know and like can die
>
> (Sarah)

For both Sandra and Vivienne, losing loved ones caused them to revise their priorities in life to place more emphasis on spending time with close others:

> It puts things in perspective . . . sometimes when I get stressed – like when you're doing an essay or an exam it's the most important thing going on in your mind then – you know – but it's actually not that important – not compared to other things like friends and family and spending time with friends and family.
>
> (Sandra)

> I'd never for once thought that when I got back from Ghana she'd be dead . . . I'm more – I've always been really close to my mum's mum and so it's kind of made me phone her more and speak to her more – make sure I see her more.
>
> (Vivienne)

In Elisabeth's case, her husband's death produced a change in perspective that had an impact on her role as a parent:

> I suppose I see life from a different point of view in that I see it now from being one person as opposed to two, you try and be more for the children.
>
> (Elisabeth)

For Sandra, the impact of losing both her friend and grandmother increased her understanding of and sensitivity towards the suffering of others:

> It changed my life in that I can understand when people go through something hard – I can understand that. I'd never had anyone close to me die and obviously that was very, very strange, but it showed me just how much things can hurt – how painful they can be. So when I hear that someone's lost someone, you know – someone losing someone, I know about all the pain and the stress and I can feel for them – I can relate to them.
>
> (Sandra)

In relation to losing his father, Stephen was aware of having come to realise and accept the loss as irreplaceable and therefore as something with which he needed to learn to live:

> I suppose the way you think about it from then on is you realise that there's always going to be – that someone significant's gone and there's going to be a

gap and that gap's never going to get filled, but you learn in a sense to deal with having that gap I think.

(Stephen)

For both Janet and Sandra, the untimely deaths of their friends left them with a sense of life's unpredictability, which, in Janet's case, made her own life feel more precious, and for Sandra served as a reminder to appreciate and take pleasure in life:

I think now – I just do want to live my life – and I do feel lucky that I'm still here and it wasn't me and it could happen to any of us, basically.

(Janet)

He was so young – only 17 – you just about never know when your time's up or someone close to you, so you've got to enjoy things – plan for the future, of course, but just enjoy everything – try not to get upset about things – try and enjoy other people – make the most of things.

(Sandra)

Summary

This chapter has illustrated the complexity and diversity of my participants' narratives of loss and how these demonstrated the inherently social nature of grief. They revealed the threat posed by the death of a loved one to the person-hood of both the dead and the living and to the social bond and fabric of people's lives. What had been lost was defined in terms of the 'deceased person', the 'self', 'others' and 'beliefs and values' to reveal how grief formed part of people's every-day social experience. This process revealed a linking of the ordinary and the extra-ordinary as narrators struggled to articulate something that constantly threatened to confound them.

Some narrators attempted to define the quality and extent of their loved one's absence. Some focused on the loss of specific attributes associated with him or her. The disorientating impact of loss reflected the role played by the deceased person as a major reference point, source of validation and guiding influence in survivor's lives, something which could be both all-encompassing as well as linked to specific situations. For some, their loved one's death represented lost potential, not only for the survivor, but also the deceased person in terms of his or her loss of opportunity. Such untimeliness and loss of potential was not only associated with young deaths.

Some participants defined their loss in terms of losing parts of the self. In some cases the linking of self with the physical nature of the body enabled narrators to convey the extreme pain of loss through metaphors of wounding and losing parts of the body. Such images captured the extent of loss and the sense of loss of integrity. Narrators conveyed how they experienced a diminishment and disrup-tion of self through specific aspects of their personalities, as well as their powers of self-control. The impact of such loss on their experience of agency and self-determination demonstrated the tension between authenticity and capacity for self-responsibility. Losing control was perceived to have an impact on one's behaviour in specific situations as well as on one's life prospects.

Indeed, loss of self could have an impact on one's behaviour, one's lifestyle, one's plans, goals and direction in life. Narratives revealed the multifaceted nature of loss and just how much could be invested in a close other. In some cases the sense of loss was perceived as permanent. It could be exacerbated by comparing oneself to others. Such definitions of loss revealed how people's experiences of selfhood were fluid and intersubjective. They drew attention to the limitations of a discourse that emphasises the unitary, rational, intentional nature of the self.

Rather, narratives demonstrated the interactive, intersubjective and negotiated nature of loss. They reflected and promoted an emphasis on individuality and diversity in relation to people's right to grieve in their own way. Such recognition of individuality and diversity, whilst promoting tolerance, could leave people feeling insecure about their own grieving style. Definitions of loss revealed how they negotiated such diversity in relation to the impact of the grief of others on their own grief, and vice versa, both those who were grieving and those who were not. The sense of loss could be affirmed, exacerbated or overshadowed by the grief of others. Experiences and interpretations of other people's responses to one's own grief, demonstrated a reflexivity that was prepared to make allowances for others' shortcomings. Lack of support from others could prompt reliance on one's own resources.

In attempting to understand and define their loss narrators drew upon the beliefs and values they held about life and death. Religious beliefs and spiritual perspectives offered some comfort but equally might evoke considerable confusion. For others, religion offered no comfort, death was constructed as final and loss as permanent. Some people were more ambivalent, in that, whilst acknowledging a hope for an afterlife, they held no firm religious belief. Some drew upon secular wisdom, such as the notion that 'life must go on' and taking account of 'the natural order of things'. For some, the experience of loss had an impact on their perspective on life, provoking a rethinking of values and priorities, such as an increased understanding of other people's suffering, an awareness of the importance of spending time with significant others, valuing one's life and taking pleasure in things. More generally, accounts reflected a context in which people were inclined to rely less on traditional religious belief or conventional wisdom and more on a self-reflexive approach to understanding and interpreting their lives.

Narratives of loss revealed how the experience of absence was intimately linked with that of presence, the one evoking the other. In attempting to define their loss narrators demonstrated how the dead retained a social presence by virtue of their absence. For to define one's loss was both poignant and restorative. The next chapter develops this paradox of absence and presence in relation to the way people materialised their loss and how this process obscured the distinction between grief and mourning.

5   Materialising loss

In this chapter I explore the way my participants experienced the material world and their engagement with it as providing powerful symbols of loss. The role played by material culture in mediating death and shaping people's experience of bereavement has been well-documented, though largely through large-scale, public forms of memorialisation (Morley, 1971; Davies, 1993; Winter, 1995; King, 1998) However there has been an increasing focus on the more 'everyday', private and personal contexts and experiences of remembering dead loved ones (Francis *et al.*, 2000, 2001, 2005; Bradbury, 2001; Hallam and Hockey, 2001; Gibson, 2004). Hallam and Hockey (2001) have further highlighted the importance of material culture in the experience of grief by adopting a wide frame of reference to include the meanings people give to the more ordinary and everyday objects, spaces and practices associated with daily living. In focusing on the meanings people attach to their experience, this approach has called into question the distinction between grief and mourning to convey a complex inter-relationship between the two, rather than one shaping the other. As already indicated, my participants made no such separation between how they felt and how they behaved.

In exploring my participants' narratives I have similarly adopted a wide stance to encompass the variety of ways in which they materialised their loss. Such materialisation did encompass the more formal ritualised social practices and the spaces and objects associated with these. In recounting these, narrators confirmed Turner's observation that the power of ritual as an event that 'makes change' and 'moves' people through the use of images, symbols and metaphors from the known world to make sense of the unknown, depends not on its external form but on participants' willingness to submit to the authority represented by ritual specialists (1969). Turner's emphasis on the symbolic power of ritual can encompass the more informal and personalised approaches that reflect the contemporary mistrust of traditional authority and the valuing of individual choice (Walter, 1999; Cook and Walter, 2005). Indeed, my participant's narratives conveyed how their sense of loss could be evoked and negotiated through engagement in the ordinary social practices that formed part of the daily business of living, including the domestic and public objects and spaces associated with these. Such materialisation included the meanings people attached to time and social space.

Viewing the body

Central to the way people materialise death are encounters with the corpse. Such encounters raise questions about the extent to which the dead body continues to represent the once living person, or the corpse as both subject and object (Hallam *et al.*, 1999). Part One of this book has explored the nature of personhood in relation to the dying body, calling into question any straightforward relationship between the self and embodiment. After death, such a relationship becomes even more complex, as demonstrated by the way my participants' conveyed their encounters with the dead bodies of their loved ones.

The therapeutic discourse has promoted the importance of viewing the body as a means of encountering and coming to terms with the 'reality' of death (Parkes, 1972; Worden, 1991). Not viewing the body has been linked to subsequent search-ing behaviour and failure to accept and face the loss and thus to adapt and move on in one's life (Bowlby, 1980). However, by taking a discursive perspective and focusing on the way people make sense of their experience, the notion of the 'reality of death' becomes less self-evident. Rather, attention is drawn to the way social reality emerges and develops through contested representations of 'the way things are' or diverse world-views (Rapport, 1993; Hockey, 1996a). This approach acknowledges and aims to capture the flux and mutability of the reality of death and indeed any social framework of meaning, such meanings being dependent on the social context of the moment.

The narratives of Roy, Fiona and Pat conveyed just how powerfully the impact of viewing the body could bring home a sense that their loved one no longer inhabited it:

I kept saying it's not Dad, it's not Dad, it's just a shell.

(Roy)

It didn't look like Nan. She was sort of quite bloated . . . and when you see somebody like that you almost wish you hadn't gone to see them and you'd remembered them as you'd last seen them.

(Fiona)

And I went to see her in the Chapel of Rest but it didn't look like her – it didn't look like her at all. That was not a good experience. I mean it wasn't a bad experience like you know traumatic. It was just like, 'Why did I come here? What was I looking for?' I was looking for Enid, but this is just a body, this is not Enid. And she didn't look like Enid anyway, she looked like a 96-year-old ravaged, injured woman which I know I'm sure she was, but there was no life there by definition really.

(Pat)

Pat's experience revealed how the corpse as a symbol of absence could provide the impetus to search elsewhere for the deceased person's presence. She conveyed how such searching was not necessarily a sign of failing to come to terms with death, as represented by the therapeutic discourse (Bowlby, 1980):

> So I must have spent two minutes there and then just walked straight out again and chose to figure out a different way to remember her.
>
> (Pat)

Rather, the life–death boundary was not so clear cut, absence evoking presence. Indeed, narratives conveyed the mutable and contingent nature of the reality of death and raised questions about what exactly it was that had died.

For Lynne, her mother's body evoked the paradoxical and disturbing nature of the corpse as 'a presence that manifests an absence' (Vincent, 1991: 165, cited in Hallam and Hockey, 2001: 14):

> I went in but I couldn't stay 'cos I was you know – out I can't stand it. Well, she just looked so awful, 'cos you thought any minute now she's going to open her eyes and you're sort of waiting for that and on the other hand you're seeing someone who's not there any more. She just wasn't there any more.
>
> (Lynne)

Lynne's reaction demonstrated how the dead body could take on a double meaning for the surviving person. In this case it was both an absence of the person who once inhabited it as well as a frightening presence that threatened to come to life.

Andy conveyed how the reality of death could depend on the temporal and spacial context. After preparing his father's body according to Sikh custom in which 'the significance of washing him in yoghurt is to make him clean to go to god', Andy was left with a profound and disturbing sense of absence:

> . . . and it was just the horriblest thing, actually, like seeing my dad inside the coffin. It was a really really hard thing to actually see. I think it kind of hit me then.
>
> (Andy)

Prior to this, Andy had already seen his father's body in the hospital where he died in intensive care. However, at this point he was unable to objectify his father's body and take in the reality of his death. Rather his father's personhood remained linked to his physical presence, demonstrating how people may view the body differently at different times and in different settings:

> And they actually told us, like, my dad had passed away. And I just couldn't believe it. I was just like, 'No, no, I 'm not hearing this right.' And Mum was, like, crying on my brother's shoulder and I was just there – like I was just in shock. I was just like, 'No this can't be true, they must have got the wrong person.' It was like, 'No, no, they're not talking about my dad.' Basically he had a cardiac arrest and they'd tried to start his heart again – and it just wouldn't

start again. Went to go and see my dad and like he just looked like he was still alive and it was, see what I mean, they've got the wrong person, they've got the wrong person – and it still hadn't hit me.

(Andy)

The experiences of Pat, Lynne and Andy conveyed how the corpse may exercise agency in the way it provides the bereaved person with the impetus to act in a particular manner, whether to leave the mortuary in a hurry, or to question whether the person was really dead (Hallam and Hockey, 2001). In Andy's case, the impact of his father's body prompted him and his brother to ask the doctor for a re-examination:

. . . and we had to get the doctor to re-examine him because he still had a pulse in him. And I didn't know if it was us that wanted to believe he still had a pulse. But he did look like he was breathing.

(Andy)

The funeral

Some people's narratives revealed how funeral rituals served as powerful symbols of absence, demonstrating the way that grief and mourning were intimately linked. Stephen reported how the experience of witnessing his father's coffin being carried into the church brought home the physical reality of his loss:

Yes – and, I think – you know, up – till at one point when it did sort of quite click in was obviously when they did carry the coffin in and then suddenly it makes it very material to you that you know that a death has taken place.

(Stephen)

Stephen further conveyed how the power of this image to evoke grief continued beyond its original context:

I would visibly – for the first three months – I would visibly cringe if I saw a funeral procession because it reminded me too much.

(Stephen)

For Brian, it was the way the coffin disappeared behind the curtains at the crematorium that was most evocative of his sense of loss, whilst for Andy it was the act of shutting the coffin:

That's the hardest bit – I've been to a few funerals and that's the hardest bit for me when they start the rollers and the coffin goes and the curtains go and I think that's it – that's the final moment and that's the hardest bit.

(Brian)

I think the worst thing was when we actually shut the coffin. I just thought, god I'm never going to see my dad ever again. I just thought, I've only got my memories of him and that's it.

(Andy)

Stephen reflected on the way that his act of placing flowers on his father's grave was such a stark and poignant reminder of his death:

You know, sort of putting flowers on the grave, that was actually a particularly sad moment as well. That was probably the worst single bit, sort of going there and seeing this grave all filled in and you kind of realise it's the finality, it's over and that's where he's going to be until, you know.

(Stephen)

These narratives confirmed the observation that 'what makes a ritual authentic is the meaning extracted from it by participants not the objects used' (Bradbury, 1999: 189). Indeed, Andy conveyed how the experience of the funeral may fail to move the participant regardless of the impact it may have on others and how such failure to extract meaning may provoke a sense of unreality and self-questioning:

And then the coffin went to the crematorium and like prayers were said at the crematorium and then he was cremated. And do you know, even when he was cremated and everyone was crying, I was just there and I couldn't even shed a tear – like – at the time I just thought, god I'm such a selfish person. I just thought, I can't cry . . . But when I reflect on it now, I think it's just because I didn't think it was true. How can I cry when I just hadn't accepted like – yeah, this isn't true? And, like, everyone was bawling their eyes out at the crematorium and I only saw half of my dad's coffin go actually into the oven – whatever they call it – I saw half the coffin and I just walked out because I couldn't see him. It was just like, is that my dad? Is that my dad going into there? That was – it was weird, really weird.

(Andy)

Yet Roy, in recalling the details of his father's funeral, demonstrated the power of outside, unplanned and unexpected phenomena to move people and lend significance to the occasion:

Dad, when he was younger, was a bit of a biker and it was just by sheer coincidence as we came out of the funeral . . . these four or five motorbike guys from the car park, they were down for a friend of theirs who was getting cremated in the next cremation. It was just the roar of the engines – it was – what are they called? Harley Davison. And it's such a beautiful sound – and I just thought, 'That sums it all up really'. So, whether they meant to, but they became part of our experience of the funeral.

(Roy)

Roy's account, along with others, also demonstrated how 'processes of ritual-isation are not confined to rigidly demarcated ritual times and spaces' (Hallam and Hockey, 2001:179). For Diane, the process of constructing a eulogy formed a private, more informal ritual activity, which served to evoke and define the loss of her mother in a way that was experienced as therapeutic:

> And I think it's quite therapeutic actually to sit down and think about the points in somebody's life and try and pull them together. So you're like typing away and sobbing at the same time. 'Cos it's the memories of the person really that kind of bring this to the fore.
>
> (Diane)

In her determination to take the opportunity to make a formal and public declaration of the person she felt she had lost in her aunt, Pat conveyed the emotional labour (Hochschild, 1983) such experience could entail:

> It was very, very hard but I wanted to say something at the service 'cos I'd found in the days after Enid died I'd managed to find letters of reference that she had been written in the 1920's and '30's that she would take to employers and they described her beautifully. So I was able to read some of those out and you know, say my piece I suppose it was – what I felt about Enid as a person – not what I felt about her but how I understood her to be – very unique and with some fantastic qualities.
>
> (Pat)

Narratives of loss reflected the growing personalisation of funerals, with clergy responding to demands as well as encouraging mourners to take an active part. For example, Janet took the opportunity to give expression to and share her sense of outrage at the unfairness of the death of her friend. Her account demonstrates how the involvement of mourners could contribute a more informal and spontaneous quality to the occasion:

> ... and I did say a few words. I had a sheet of paper which I'd written but I couldn't really follow it very well. It was just like he's such a good person and it's not fair that he's not here today and it was just the fact that he'd never reached his 18th birthday and it didn't seem fair – there's no justice in the fact that he didn't get to his 18th – and all the things he wasn't going to get to do – that was just what was going through my head.
>
> (Janet)

Roy recounted how, as a musician, he had been entrusted with choosing the music for his father's funeral, giving him the opportunity to choose those pieces that had the power to evoke loss and the expression of emotion. Such criteria reflected a discourse of romanticism and the therapeutic value placed on emotionality, to which I drew attention in the last chapter (p. 103):

'Cos Mum asked me if I'd chose the music because I'm a musician and I suppose she thought, 'Well, Roy would know what Dad – or what should be played.' So I picked the ones that would evoke emotion – and it certainly did. We were all blubbing when we were in there. As soon as you heard the music coming through. Moonlight Serenade and Eva Cassidy definitely. Very powerful they were.

(Roy)

Everyday reminders

The experience of loss could be powerfully evoked through routine activities that formed the daily business of living, such as driving. Linda conveyed how the experience of her father's absence gripped her very forcefully when she was engaged in the routine activity of driving her children to school:

I was doing something really ordinary like driving the kids to school and this thought popped into my head that I couldn't remember what he sounded like and by the time I'd dropped the kids off at school and was coming back I think I was quite hysterical, that I actually couldn't remember what he sounded like.

(Linda)

In some cases objects and places that once evoked positive feelings could become painful to encounter, as conveyed by Tania in relation to her mother:

But I also found two significant things that I've always liked when I've gone back to Newcastle – I love the Angel of the North and I love crossing the Tyne – but I've found those two things quite hard – I get to the Angel and, you know, and I do find that hard.

(Tania)

Indeed narratives revealed how a person's social presence extended beyond the body to encompass objects, spaces and activities with which he or she had become associated. These would then become powerful symbols of absence, as represented by Lynne's mother's flat or 'living space':

That was awful when I first went up and you . . . there was just this great empty floor.

(Lynne)

For Sandra, the impact of her grandmother's living space revealed the power of the material environment to deceive and how absence and presence are mutually evocative:

Walking into her room and knowing she'd been sitting there every day – she'd be sat watching TV – that was very strange – you'd just expect her to be there and she wasn't.

(Sandra)

In relation to her friend's absence, she conveyed how this was powerfully evoked through the material environment of the classroom. As a space that was associated with her friend's joviality, Sandra now experienced this as having taken on an atmosphere of coldness:

> And we all sat in the same seat every week. So we got back to economics and there was just an empty seat. And it just seemed really cold, not just visually but in the whole atmosphere. It just wasn't the same. And eventually we did get a few jokes back in the classroom but it was never the same. And that was really difficult.
>
> (Sandra)

In some cases a sense of loss could be evoked unexpectedly through associating loved ones with particular pieces of music, as experienced by Brian:

> I came home, put on the TV to watch the Challenger cup and they played Abide With Me and I sat and cried. That was the first time when I thought I'm never going to see my granny again . . . I really really missed her madly 'cos that reminds me of her.
>
> (Brian)

For Andy, such association evoked the painful nature of the passage of time since his father's death and the impact this had had on his life during that period:

> From time to time I listen to, like, the religious hymn CD . . . And I'm just listening to that and I just sat on the bed and looked at my dad's photo and started bawling my eyes out. And I thought, 'Oh my god, a year today, what did I go through?
>
> (Andy)

Anniversaries

Several accounts conveyed the impact of specific key times and the way these may serve to intensify the experience of loss. Such times included both the collectively held festivals of Christmas and Easter, as well as those that were specific to the deceased person, including those marking birthdays as well as those marking the death. Janet reflected on the impact of both the anniversary of her friend's death and his birthday, the latter being experienced as more painful. Her account also conveys how the passage of time may be intimately linked with the grieving experience:

> The first one was really harsh – it was in the paper – his mum put a memoriam thing in there. That wasn't very nice. But I mean his birthdays I think are harder 'cos that sort of hits more so – like I wonder what we would be doing now? But I remember after it happened – the anniversary – like the week anniversary

and the month anniversary and the two month anniversary of when it all happened, those days did – they were really hard – they hit quite hard.

(Janet)

Christmas and birthdays with their festive associations could be particularly difficult, as conveyed by Susan in relation to her aunt:

Like Christmas – Christmas is quite hard. And her birthday is very hard.

(Susan)

Fiona anticipated how Christmas and Easter and other family occasions would no longer be the same without her father:

But as time goes on and like Christmas is here and then it's going to be Easter and we used to go camping as a big family and things like that probably won't happen as often now because Mum won't be able to drive the car to take the caravan.

(Fiona)

Stephen recalled how one of his father's birthdays evoked a sense of having lost him and the potential of their relationship prematurely:

And I remember thinking, ooh March 8th, it's my father's birthday, he'd be 76 and 76 isn't that old – and it was because it was when I was doing something academic and my father was an academic, I thought it would be nice to have someone like that to talk to.

(Stephen)

These accounts revealed the social nature of loss through the way the meanings attached to both the passage of time as well as specific times and dates represented poignant reminders of how integral to one's life the deceased loved one had been and without whom one's life would never be quite the same again. They conveyed the way such reminders involved negotiating the painful paradox of simultaneous absence and presence.

Summary

In recounting the way they materialised their loss, narrators obscured the distinction between grief and mourning to highlight the complex nature of the relationship between the two. This relationship between inner experience and outer behaviour reflects that between the individual and society in that, although we may behave in culturally specific ways, the meanings we attach to such behaviour are mediated by our own personal agendas and priorities. In focusing on the process of meaning-making, a wider definition of what constitutes ritual has drawn attention to the diversity of death-related practices through which people make sense of death.

The impact of loss was conveyed through the meanings people attached to both formal and informal rituals, such as viewing the body, watching the coffin disappear, scattering ashes, and placing flowers on the grave. Viewing the body could evoke a powerful sense of absence. It could be experienced as disturbing and paradoxical in relation to the extent of its subjectivity and objectivity. Such responses conveyed how viewing the body could form part of a process of searching for and recovering the personhood of dead loved ones and how searching was not necessarily a failure to come to terms with the 'reality of death'. Rather, narratives challenged any rigid distinction between life and death, raising questions about what we mean by the reality of death and what it is that has actually died. They conveyed how the corpse may exercise agency.

Narratives confirmed the importance of focusing on meaning-making to reveal how participation in a loved one's funeral may be experienced as deeply moving or else fail to evoke meaning. Using a wide frame of reference allowed the significance people may attach to outside, unplanned, unexpected phenomena and more informal ritual activity to be captured. It revealed how ritual was not confined to formal, public occasions and spaces. Evidence of the growing personalisation of funerals was reflected in the way narrators reported taking the opportunity to make their own contribution to the occasion. The emotional labour such contribution could involve was also apparent.

Some participants conveyed how loss could be evoked unexpectedly when they were engaged in a routine activity such as driving a car. The impact of more ordinary aspects of material culture was revealed by the way in which the deceased person's identity was evoked by objects, activities and spaces with which he or she had become associated. Those that once held positive associations could take on very negative qualities and become painful to encounter. In some cases music was a potent reminder of loss, whilst the passage of time and specific key times, both collective festivals as well as personal anniversaries could intensify the sense of loss.

In materialising their loss people conveyed the poignancy of the way absence evoked presence and vice versa, to highlight the more distressing and disturbing nature of this paradox. The following chapter continues this theme from the perspective of continuing presence and the way my participants conveyed their experiences of rediscovering loved ones to emphasise the more restorative dimension of making sense of death. It considers such experiences in relation to what they reveal about the way we relate to and treat our dead in contemporary British society.

6   Rediscovering presence

This chapter highlights the way that grief may encompass not only the experience of loss and absence but also the regaining of presence. It illustrates how the bereaved people I interviewed experienced and treated deceased loved ones as remaining part of their ongoing lives. It focuses on their narratives of rediscovery and how these provide further insight into the nature and meaning of the continuing relationships between the living and the dead. I have described how, during our interview conversations, the interview space became imbued with the deceased person's presence. Thus it was not only the details of people's narratives, but the interview process itself that demonstrated how someone may die in a medical and biological sense yet remain alive in a social sense.

I have already drawn attention to the way narratives reflected the dynamic, social and interactive nature of the bereavement experience, in which narrators used available cultural forms to express meanings that were personal to them. Any attempt to categorise such experience runs the risk of representing this in terms of a neat, coherent, overarching model that fails to reflect the way people actually experience and live their lives. A frame of reference that attempts to discover and impose a single, or even multifaceted, overarching explanation of the way people grieve, however flexible, cannot capture the interplay of divergent discourses and the fluid, reflexive, contested and contingent nature of the way people construct their worlds (Hockey, 1996b).

Although bereavement may initially form an overriding focus in a person's life, it will still interact with other agendas and priorities, which may compete for attention. The deceased person may continue to live on for some and not for others. His or her continuing aliveness and presence may fluctuate for the survivor and it may be both welcome and unwelcome or a mixture of both. It may be experienced as a permanent part of the survivor's identity, something which one recent, more flexible psychological model of bereavement does not fully capture (Stroebe and Schut, 1999, 2001). As such, the Dual Process Model (DPM) promotes a dynamic, regulatory coping process of 'oscillation' between 'loss-orientation' and 'restoration-orientation', by which bereaved people at times 'confront' and at other times 'avoid' their loss. Some people and certain cultures may emphasise one or other of these orientations, whilst others oscillate between the two according to their own personal rhythm.

The DPM thus moves away from constructing bereavement as a linear process of stages or phases to offer a more dynamic and flexible approach that allows for individual, social and cultural differences. However, it still places more emphasis on individual psychology than social context, identifying core features that characterise 'healthy adjustment'. It implies that grief has a time scale. As a time-bound process of 'oscillation' between the demands of the living and the dead, it does not fully capture the way that, for some people, a deceased loved one may become a more permanent and integral part of their day-to-day lives and sense of identity.

For example, Littlewood's study (2001) of a group of widows reports how these women 'were expressing the ability and desire to conduct an ongoing relationship with the person they knew to be dead' (2001: 85). These women had no intention of 'resolving' their loss or giving up their attachment to their dead husbands. So for them the notion of moving between facing and avoiding their loss or between grief work and coping tasks does not really fit; nor does the notion of adjustment to the 'real' world without the deceased. In terms of the literature they had adopted a position of 'chronic' grief. Yet they were not expressing any belief or hope that their husbands would return to them or 'avoiding the reality' of their deaths.

Similarly, in my own study, Pat conveyed how, after six years, she still experienced her aunt as a constant companion and an integral presence in her daily life:

She's so deeply embedded in my consciousness – that yeah there probably isn't a day that goes by that I don't think about her.

(Pat)

Though Pat's narrative represented a snapshot that was inevitably subject to change over time, it still demonstrated how at that point in time her experience could not be encompassed by a model of oscillation. Such examples point to the limitations of any model, however flexible.

The approach I have taken of organising people's narratives around the predominant areas of focus embedded within them has allowed me to explore and illustrate a number of key discourses in a way that conveys the varied and individualised forms these can take. Though it can be argued that my threefold narrative structure still amounts to a model, I make no universal claims for this structure. Rather I present a 'view' that is based on my shared encounter with a small group of bereaved individuals and that reflects a style of interviewing that invited people to tell their stories. Following the anthropological tradition, my aim has been to learn about the general through the particular, or to demonstrate how culture speaks through the individual. This approach has required an attention to subtlety through the detailed examination of a small number of cases, in order to be able to capture the diversity, complexity, contingency and ambiguity of experience. Rather than making definite statements about how things are, I offer a possible way of looking at something that can enlarge our understanding.

In relation to narratives of rediscovery and the way participants negotiated presence, diversity was particularly apparent, something which may reflect the way the continuing bonds discourse in contemporary British society is not grounded in traditional or religious frameworks. As already indicated, such bonds have been marginalised by the dominant discourse of 'letting go'. In the absence of well defined cultural structures people have more scope to improvise and construct their relationships with dead loved ones in idiosyncratic ways. This chapter draws attention to the social nature of such bonds in terms of the continuing agency and influence of those who have died on the nature and direction of the lives of those they leave behind. Indeed narratives of rediscovery illustrated how the dead have a presence that is not only an inner representation, but also sensory and material (Hallam *et al.*, 1999).

In highlighting the way personhood and agency may survive beyond embodied existence, this chapter further explores and develops some key themes from previous chapters, to include personhood, agency, embodiment, society, individuality and relatedness. As indicated, understandings of these concepts that exclude the human encounter with mortality are inadequate in the way they focus attention on the living, healthy, performative body to the exclusion of the dying and dead body (Hallam *et al.*, 1999). Indeed, my participants represented self-identity, personhood and agency as relational and intersubjective and as defying the temporal and spatial boundaries between the living and the dead. As will be illustrated, their narratives conveyed the way people negotiated such experience within a culture that has tended to prioritise separateness, independence and control.

The nature and meaning of continuing bonds

Now that understandings and norms about the experience of bereavement have shifted away from an emphasis on relinquishing ties with deceased loved ones, it has become possible to explore the nature and meaning of the bonds that are forged beyond the grave. The narratives of those I interviewed revealed how they were fostering links with deceased loved ones that represented a variety of meanings for survivors as well as conveying particular cultural preoccupations, norms and values. These cultural emphases have been identified as 'mutuality', 'contact initiated by the deceased person', 'continuity and change', 'rediscovering the deceased person', and 'respecting the deceased person's wishes'. These themes are explored and illustrated through the highly individualised narratives of my bereaved participants. They reflect how dead loved ones retained personhood and agency by virtue of their relationships with the living, to convey an experience of social being and significance that depends not on embodiment but on relatedness and interdependence.

Mutuality

The nature of the relationship between the living and the dead in a Western context has been represented as one-way, in that the living can do nothing for the dead although the dead can connect the living to transcendent realities and help them to be better persons (Klass and Goss, 1999: 548). This emphasis has been linked to a religious tradition of Protestantism, which has promoted the separation between the living and the dead, as well as the cultural valuing of autonomy and a context of consumer capitalism, features that lie at the root of the severing ties discourse. Thus, inhabiting a higher, spiritual plane far removed from the earthly plane of existence, the dead can offer a critique of consumerism and help the living to be better persons (Klass and Goss, 1999: 548). Studies conducted in a US context, found that bereaved parents and students experienced their deceased loved ones as taking on the role of supporting their better selves and personifying co-operative, caring values (Klass, 1988; Marwit and Klass, 1996). However, they did not experience themselves as reciprocating in any way.

The following representations of continuing bonds in the UK context revealed a different emphasis in which relationships between the living and the dead were characterised by an interdependency that included sharing and reciprocity. The way people talked about their experiences emphasised relational rather than individual intentionality and achievement. Their narratives conveyed an intersubjective experience of identity, personhood and agency, in which the relationships between the vulnerable living and the disembodied dead provided mutual support, validation and empowerment. Such mutual reinforcement served to validate both the bond itself as well as the personhood of both parties.

The mutuality of continuing bonds was reflected in the way deceased loved ones were represented as involved in the lives of those they had left behind. Such involvement extended to sharing in, as well as contributing to, their well-being and receiving reinforcement through the relationship. Andy conveyed how his bond with his father enabled him to 'rise above' the family squabbling that threatened to spoil the occasion dedicated to scattering his ashes. He further conveyed how his efforts represented a source of pride for them both:

> When I was in India my mum was squabbling with my aunt from Canada and my brother was squabbling with me and my sister, my brother was squabbling with my aunt and I thought, this is supposed to be time for my dad – you shouldn't be squabbling . . . how ridiculous . . . and I felt proud of myself and my sister because we were making so much of an effort – and we thought, my dad's looking down at us and he's probably thinking, 'You're doing well you guys', like, 'You're making me proud'.

> (Andy)

Narrators experienced their loved ones as involving themselves in more ordinary, everyday aspects of the lives of the living. Julian reported how he sometimes experienced his grandfather as sharing his pleasure in making certain acquisitions; whilst Stephen reflected on the pleasure his father would have taken in his studies, having been an academic himself:

> Yeah – I sometimes see his – you know, I feel that if I do something good, like buy a boat, buy a narrow boat, that he's pleased for me – you know?

> (Julian)

'Cos basically, I think my father – 'cos my father was an academic and my father had a PhD, I think he would have been quite pleased with the idea that at some point I would be doing this now.

(Stephen)

Some accounts conveyed how continuing bonds were characterised by mutual affection and appreciation, as Andy illustrated by means of a dream:

... and my dad walked through the door ... and like he looked at me and I looked at him – and he said, 'Thank you for everything you've done – you've been wonderful.' And then, like, he started to walk past the door and he turned back round and I walked back and gave him a huge hug.

(Andy)

Brian conveyed the mutually reinforcing nature of his bond with his grandmother with reference to her supernatural powers of seeing and knowing. His belief in her omniscience was a source of comfort to him. For these powers allowed her to 'see into' him and thus validate and appreciate how his behaviour at her funeral demonstrated the affection he felt for her:

And I've no doubt that she was watching her own funeral and from that point of view she knows how much I loved her and felt for her 'cos just by the way I acted at the funeral – it was completely natural.

(Brian)

He further conveyed how their bond was based on a mutual understanding of one another that served to affirm his modest style of memorialising her:

I'll only get one flower ... I mean I could go and pick a daisy and take it and I don't think my grandma would be offended, because it's the thought that counts and if I wanted to pick her a flower, whether I pick a daisy on the way or whether I've bought a £50 bunch of flowers, it's irrelevant because it's the thought that counts.

(Brian)

Stephen, too, drew upon a discourse of supernaturalism to convey the mutually reinforcing nature of his bond with his father whom he experienced as having mysteriously intervened to help him with his studies:

There's one book that I've been chasing around for quite a long time to do with my thesis ... and it's been out of print for a while and, you know, I've always thought to myself it would be really really good if I could get hold of my own copy of it. Walked into the LSE bookshop ... and I went to the second-hand book section and there was one second-hand copy. So basically it was almost thinking, 'Ooh, did my father sort of mysteriously have that put on the shelf for me to buy because he would know that you know that would be a book that I was really really after?'

(Stephen)

These supernatural constructions not only problematise theories of individualised, embodied agency, but also convey an enhanced agency by virtue of the deceased person's disembodied status. The way people negotiated such unusual perceptions and experiences will be discussed more fully in the next section.

Andy reported how he experienced his father as instrumental in furthering his studies and securing his place at university, to the extent of representing a 'driving force'. He conveyed how his achievement was mutually reinforcing:

> Like my dad passing away kind of motivated me more to concentrate more on my college work. Like I've always worked hard – like during my A levels – it was just a sort of driving force ... But I think because I worked so much harder and it was such a driving force, that's probably why I'm here. And it's probably made my dad proud.

(Andy)

These examples revealed how mutuality encompassed the deceased person's agency in furthering the future direction of the lives of surviving loved ones. Experiences that had the appearance of individual actions based upon individual intentionality were represented as joint efforts and shared achievements, the body of the bereaved person forming the site of their mutual empowerment (Hallam *et al.*, 1999).

The mutual nature of continuing bonds reflected the way dying people may try to ensure their continuing presence and influence in the lives of those they leave behind (Matthews, 1979). Fiona conveyed how her deceased father had created a unique opportunity for her nephew, who had been entrusted with scattering his uncle's ashes according to the instructions he had given before he died:

> Actually, I've just seen some photos, 'cos while Rick was scattering the ashes, 'cos I think it was in St. Carlos water ... a few of them went out on, like, a little dinghy and while Rick was scattering the ashes in the water someone was taking pictures ... And I think it was quite good for Rick as well, you know, something that he'll remember for the rest of his life and he met some people out there that knew Dad.

(Fiona)

In some cases the experience of disposing of the deceased person's remains was linked to abandonment to evoke a concern to safeguard a loved one's social being. Both Lynne and Jane conveyed how they sought to ensure that their mother and friend respectively did not suffer abandonment to reveal a discourse of care and protectiveness.

But I just thought no she must feel very lonely down there somehow – 'cos she was very – absolutely potty about her dog so we put the photograph of her present dog – well, he's still around – and the previous one in the coffin with her for company.

(Lynne)

Janet struggled to make sense of her desire to 'be there' and provide companionship for her friend in the absence of any belief in an afterlife, demonstrating how such impulses did not depend upon religious belief but rather reflected a continuing emotional attachment to both the body and personhood of the deceased loved one (Hockey and Kellaher, 2005):

But it's just weird thinking that he's there and he's got, like, no-one looking after him or anything, like night after night – it's just such a cold horrible place, really, a graveyard . . . I suppose it's conflicting – because I feel I don't believe in life after death, yet on the other hand I don't like to think of him being there and not having anyone – like at night.

(Janet)

It has been suggested that such concern about the dead being left 'alone' in an institutional space reflects a current shift away from the modernist approach of separating the dead from the living to a desire to integrate deceased loved ones into the lives of those they have left behind (Hockey and Kellaher, 2005; Kellaher *et al.*, 2005). In other words such a discourse of care encompasses a more fluid perception of the boundary between the living and the dead (Howarth, 2000, 2007b) It reflects a more intersubjective experience of self and agency, which reveals the mutuality of people's continuing bonds. For these narratives conveyed that, in taking care of deceased loved ones, survivors were also comforting themselves.

Contact initiated by the deceased person

The notion that, unlike relationships with ancestors in traditional societies, individuals in modern societies have more control over continuing relationships with the dead has been called into question (Hallam *et al.*, 1999: 157). Attention has been drawn to the way the dead may sometimes make their presence felt by the living. Indeed, some of my participants' narratives have revealed how continuing bonds were not only dependent on the intentions of the living but could be experienced as having been initiated by the dead themselves, sometimes via the senses, such as through physical contact or hearing the person's voice. Such experiences could occur unexpectedly in the ordinary course of events, both at night and as part of day-time activities. They revealed how continuing bonds could be shaped by the deceased as much as the bereaved person.

In recounting these unusual experiences, narrators negotiated the competing discourses offered by modernist scientific rationality and those offered by religion and spiritual or supernaturalist perspectives, sometimes switching from one to the other. The view that dominates scientific discourse is that these experiences are imaginary and illusory, evoked by the way bereaved people may search for the deceased in the early stages of grief (Bowlby, 1961, 1980; Rees, 1971). In contrast the supernaturalist perspective allows them to assert the reality and convey the power of such experiences (Bennett and Bennett, 2000).

It has been noted how few people feel comfortable psychologically or socially with unusual experiences that fail to conform to societal norms (Howarth and Kellehear, 2001). The process of trying to make sense of these inevitably evokes social uncertainty about other people's responses, both anticipated and actual. In order to manage such uncertainty people are likely to 'negotiate their trust and safety with strangers cautiously and conditionally' (2001: 85), as demonstrated by some of my participants. As a stranger who was also a researcher, I was likely to be associated with rationality and scepticism. Thus my participants would tend to insert some qualification of the 'reality' of their experiences which, in some cases, had the impact of diluting their power and significance. Yet it also allowed them to share these 'incredible' experiences with me whilst at the same time protecting their own credibility. Furthermore, such experiences tended to be revealed towards the end of the interview, almost as an afterthought, suggesting that people do not share them easily.

Elisabeth asserted the reality of her experience of physical and verbal contact with her husband, something she found both reassuring and comforting. Yet, at the same time she acknowledged the more conventional line that relegated it to the imagination:

> I tell you what I did experience one night, was – and I'll swear it was him – there was one night when I felt a tap on my shoulder – I was asleep and he said, 'It's alright, love, it's only me, but everything's fine'. And I swear to this day that I wasn't dreaming . . . I didn't know whether it was my imagination or not but I'm sure it wasn't I thought, well, perhaps he's telling me it's ok, you know, get on with life and don't worry
>
> (Elisabeth)

Sandra represented her experience of sensing the presence of both her friend and her gran as their way of providing her with support and comfort in the early stages of her grief. She drew upon the image of the soul surviving beyond the body and inhabiting a spiritual realm in order to try to make sense of and convey the profound nature of this experience. Yet, at the same time she acknowledged the more conventional, 'commonsense' perspective through which it was likely to be pathologised:

> I felt like he was there with me. He hadn't left yet so I had him for a little bit longer. I kind of felt I know he was going to go – that his soul wasn't going to be around forever, but I kind of felt he hadn't just gone, just totally disappeared . . . and with my gran I had the same thing . . . and sometimes it sounds really

loony and I'll think am I making this up – did my mind just construct something because it helped?

(Sandra)

In Jason's case, sensing his grandmother's presence was not a 'one off', but an ongoing series of visits which were characterised by her gestures of care and attention towards him. Whilst acknowledging the apparent 'strangeness' of his experience, Jason demonstrated a familiarity with a supernaturalist discourse. Indeed, any concern he may have had about my reactions soon gave way to a readiness to share with me his experiences of what had become a very comfortable and familiar culture to him, his family background consisting of psychics and mediums:

Both my grandmother and my mother, I know this may sound strange, but they visited me after they had died. My grandmother over quite a period of time she kept visiting me . . . well, she'd open the door and come into the room, she'd click the window open, she'd switch the light on underneath my bed . . . and she'd blow on my forehead, because when I was a small boy and it was very hot at night she used to blow on my forehead to keep me cool. So I knew it was her.

(Jason)

Pat described how she sensed her aunt's presence through a form of physical contact that was particularly characteristic of her. The powerful and transformative impact it had on Pat served to validate its reality regardless of any rational attempts to explain it away:

. . . and then I just lost it and started crying and it was in the middle of Waterstones which was a little embarrassing, but there we go, and I felt this – I felt a hand on my back which was what Enid always used to do when I'd leave, she'd just put her hand on my back and kind of gently stroke – she wasn't a huggy sort of person and I just felt this hand on my back, this stroke and I just heard, 'It will be ok' – you know and things just kind of came to – all the rage and the rawness and everything else just like a deflated balloon. I don't know if I've conjured her up – it doesn't really matter – it works so.

(Pat)

Indeed, in the absence of a material body and the boundaries associated with material existence, the dead were free to make contact with the living in more subtle and mysterious ways, choosing both their timing and their vehicle. In recounting her experience of her mother's continuing presence, Linda conveyed how the dead may respond in answer to the unwitting invitations of the living:

I was with two of my sisters and we were having breakfast and . . . my mother had always loved her music and she was a lovely singer and she always used to sing *Summertime* and there were always family parties and people had their party pieces and . . . I had this aunt Lucy . . . and her party piece was always *Robin's Return* . . . And while I was texting someone, my sisters were saying, 'We wonder how Mammy's getting on now,' really, and 'I wonder if she met Lucy?' . . . and we were kind of having that sort of conversation and we were listening to the radio and suddenly *Robin's Return* came on the radio followed by *Summertime.*

(Linda)

As well as initiating contact, the dead may withdraw their contact, regardless of the wishes of the living. Linda and Jason revealed how continuing bonds were dependent on the dead as well as the living for their continuation:

When she died I kind of felt, 'Oh well, she's around', for that couple of weeks afterwards I really did feel that she was around. But then this real absence – do you know what I mean? And a real silence, you know.

(Linda)

So that with Vera I go to the special places that she used to go to. And then I'm in immediate connection with her. But sometimes I can't get hold of her also – she's busy on the other side doing things.

(Jason)

Continuity and change

Narratives of rediscovery revealed how the nature of a loved one's continued presence often reflected the role he or she used to play whilst still alive, further emphasising both the intersubjective nature of self-identity and the integration of the dead into the lives of the living. For such continuity enabled people to view the world through the eyes of deceased loved ones and provided a resource for negotiating the disruptive impact of bereavement on their social worlds. Though death may demand that the forms of people's relating change, their character and meaning may continue (Hockey, 1996a).

For Fiona, her sense of connection with her father took the form of the remembered practical guidance and know-how that characterised her relationship with him while he was still alive. In sharing this connection with other family members she also ensured her father's continued presence within the family unit:

Like, if I'm driving my car, like last night, we had our Christmas meal last night and we [i.e. family members] were talking about driving in the fog and bad conditions and I was saying that I just remembered Dad saying to me if it's very foggy and you can't see then just follow the line of the curb, you know follow the white line and you'll be fine so

(Fiona)

Lynne conveyed how her mother continued to occupy a significant place in her thoughts and exert a profound influence on her present life, providing her with a tried and trusted reference point:

> I still think about her a lot. She will always, you know, she would always be a very important part of my life and I still do things and think, 'Oh what would Mum think of this?'
>
> (Lynne)

Pat revealed how her aunt continued to provide her with moral guidance:

> ... like she shaped my life – continues to do so ... she's a kind of Good life, Good living with a Good capital G – living, ethics and morality and yeah ... an emotional standard.
>
> (Pat)

Pat's narrative, along with others, conveyed how continuity could be defined in terms of realising the extent to which the deceased person had shaped one's life. Jane appreciated the extent of the practical instruction she had received from her great grandmother and Pat recognised the lasting value of what her aunt had brought into her life:

> She taught me loads as a child. I know about finances because she set up an account for me as a child and put money in – you know little things.
>
> (Jane)

> I recognise what she brought to my life, you know, and that was a sense of family ... I only know half of what I know about this city because Enid told me about it.
>
> (Pat)

Activities that promoted and extended generational ties, represented another source of continuity, as Adrian conveyed in recounting his experience of taking his sons to visit their deceased grandfather's place of birth (Francis *et al.,* 2005):

> ... but I've been taking my two youngest down there every year, ... my two boys, they've been going since they were babies, at least once a year, so it's really part of their – who they are and I want to keep that connection because it's also my roots.
>
> (Adrian)

Continuity could be maintained in more practical ways, such as Roy's decision to keep his father's details on his mobile phone, thus preserving the parental couple:

> No, I won't change it on my mobile where it says 'm and d', it will just stay 'm and d'. I'll know it's Mum and Dad, but it's Mum. Whether I change it in a year's

time or two year's time I don't know . . . 'cos Mum now epitomises all those strong memories I have of Dad. When I talk to Mum I'm talking to Dad at the same time.

(Roy)

For Tina, keeping her mother's details on her mobile phone was a source of ambivalence, its presence evoking absence. Though she felt unable to remove the name, she found it upsetting when she saw it there:

I still have on my mobile phone 'Mum and Dad' – I can't take it off – I can't – yet I don't like it when it comes up because it throws me. I do want it to come off yet I can't take it off.

(Tina)

Some accounts revealed how losing a loved one could change the nature of one's relationship with that person to reflect an increased sense of protectiveness towards his or her memory. Marianne conveyed how she became more protective of her mother's memory, whilst Julian reported how his relationship with his grandfather had softened. In so doing, they provide further examples of an implicit discourse of care:

I used to be quite evangelical about my mum's alcoholism and tell everyone while she was still alive because it was saying normally, lovely people can be alcoholics. Now that she's died I'm not doing that anymore . . . I feel more protective of her memory, more selective.

(Marianne)

My relationship with him was sort of one of fear really – but now it's more endearing – it's more loving now.

(Julian)

Rediscovering the deceased person

As well as representing continuity and sometimes change, continuing bonds included discovering more about the deceased person, to further define and enhance his or her personhood and the relationship itself (Walter, 1996; Riches and Dawson, 1997). This could occur via the person's effects, or through communicating or being with others who knew him or her. Pat reported how she continued to discover more about her aunt's public life through meeting people who had known her. Letters of condolence provided a further source of information through which Pat also discovered what *she* had meant to her aunt:

. . . and you know that was quite interesting getting to know Enid's public life 'cos she never told me anything about that . . . got to know what she did long after she died and even still, like two years later I was still finding out little bits of stuff like that which was interesting.

(Pat)

So I had all of these letters from people who I'd never met who were expressing condolences and they were talking about how Enid used to talk about
meeting me and some of those letters were also saying, you know, you gave
her a family again.

(Pat)

For both Patrick and Adrian, the funeral represented an occasion of discovering
more about their fathers through being with others who knew them. Patrick reported
how the large turn-out of people bore witness to his father's caring nature and the
extent of its impact on the lives of others:

I think his funeral taught me more about how he'd – affected so many lives –
so his funeral taught me how much he cared about other people . . . having so
many people come up and say that he'd really touched their lives, that was nice.

(Patrick)

Adrian's experience of the funeral allowed him to enter his father's social world
in a way that provided him with the impetus to further engagement with other
people who had known him:

We took half his ashes back to Spain . . . and we had a service there in the local
church in his home town and that was packed too – I couldn't believe it. I didn't
know – I recognised everybody but the problem was I don't know the names
of half of these people and it feels awful you know, 'cos I want to go and find
them and talk to them, you know these people that I've seen over the years
. . . through my dad – I mean it was my dad's world and I sort of entered into
that.

(Adrian)

For Marianne, making contact with her mother's side of the family represented
a positive source of discovering more about the kind of person her mother had been:

It's really nice to have her older sister to go to and talk about my mother and
hear about her childhood . . . I think she was a lot more confident than she was
when I became really conscious of her – adventurous she was in a quiet way.

(Marianne)

Respecting the deceased person's wishes

Narratives of rediscovery revealed how deceased loved ones played a significant
role in shaping their funeral and disposal arrangements as well as bereaved people's
styles of grieving. My participants' concern to interpret and respect their loved
ones' wishes reflected the social and relational nature of personhood and agency.
Such concern, and its expression in the efforts people made to implement these
wishes as far as possible, represented a further expression of a discourse of care as

an aspect of continuing bonds. Narrators conveyed the mutuality or shared comfort this involved. The deceased person's wishes, their likes and dislikes, whether expressed or anticipated, provided an important measure of the appropriateness of bereaved people's responses and behaviour, something which may reflect the paucity of guidelines in a culture that promotes personal choice and freedom. As noted by Walter (1999: 142), in spite of the value placed on individualism, the absence of cultural prescription can leave people feeling at a loss.

Susan and Vivienne invoked the authority of their great-aunt and great-grandmother, respectively, on the basis of their knowledge, understanding and experience of them in order to evaluate and affirm their families' styles of grieving:

> We kept thinking maybe she didn't want us to cry and she wouldn't have really wanted us to be sad – and she wouldn't – like my mum carried on working, she would never have wanted my mum to stop her work because she thought it was wonderful that she did Marie Curie nursing.
>
> (Susan)

> It was quite a kind of cheerful – she had a good life she wouldn't want you to all be sitting here moping – she wasn't that kind of person.
>
> (Vivienne)

Stephen and Julian similarly invoked the authority of deceased loved ones in order to retrospectively validate their own actions:

> You know I sort of think to myself, my father would have liked me to use the example of his death in someone else's PhD thesis.
>
> (Stephen)

> I think Granddad would be happy that I'm working and not hitch-hiking around the world. I suppose he would be happy that I've got a girlfriend and he'd probably be happy if I got another girlfriend next week being a 'Jack the Lad'.
>
> (Julian)

For Tania her sense of knowing what her mother would have wanted provided her with a sense of direction:

> I know what my mum would want – she'd want all of us to be fine and, you know, the grandsons to have a good life and everything, and I think that is what I take forward.
>
> (Tania)

Diane conveyed how taking the trouble to ascertain and carry out a loved one's wishes formed an important part of coming to terms with his or her death:

> . . . because people do have, I think – deep down wishes that they often don't vocalise because it involves talking about them not being around any more. But

they do have really really strong wishes. I think there's a sense – you come out the other end of it if you feel you've done everything you can possibly do towards fulfilling those wishes – as far as you can possibly grasp what they want.

(Diane)

However, identifying the deceased person's preferences was not always a straightforward matter, reflecting the complexity of human nature. Susan conveyed how her great aunt's wishes included competing tastes, presenting her with the need to negotiate these in relation to the style and character of the funeral:

We wore black or dark colours, my mum wore navy. And I think – part of me kept thinking, I'm not sure if she'd really want us to wear black, because she loved clothes and she loved pretty things. But on the other hand if we'd not worn black I think it would have felt wrong really. I think she was quite traditional just because of the age that she was.

(Susan)

Also, divergent interpretations of the deceased person's wishes could provoke family disputes, as conveyed by Vivienne. Drawing on her own knowledge and understanding of her grandmother she questioned the behaviour of other family members as being contrary to what her grandmother would have wanted:

. . . and then my aunt decided she wanted to do it on another lake, but my dad said no this is where my gran would have wanted to have her ashes scattered. So that was another thing – and that also annoyed me because she wouldn't have wanted to be looking down or whatever – you know she'd be upset if she thought it was going to cause these problems and arguments and stuff.

(Vivienne)

In cases where the deceased person's wishes were expressed, people took pains to ensure that these were carried out as fully as possible, as illustrated by Fiona in relation to her father having made it clear that he wanted people to celebrate rather than mourn his death:

'Cos Dad had said this for years and years and years that when he finally dies he doesn't want people grieving, doesn't want people mourning and wants people to be happy and you know celebrate his life and wear bright colours and we tried to stick to that as best we could, so.

(Fiona)

Fiona further reported how her father's express wish for his ashes to be dispersed overseas was adapted to ensure that the family played a role in this. Her unspoken assumption that her father's wishes were being carried out even more fully than he had anticipated, reflected perceptions of the nature, rights and obligations attached to family relationships. It also conveyed how respecting the deceased person's wishes could reflect the need to sustain family ties and integrate the dead within the lives of survivors:

> He always said that he wanted his ashes scattered in the Falklands and he always joked about putting them in a brown paper envelope and posting them off to the Falklands and his friends out there would do the duty of scattering his ashes, but it actually turned out that Rick was able to go, my nephew.
>
> (Fiona)

The deceased person's express wishes could sometimes override those of surviving loved ones, as reported by Adrian in relation to his father's disposal:

> Well, yeah, he had specifically told us that he wanted to be cremated, although I know my mother would have preferred a burial, but she went along with his wishes to be cremated after they'd done a post-mortem.
>
> (Adrian)

Fiona conveyed how anticipated wishes could be combined with express wishes to the enhancement of her father's funeral in a way that celebrated and affirmed his personhood:

> 'Cos Dad used to do line dancing and we decided that Dad would have thought it quite fitting and quite funny if we had his stetson hat and holster on top of the coffin. So we had a nice display of flowers and also his hat and his line dancing stuff as well. So that was quite nice 'cos that was very Dad and sort of put a bit of humour into it.
>
> (Fiona)

Several people reported how they appreciated their loved ones' express wishes in relation to funeral and disposal requirements, to emphasise the supportive nature of their presence in the immediate aftermath of their death. For example, Marianne acknowledged how helpful it was for her father to know what her mother wanted for her funeral:

> ... because she'd been able to communicate what she wanted about her funeral, that she wanted to be cremated and she didn't want a gravestone, well, not a standing one, but a lying one and that was immensely helpful to Dad to know all these things.
>
> (Marianne)

As already discussed in Chapter 2, Pat conveyed her appreciation of the way her aunt had left clear and detailed instructions for her funeral and disposal. These instructions included a Methodist funeral service at the church where her aunt's father had once been a minister and the present minister, a woman, was experienced by Pat as 'fantastic'. Indeed, Pat conveyed how following her aunt's instructions had saved the day in avoiding potential family conflicts:

> But she left very clear instructions that she wanted whoever was the minister of that church to adjudicate or, you know, to do the service and that was the kind of old family link and her name – her first name was Anne – I've no idea what her surname was – and she was fantastic actually. She was absolutely fantastic, 'cos I told her about the family conflicts. She managed in the service to kind of steer around some of that.
>
> (Pat)

Fiona conveyed how her father's instructions turned a sad occasion into one that could be enjoyed and that he himself would have appreciated:

> It was actually just a really nice day and my nephew Rick, who's the youngest of the nieces and nephews, he was asked by Dad, I think, to do the Eulogy . . . which was nice as well 'cos it was something Dad wanted . . . So that was really nice and my sister read a poem out which was really nice. So, considering it was a funeral it was actually quite a nice day and I think Dad would have really liked it.
>
> (Fiona)

Express wishes could also be experienced as imperatives. Lynne reported how her mother had reinforced her wish to be buried and not cremated with the threat of returning to haunt her:

> She did say she had to be buried and not cremated. And she said if you cremate me I'm going to come back and haunt you. And she probably would have too. So she was buried – and that was a relief.
>
> (Lynne)

Respecting the wishes of the dead could thus represent a means of keeping the dead in their place to convey a less comfortable, more disturbing dimension of the relationship between the living and the dead (Hallam *et al.,* 1999: 160–182).

Summary

This chapter has identified and illustrated the mutual nature of continuing bonds, how these could be initiated by the deceased person, and how they were characterised by continuity and change, recovering and rediscovering deceased loved ones and respecting their wishes. In so doing it has revealed a discourse of care that was both implicit as well as explicit. It has highlighted how, in sharing such experiences, narrators represented the experience of selfhood and agency as relational and intersubjective, to convey a far more complex and nuanced understanding than that encompassed by a unitary, embodied, rational, intentional self-hood (Hallam *et al.,* 1999; Lawton, 2000).

The mutual nature of continuing bonds encompassed sharing and reciprocity. Some individuals reported how they shared feelings of pride and pleasure with their loved ones and experienced a sense of mutual support, understanding and affection. The reciprocal nature of bonds was conveyed in terms of agency being exercised on both sides. In some cases the deceased person's agency was enhanced by virtue of his or her disembodied status. Thus the dead had a hand in the future direction of the living by providing support, energy and opportunity, whilst the living provided comfort, protection and companionship for the dead. A concern to ensure that loved ones were not left alone in an institutional space revealed a discourse of care. These narratives revealed how, in taking care of their loved ones, survivors were also taking care of themselves. Such mutuality demonstrated that continuing bonds in contemporary Western societies are not necessarily one-sided. By emphasising the unique personhood of deceased loved ones, they revealed how individualism and relatedness could be mutually enhancing rather than exclusive.

Communication could be initiated by the deceased person as well as the bereaved. It could occur unexpectedly, via sensory experiences in which the body of the bereaved person formed the vehicle through which the deceased person exercised agency. Whilst narrators represented these experiences as comforting, supportive, empowering and transformative, they also questioned their validity and reality. They juxtaposed the competing discourses of rationality and super-naturalism, negotiating these to try to preserve both the power and significance of the experience, as well as their own credibility. Music and dreams provided other means through which deceased loved ones made their presence felt. Such presence could be experienced as disturbing rather than reassuring. It could be withdrawn by the deceased person regardless of the wishes of the bereaved.

Continuing presence was represented as reflecting the role the deceased person had played for the narrator whilst alive, thus preserving continuity. For some, their loved ones continued to provide practical, reliable and moral guidance. Such continuity was reinforced through realising the extent to which their lives had been shaped by the deceased person. Preserving continuity could take the form of encouraging generational ties. For some, continuity was maintained in more practical ways, such as retaining their loved one's details on a mobile phone. In other cases narrators reported that the nature of their relationship with their loved ones changed after they died to reflect an increased sensitivity towards their memory and an implicit discourse of care.

For some, continuing presence included discovering more about their loved ones in ways that further defined and enhanced both their unique personhood and the relationship itself. One person discovered what she had meant to the deceased person. Such discovery occurred through coming into contact with his or her personal effects, and through communicating and engaging with others who had known him or her. For some, the experience of the funeral provided them with an enlarged perspective of their loved ones through providing them with access to their social worlds and the part they had played in the lives of others.

Narratives of rediscovery revealed a concern to respect the wishes of deceased loved ones, both express and anticipated. As well as reflecting the way people may attempt to ensure their continuing social presence after death, such wishes provided guidelines for bereaved people's responses and behaviour in the immediate aftermath of death. The way the deceased person's authority was invoked demonstrated the social and relational nature of personhood and agency. Narrators drew upon their knowledge and understanding of their loved ones to construct their likes and dislikes. 'What he or she would have wanted' provided a means of both validating their own behaviour as well as honouring the deceased person's memory, emphasising the mutual nature of the relationship. Such concern with identifying and implementing their loved one's preferences reflected a further dimension of a discourse of care in people's continuing bonds that provided comfort for both parties. However, ascertaining such wishes could involve negotiating competing preferences, as well as provoke family disputes over differing interpretations of his or her wishes.

Express wishes in relation to funeral and disposal requirements were considered particularly helpful and supportive. Narrators described how they took great pains to ensure that a deceased loved one's express wishes were carried out, and were prepared to have their own wishes overridden. However such wishes could be modified to ensure that the family played a key role, as well as combined with anticipated wishes to the enhancement of the occasion. One participant conveyed how the dead could be perceived to possess the power to enforce their wishes by threatening to haunt the living, suggesting that respecting the wishes of the dead may encompass concerns about keeping the dead in their place, or maintaining the boundaries between the living and the dead. This example demonstrates the complexity of continuing bonds and, as illustrated in Chapter 5, the mutable nature of the life–death boundary.

7 Locating and sustaining presence

This chapter explores the variety of ways in which my participants sought to maintain the continuing presence of their dead loved ones in their ongoing lives. It has been noted that, in the absence of their physical presence, it can be important for bereaved people to find places that deceased loved ones can inhabit (Berger, 1995). Indeed, people conveyed how, in the absence of the physical body, deceased loved ones were free to inhabit a variety of forms. Though they talked about more formalised memory-making activity, their narratives tended to emphasise the informal, day-to-day dimension of locating and sustaining the presence of dead loved ones, as conveyed by Fiona as she remembered her father:

> There's things he's told me or places we've been or if I'm sat at home and I can see his picture on the window sill or programmes I know he used to watch, like The Bill or things like that.
>
> (Fiona)

Narratives of rediscovery captured the sometimes spontaneous and unexpected ways in which such presence could be evoked. Presence and contact was experienced and located inwardly via mental, emotional and imaginative activity. Such experience was negotiated through beliefs about life and death. Presence and contact was also evoked more 'outwardly', through 'social and cultural activity' in the form of 'conversation' and 'material culture'.

Mental, emotional and imaginative activity

I have already drawn attention to the social nature of the self and the diminishing impact that losing a significant other may have on one's sense of identity. However my participants' narratives revealed how loss evoked presence so that deceased loved ones could be experienced as continuing to form part of and even enlarging the self. The person's presence could be located in the mind and sustained through thinking about them, as expressed by Pat in relation to her aunt:

> . . . but there probably isn't a day that goes by that Enid isn't in my mind in one way or another.
>
> (Pat)

In contrast to the way that Enid formed a constant presence in Pat's mind, Lorraine conveyed how the dead could put in unexpected and unanticipated appearances:

> You know, people do stay in your mind don't they? I mean they pop up – there's the kind of pop-up ones who kind of come out of nowhere.
>
> (Lorraine)

Both Pat, in relation to her aunt, and Jason, his partner, emphasised their own role in actively bringing the person to mind:

> There was many a night I'd just lie in bed and think what would Enid tell me to do, what would Enid tell me to do? So she's kind of become this like person I can talk to.
>
> (Pat)

> I don't just talk in my head. I usually go into a meditative state and connect with her, visualise her. Every so often I do that with people. I do it a lot with Vera.
>
> (Jason)

Presence could be experienced at a more visceral level, as conveyed by Andy in relation to his father:

> And I do have days when I still feel that his presence is still around me, he's still looking down at me . . . and it feels comforting – comforting.
>
> (Andy)

Some people conveyed their experience of presence through images of embodiment or incorporating the deceased person within or as part of the self. Stephen experienced his father as living on inside him:

> I'm quite conscious . . . that I'm very similar to him and so there's almost a feeling that in some sense he still lives on, but he lives on through me not just in a genetic way but actually in a kind of more personality way because we do things that are frequently quite similar and I might be doing something or saying something and then I suddenly think to myself, that's what my father used to do. And so you do feel a kind of element of – you almost feel as though the person's a little bit alive but still living inside you.
>
> (Stephen)

For Brian his grandmother's continuing presence inside him was a source of amusement in the way it evoked her characteristic 'quirky whistle', whilst for Tania, her sense of identification with her mother was comforting:

> My granny has passed away but she will always live on within me you know. I mean I even smile when I think about the way she whistles now because it's just such a quirky thing to do.
>
> (Brian)

> I kind of feel she's more part of me now – and what I like is the realisation of just how much I'm like my mum . . . I don't know, I get a lot of comfort from that. I like some of the strengths I've got from her.
>
> (Tania)

Lynne conveyed how a loved one's presence could be located in other related selves. She reflected on the way specific aspects of her mother's character lived on in other family members:

> . . . but I think my niece has got her strength 'cos she's an incredibly – if she wants something she goes out she gets it – she's been very successful and she's got great inner strength which I think my mother had as well, so I think she takes after her more than anybody else. I'm trying to think about my children – well, I think my elder son has got her obstinacy.
>
> (Lynne)

Beliefs about life and death

In making sense of such continuing presence, my participants would find themselves reflecting on their beliefs and understandings about life and death. These demonstrated the diversity of belief systems in a culturally plural society in which images and ideas were often divorced from their traditional roots and reconstituted to reflect individual experiences, needs and inclinations. They conveyed a tolerance of other people's beliefs. Thus the eclecticism of Adrian's spirituality enabled him to acknowledge the appropriateness of his father's funeral taking the form of a Catholic mass. This eclecticism reflected the emphasis on personalised funerals that celebrate and affirm the deceased person's uniqueness:

> I mean, I would say I'm spiritual – I mean, if you asked me what religion, what faith are you, I would say I just have a spiritual element to me and I have actually drawn on many many different – I mean, I was quite happy for my dad to have a Catholic mass and that seemed very appropriate.
>
> (Adrian)

In some cases such personalised beliefs were presented as offering comforting possibilities rather than fervent convictions, as conveyed by Sandra and Brian:

> You know you can believe that when you die you can be around for people that need you and then when you're not needed any more, you can go and watch over people and take care of them and maybe you can all get reincarnated together. It's very idealistic . . .
>
> (Sandra)

> It's just a bit of hope to cling on to, that these people are still there and they are listening to me and they can hear and every time I visit the grave of a

relative I'd like to think there's a little buzzer switch that goes off somewhere
so that they know that I'm there and they can come and have a look, you know.

(Brian)

Both Stephen and Brian acknowledged how belief in an afterlife served to
validate and reinforce their continuing bonds with deceased loved ones:

So sometimes when something kind of quite nice happens to you, you're almost
thinking, sometimes, you know, is this little signs from beyond the grave to a
certain degree happening? Which I suppose in a sense is a way of, I suppose,
of almost, kind of, maintaining a relationship with somebody for you, even
though there's nobody there now for the relationship to be maintained with.
And, you know, that's something that I definitely do. If I have something nice
happen to me then you kind of say, maybe somebody up there's sort of put in
a good word for me.

(Stephen)

I think that's what the general basis of bereavement is – is that you never let
them properly go – I mean that's in any religion that you just don't let them
go, they're always there somewhere, whether it be a picture on the mantel-
piece or ashes on the cabinet in the living room, or anything really.

(Brian)

However, the implications of continued existence in an afterlife could generate
ambivalent feelings about the life–death boundary. Though taking comfort from
believing that her father was still around, Fiona expressed some anxiety with regard
to the possibility of any sensory experience of his presence:

. . . even though I'd like to think that he's out there somewhere in spirit form,
if I actually saw him it would be actually quite frightening. So I don't know if I'd
really want to sense something. But it's just sort of comforting to know that
he's out there somewhere and watching over me.

(Fiona)

For Stephen such belief involved negotiating the competing discourses of
rationality and spirituality:

. . . and it's the kind of thing that on the one hand my head says obviously I'm
just talking to a grave and my father's in there somewhere, but there's probably
not that much of him left now, but at the same time you do sometimes wonder,
you know, if there is an afterlife up there is he in some sense standing over me
and can do things for me?

(Stephen)

Such beliefs could be represented as certainties, as in Sandra's experience of the
continuing presence of both her friend and grandmother:

But I know they're watching and just with me in a way – they haven't just gone and disappeared.

(Sandra)

For Jason such certainty included a detailed description of the 'other side'

Well, it's the astral plane and it's got many levels. So people gravitate to the level they're sort of at. It's like here but it's different because they're not in dense physical bodies, and they have jobs, they have whole lives that they carry on, they do all sorts of things . . . it's like very similar to our existence here except much more free.

(Jason)

Others felt that continuing presence did not depend on belief in an afterlife. Rather they emphasised the power of memory to sustain such presence, as conveyed by Vivienne in relation to her grandmother:

I don't think she's around in any physical sense. I just think she's around in people's experiences and memories of her.

(Vivienne)

For both Janet and Vivienne, continuing presence depended on the living continuing to bring the dead to mind. Remembering the dead was therefore an imperative, reflecting humanistic values:

I'm not really religious and I don't – I don't know, I don't really think of an afterlife, but I – it's kind of you don't want to forget someone's memory and you don't want to forget that they're there and so it's kind of nice to think – I think it's nice to still have an idea of their presence and that you can't just forget them so you still have to think of them and the things they do.

(Janet)

I don't imagine her looking down on me or anything, but like if the family's having problems about her I kind of get the feeling that if, you know, she knew what was going on it would upset her. I guess it's just the not forgetting about her kind of thing. Thinking about her. You can't just forget people.

(Vivienne)

Conversation

I have already drawn attention to the role of conversation in constructing a memory of the deceased person that is comfortable to live with (Walter, 1996). The interview itself demonstrated this process to the extent of evoking the presence of deceased loved ones. Indeed, the opportunity people took to consider and appreciate what deceased loved ones meant to them served to reinforce and sustain their continuing bonds. The role of conversation in this process was confirmed by Lorraine, who reported how talking to others about certain topics could bring home to her just how much she had learned from her involvement in the care of her godson:

> Like I said, quite often he comes up because it's something about something I learnt from the relationship with him that's triggered off. It could be something very practical like you know, you might be talking about children with needs and something about that and you think, 'I have this store of information'. He was my landmark in knowing that or learning that particular insight.
>
> (Lorraine)

A discourse of care was apparent in the way some people conveyed how such conversation took the form of protecting loved ones' memories by trying to counter any misunderstanding or misrepresentation of them by others. Marianne reported how she would talk at length about her mother to her friends to ensure that they gained an accurate picture of her. She also found herself challenging what she felt was her father's distorted version of how things were in the family whilst her mother was alive:

> Somehow it was really important to me that they would understand who my mother was.
>
> (Marianne)

> And Dad kind of sometimes makes it sound all kind of happier than it was. Once or twice I have said it isn't actually how I experienced it at the time and I don't think it was how you experienced it at the time either. So I have a certain sense of keeping my mother's memory alive in the family that I find difficult.
>
> (Marianne)

Tania similarly challenged what she felt was her father's inaccurate portrayal of her mother:

> And he started to put almost a kind of pathetic quality onto her and I'd say that's not Mum.
>
> (Tania)

Fiona and Diane illustrated how talking about their loved ones could arise spontaneously as part of normal conversation:

> He'll come up in conversation like, 'Dad would have done this' or 'Dad would have said that' or you know pass comments about him. So he is still talked about.
>
> (Fiona)

Most people acknowledged the value of talking to others about deceased loved ones. Yet accounts also revealed competing social norms in relation to the extent to which the dead could be talked about. Diane conveyed how including them in everyday conversation may enhance a sense of their continued presence for surviving loved ones. However, she also revealed how people may still avoid talking about and thus exclude the dead:

> . . . and I happened to say the other day, I think my father came round for a meal or something and we were waiting for my mother-in-law to arrive, and I said something like 'Mum wouldn't have done that, she'd have done such and such', and he laughed – and he said 'Do you know, no-one ever mentions Mum in conversation but you' – and he said, 'it's so nice'. Because he feels she's still with him.
>
> (Diane)

Diane's experience may reflect what has been perceived as the cultural reserve of English people who may feel obliged not to intrude on the 'private' grief of others (Walter, 1999). Yet it has been argued that such reserve only applies to the 'England of the white middle classes' (Howarth, 1997: 95), and that reluctance to talk about the dead may have more to do with fearing them (Hallam *et al.,* 1999: 160–182).

Other accounts revealed how people negotiated these competing discourses of 'inclusion' and 'exclusion'. Marianne sought out her mother's sisters, for whom her mother remained more present than in her immediate family, whilst Tania and Susan resorted to talking about their loved ones to others as if they were still alive:

> Yeah, and I go and see her older sister now – and the older she gets the more she looks like my mum . . . her and her younger sister talk about Mum a lot more – she's more present for them than she is in my family.
>
> (Marianne)

> I still talk about my mum and dad . . . and I have talked to people about my mum as if she's alive.
>
> (Tania)

> . . . but I don't think people really realise that she's passed away, because I do sometimes say 'My aunty Doreen would do that' or 'My aunty Doreen grew those flowers', or something along those lines. And I wouldn't then afterwards say, 'Oh, she's not with us anymore'. I'd never say that.
>
> (Susan)

In contrast Pat revealed how she was not prepared to compromise in relation to talking about her aunt regardless of what other people might think:

> I've probably mentioned her to some people, I don't know, every two or three weeks – she's very present – people probably tire of that but who cares?
>
> (Pat)

Narratives of rediscovery revealed how deceased loved ones could be 'talked to' as well as 'talked about'. Such conversations could be frequent and continuing, forming part of the ordinary course of daily living. Jason conveyed how he engaged in an ongoing dialogue with his partner in order to try and make amends for his perceived shortcomings whilst she was alive:

> I talk to her a lot actually. Yeah I do talk to her. Mostly I say how sorry I am and that I could have done it better.
>
> (Jason)

For several people these conversations involved sharing the day-to-day events of one's life with the other, as reported by Tania in relation to her mother:

> It's more the, 'This is what I'm doing, Mum', that sort of thing. It's sort of a – I'll often talk to her.
>
> (Tania)

Such sharing could be separated from the ordinary business of living, and take place in the memorial space of the cemetery. Both Stephen and Elisabeth located their conversations with their father and mother respectively, at their gravesides:

> . . . and when I go down to Devon I will go for a walk in the afternoon and usually I will pop up to the cemetery and just see what's going on . . . and I will go in and just I suppose talk to him for five or six minutes . . . I just say to him – if something's going on in my life you know.
>
> (Stephen)

> When I go to the grave I tell him, you know, what the children have been doing and what I'm doing and, you know – have a conversation with him, yeah – I do – I don't know if that's normal or whatever but – I suppose it's a way of perhaps getting things off my chest as well – if I've got nobody else to talk to, I can just go and talk to him.
>
> (Elisabeth)

As already discussed in relation to 'sensing presence', narratives revealed how sharing such experience with another, as in the interview situation, could evoke competing discourses of rationality and supernaturalism (Bennett and Bennett, 2000). Thus Elisabeth, whilst acknowledging the therapeutic value of such activity, called into question its conformity to existing norms. Both Brian and Andy conveyed how such behaviour may be considered a sign of pathology:

> I mean, I visit both my grandfathers' graves and I do sit and talk and I don't think I'm mad – but I think it's a way of dealing with things, you know, because the physical has ended but they're still there.
>
> (Brian)

... and I was just sitting there in the peace and quiet and I was just talking to my dad. I was talking out loud and it was like, 'What am I doing?' And I thought, if someone's around, if security comes around they'll think, 'God, he's gone mad'.

(Andy)

Material culture

The last chapter explored how people materialised their experience of loss and absence through formal and informal ritualisation and memory-making activity, calling into question the distinction between grief and mourning. It highlighted how loss could be evoked by more ordinary, everyday objects, spaces, times and activities. In relation to the experience of continuing presence, aspects of material culture could take on a special significance, not only as reminders of the deceased person, but as sites of his or her presence and agency. Material culture thus formed an extension of personhood, destabilising the boundaries between subject and object (Hallam and Hockey, 2001).

Viewing the body

As already illustrated, viewing the corpse could evoke a powerful sense of absence for bereaved people. However some accounts posed a challenge to the common-sense assumption that the corpse offered unequivocal proof of social as well as biological death. Both Fiona and Elisabeth revealed how the physical remains of their father and husband respectively, could evoke a recovery of presence. Their accounts conveyed how the behaviour of bereaved people towards the corpse may contribute to its personalisation and demonstrate its capacity for agency (Hallam and Hockey, 2001):

But we went in and he did look like Dad and he did look like he was just asleep. And we just stood around, not – we weren't laughing at Dad we were sort of laughing with Dad thinking he's at rest now. He looks very peaceful and you know – we'd like to think he's sort of stood with us watching us and laughing with us . . . in a way it was quite nice to see him like that because how he was in the hospital was quite difficult – whereas he looked like Dad again.

(Fiona)

. . . and the grandchildren came down with me once because they wanted to see him. And we actually dressed him in t-shirt and jeans rather than the white silk sort of things they put on.

(Elisabeth)

Elisabeth's account further revealed how she came up against the modernist imperative to 'let go' and 'move on'. Her demonstration of affectionate behaviour towards her husband's remains was experienced as inappropriate and disturbing by close others in the way it defied the boundaries between the living and the dead:

I just wanted to hold him and be with him but my mother and my eldest daughter were really worried about me ... they said, 'It's just not right – you're always up there at the cemetery or down at the funeral parlour'.

(Elisabeth)

Yet for Elisabeth her husband's remains were so powerfully evocative of his presence that she expressed wanting to throw herself on his coffin during his burial.

The funeral

Adrian illustrated how the funeral, as a more formal, public, ritualised and socially acceptable practice provided a wider platform for locating and sustaining the deceased person's social presence. His account reflected a growing emphasis on self-styled funerals to celebrate the person's unique selfhood (Cook and Walter, 2005), conveying the sense of responsibility this placed on those left behind to ensure that their deceased loved one was not misrepresented. Thus he described the embarrassment that he and his sisters experienced through having chosen an inappropriate reading for their father as a result of having based their choice of text on just a few of its lines without reading the whole:

So when it came to the service and Father Alan read out this reading about separating the sheep from the goats and the righteous from the unrighteous, we just cringed because it was so inappropriate for our dad. It was just completely the wrong thing and my sister was sitting next to me and saying, 'This is the wrong one'.

(Adrian)

However, Adrian also reported how a further reading served to redress the situation:

I read a bit from Graham Greene, which was my dad's favourite English author and ... it set right the – the things that had gone wrong prior to, you know – it put my dad in a better perspective than separating the righteous from the unrighteous which is, of course, in his eyes, nonsense.

(Adrian)

Memorialisation

In relation to more private memory-making activity, narratives revealed how the experience of absence could be transformed into one of highly personalised presence by creating spaces that represented focal points for continuing contact between the living and the dead. Cemeteries, as bounded spaces set apart from the hustle and bustle and routine of daily living, have been reported to provide environments of peace and timelessness in which to remember dead loved ones (Francis *et al.,* 2005). Whilst designated as public places, cemeteries could still offer a sense of privacy. Pat conveyed how such a space, far from evoking pain and distress, could provide a sense of safety:

> I go down to the cemetery a lot. It's not kind of like going down there to look at the grave stone and like beat my chest and grieve, but it's a very peaceful and beautiful place and, you know, I have fond memories of that cemetery and it feels like a very safe place.
>
> (Pat)

Both Adrian's and Janet's accounts revealed how the communal, institutional space of the cemetery could be personalised. Adrian and his family placed some of his father's ashes in a cemetery plot overlooking the racecourse he had frequented whilst he was alive:

> And the other half we've still got at home on the table, but we were going to choose a plot in Cheltenham cemetery – which we did last week and it's local where me and my mum lives and my other sister lives in the next town along, and my other two sisters are in London . . . well it looks out over the hills and you can see the racecourse and my dad was a great racing fan.
>
> (Adrian)

Janet's account reflected the way that consumer goods may be used to create highly personalised grave displays that represent an enduring sense of personhood (Hallam and Hockey, 2001: 209). Such displays tend to combine objects already belonging to the deceased person with new items contributed by others to complement them:

> Like on his 18th birthday we went down and there was an empty can of Fosters and we put some daisies at the top of it – a record, which was one of his favourite records – that went down there. There were lots of pictures – and there were things obviously from when we didn't know him, when he was obviously very young because we hadn't met until we were 12 years old and, like, things like his dad and his uncles and aunties back in Bristol had brought down, like cricket balls and things like that, because he used to play cricket. So all stages of his life were sort of represented down there.
>
> (Janet)

For others, alternative memorial spaces were considered more appropriate to reflect the deceased person's identity. Adrian and Michael chose to place their parents' cremated remains in local beauty spots that held significance for their lives. Their accounts demonstrated that being able to remove cremated remains from crematoria may offer bereaved people more scope to create personalised spaces and provide loved ones with their own 'spot' or, in Adrian's case, more than one spot. Adrian reflected on the beauty and appropriateness of one of the two sites where his father's ashes had been placed, the one located at his place of birth:

So he's got his spot which is beautiful – I mean it really is quite spectacular up there – 360 degrees – it's . . . right in the heart of the Pyrenees. All around is big mountains, snow-capped mountains . . . it's really, really very beautiful and that was where he was born and, you know, he used to run up there as a kid and . . .

(Adrian)

Michael's account demonstrated how such personalised memory-making could encompass both personhood and relatedness and how the cemetery may be rejected in favour of somewhere that was perceived to offer more scope for such expression:

I still had some of my father's ashes so I was able to put the two together and I made a cross which – it's just a marker really, a place they knew, a nice spot because it's a lovely view over the town and it's a place I can go and visit, because I didn't like – even if I had decided to, I don't think I'd have wanted to have a stone in a graveyard. The idea of burying ashes where you want is more appealing to me than a sort of communal graveyard if you like – because it's chosen by me and it kind of in someways fulfils the need of my mother to be up high – a sense of a view and where I can sit – there's a bench there.

(Michael)

He revealed how his choice of site forged a link with the wider social environment and provided the dead with a more integrated social presence. Furthermore, such memory-making activity served to enhance the site for the enjoyment of others, demonstrating that the expression of a very personal need could incorporate a wider social benefit:

But the other thing was that my father and mother loved daffodils so I've planted some daffodils upon the cliffs as a sort of way of not just as a memorial but also just to sort of give something by way of, kind of, make an expression really – beautifying the environment really and nobody can see the cross, it's hidden away in the bracken so it is quite private in that sense – and I did a carving on there – just a personal thing.

(Michael)

Patrick conveyed how a 'natural' setting may be more meaningful for people than a cemetery, which may be associated with decay as opposed to the regenerative power of the natural world:

They bury you and plant a tree, which is really nice so – I'm going to go and visit the site in April and have a look at the tree – which is nicer than going to a graveyard because graveyards just deteriorate – every time you go and visit the grave it's a bit older and a bit falling apart, whereas this little sapling forest, every time you go and visit it's going to be a bit bigger and the trees will be bigger and it'll be nicer and eventually we won't even know which tree's his . . . and he's kind of rejoined the world of nature in a spiritual sense.

(Patrick)

He further reported how a more 'natural' setting resonated with his father's identity:

> ... and also Dad was always out in the countryside anyway 'cos of the scout camps – so rather than being in a city in a graveyard it's really nice to have this little spot.
>
> (Patrick)

Some people appreciated the way memorial spaces provided a material focal point for evoking presence (Hockey and Kellaher, 2005). Janet reported how visiting her friend's grave was not a matter of duty but an expression of continuing emotional attachment to his memory:

> I mean I don't go there to speak to him or anything like that ... it's not like I feel a duty to go there – I want to go there – but I don't know why, because it's not like once I get there I talk to him or I feel I'm closer to him. I suppose it's the one place I can go and it's where I remember him most. I mean – it's quite, like, emotional going there.
>
> (Janet)

Some participants conveyed how they appreciated having a place that could be revisited, that offered scope for personalisation, tending, enhancement, spending time there and provided an enduring symbol of the deceased person's presence. In so doing, they confirmed findings from a recent study of ashes disposal, which has drawn attention to the role of time and imagination in creating 'environments of memory' (Hockey and Kellaher, 2005; Kellaher *et al.*, 2005), as illustrated by Michael and Adrian:

> Well, it's nice to go there and just spend a bit of time there and I can do something practical because I've already planted – three times I've planted flowers there, and it's nice to see them come up and I hope some more will come up this year. So it's a way of keeping something alive, if you like.
>
> (Michael)

> It was a lovely lovely thing – after the service we all walked up the little hill just behind the cemetery and we dug a hole and planted a holm oak ... and because of the altitude it doesn't grow into a tree but it remains more like a bush and it sort of fits in with the surroundings and so that's going to be lovely – it's somewhere to go back to each time we go and to look out from there – and all his friends came up.
>
> (Adrian)

Elisabeth, in describing how her grandson maintained a continuing bond with his grandfather, revealed how such focal points for remembering deceased loved ones could provide a link between the generations (Francis *et al.,* 2005):

He'll go up to the grave and put flowers on it at Christmas and on birthdays and what have you, and he's talked to him as well, which is quite interesting – sometimes he'll say 'What did Granddad look like?' and we'll get a photograph out and show him and, you know – he doesn't want to forget him.

(Elisabeth)

In the absence of a focal point, the linking of generations could also be achieved through the involvement of a younger member of the family in the deceased person's disposal wishes, as reported by Fiona and already discussed in the section on 'respecting the wishes of the deceased'. However, Fiona regretted the absence of any focal point for her father's memory, consoling herself with a discourse of emotionality and intimacy which located the deceased person within the survivor as a constant and more integrated presence:

So I was sort of thinking well for Dad to be buried was quite nice 'cos then there's always somewhere to go and see him or visit him and take something. But that wasn't the case and, you know, people say your memories are in your head anyway, and going to visit a grave doesn't necessarily mean you're going to visit them, because they're with you all the time anyway.

(Fiona)

Such integration was represented by Diane in relation to her father's decision to keep his wife's ashes at home with him. However she also added that the ashes were 'not on general display', reflecting the influence of the modernist discourse of separation and the anticipation of social disapproval in relation to taking a more intimate stance (Hockey and Kellaher, 2005; Kellaher *et al.*, 2005).

So then he suddenly came up with this idea that as both my brothers make furniture – and he decided he would have a casket made so he would have her ashes kept at home in this casket so that when he died he could have his ashes put in with it and we could go and scatter them somewhere in a place of our choice.

(Diane)

In recounting such experiences participants revealed an implicit discourse of care in the way their choice of disposal and the ways they maintained and interacted with disposal sites reflected the personhood of deceased loved ones. They conveyed the significance that could be given to those sites to which one may then become very attached (Klass, 2006).

Places, times and activities

The way that places and times that had been particularly important to the deceased person when they were alive could so powerfully evoke their presence, was conveyed by both Jason and Lorraine. Jason identified a particular place in the countryside as representing his sense of connection with his partner, whilst Lorraine reported how she was able to sense her friend's presence when tending the allotment she had taken over from her:

> Well Vera used to have some special places . . . and we used to meet up at a spot on the Mendips quite a lot. It was sort of like our special place and I go there still fairly often and meditate there and it's very isolated and I can sit up there for two or three hours and there's nobody comes, you know, it's very secluded and you have to walk for miles to get there. And Vera and I used to go and meditate up there on a full moon and so I still go sometimes on a full moon and sit up there, connect with Vera . . .
>
> (Jason)

> I used to do her allotment for her towards the end 'cos she couldn't physically manage, but wanted to do it . . . so I actually took on her allotment and when I'm on it – it's funny you know, there are particular places on the allotment where vividly she's always there beside me, because she was there before she got ill.
>
> (Lorraine)

Engaging in activities associated with the deceased person could provide a powerful source of connection with him or her. Such connection could be experienced as enhancing one's enjoyment of the activity, as in Andy's case in relation to his father's religious observance:

> And when my dad passed away I held onto my faith again. I think like because my dad was so religious and believed in faith so much, it really put me in touch with my faith and I don't want to lose that faith again . . . and I look forward to going to the temple now – I really do.
>
> (Andy)

Such activities included creative pursuits. For Sarah, her ability to paint was something she had shared with her grandmother while she was alive and from whom she continued to receive inspiration after she had died. Her sense of difficulty in putting such experience into words, pointed to the inadequacy of available discourses to encompass a more intersubjective experience of agency:

> It's just when you're painting you realise that you've got to have got that from somewhere – the ability to draw, to paint, and I guess you think of her style . . . I don't know, you think about her drawing – I mean it's a point of inspiration when you think you can't draw, then it sort of spurs you on and you think you know you can draw 'cos Granny could draw. I don't know how else to explain it – it's almost like meditative when you're drawing . . . it's not necessarily like a conscious action. So it's hard to explain how it links to Granny apart from the fact that she painted as well.
>
> (Sarah)

Marianne conveyed how the fruits of her mother's 'patchwork' activity, something that had become a shared activity before she died, represented a very personal and intimate connection with her:

> And my mum did a lot of patchwork and about two years before she died I took it up with her and then partly independently and the weekend of her birthday when I went back, that's what we did. So I have all her fabric collections – and I think that to me is very much my link to her.
>
> (Marianne)

Patrick reported how his father's death had inspired him to learn to play the guitar, as a result of which he had written a song about him:

> And I've written a song about him. I'm learning the guitar.
>
> (Patrick)

In Adrian's case the fruits of his father's creative activity, in the form of poetry, offered a means of locating and sustaining his social presence beyond the immediate family. It also provided a potential project by means of which Adrian could integrate his father's presence into his own future plans:

> . . . it would be lovely to do something with his writings and his work so that he'll – not just live on in our family but . . .
>
> (Adrian)

Roy reported how he had made use of the internet to locate his father's social presence in a medium that would sustain this both temporally as well as spatially:

> And in fact he's on the internet now. I've done a family history so his name is now on the internet and to me that means he'll go on forever. I'm not saying that's a new religion but that to me means the memory of him will be there.
>
> (Roy)

Participants' narratives revealed how the deceased person's presence could be evoked by and located in ordinary, everyday spaces and activities. Jane reported how her great-grandmother's presence was evoked when making the bed:

> When I'm making the bed I'll think oh yes Great-gran taught me to do that.
>
> (Jane)

The deceased person's home and its locality could be powerfully evocative of his or her presence. Susan and Pat revealed how driving past the homes of their loved ones provided a means of sustaining their presence and affirming their relationship with them:

Every time we drive by the road she lived in – the house has been sold now . . . and every time we drive past the road we still say, that's Aunty Doreen's road. We haven't stopped calling it that. I think it will always be her road.

(Susan)

I drive by her house every now and then, and again that's just kind of like some connection with her.

(Pat)

Objects

Narratives of rediscovery illustrated the capacity of material objects to mediate continuing personhood and sustain the bond between the living and the dead, revealing the variety of objects that could be cherished as 'keepsakes' (Ash, 1996; Hallam and Hockey, 2001; Gibson, 2004). For example, Vivienne retained a postcard from her grandmother, Brian treasured the writing bureau that he chose from his grandmother's effects, Roy retained his father's record collection and some participants treasured their interview transcripts.

The way people engaged with such objects revealed how presence could be actively encouraged. Some people reported how they actively transformed certain objects into memory objects by displaying them in a manner and location that enhanced their specialness and significance, whilst keeping them close at hand. Fiona described how she had framed and displayed some photographs of her father in her home:

You know I've got pictures of him up at home now which I didn't really have before so I've found some nice photos and put them in frames.

(Fiona)

Both Adrian and Jane described how a very private location could enhance the value of such objects, such as Adrian's bedroom and the room that most represented Jane's relationship with her great-grandmother while she was alive:

I've got a little photo of him right by my bedside and his mother's rosary which is nice to have.

(Adrian)

I've got a really nice picture of her when I was a child with her. And it's really nice and I've got that in my room at my gran's house.

(Jane)

Lupton has highlighted how objects that enclose the body, such as clothing and dwelling places, and those that people interact with on a daily basis and express relations with others, such as postcards and letters, may acquire a heightened emotional charge (1998:144). Elisabeth and Stephen revealed how items of clothing that once belonged to the deceased person could evoke a sensory experience of that person's presence:

> I've still got the clothes he died in . . . I just still smell him and see him.
>
> (Elisabeth)

> In the hall there's one of my father's coats that my mother sort of decided that after my father died I might quite like . . . and sometimes when I'm in the hall I see it and just go over and sort of pick up the sleeve and smell it and it just reminds you.
>
> (Stephen)

Other accounts revealed how items of jewellery and clothing could provide a very intimate experience of the deceased person's presence, as conveyed by Pat:

> I have her gold necklace which is a very thick gold chain which I wear that she wore every day that I ever knew her and she'd given that to me.
>
> (Pat)

By wearing her aunt's gold chain, Pat retained a constant and open link with her, whereas Susan's treatment of her great aunt's coat conveyed a more hidden and intermittent, though readily available, source of contact, that allowed her to both retain and let go of her aunt's presence:

> And the coat I inherited – the fur – I put it away, you know, like in plastic cover and I don't think I'll probably wear it at the moment. But I'll always keep it. You know every time I open the wardrobe when I'm at home I always think of her then.
>
> (Susan)

These examples showed how deceased loved ones themselves could have a hand in securing their continued social presence and reinforcing ties with the living through the way they chose to distribute their possessions (Matthews, 1979). Indeed Pat's aunt secured a firm presence in Pat's home as a result of having left Pat the money that enabled her to buy it:

> She also had left some money which enabled us to buy the house that I live in now so you know . . . it feels like she's actually here.
>
> (Pat)

Summary

Continuing bonds were located and sustained through mental, emotional and imaginative activity. The deceased person could be located in survivors' minds and sustained through thinking about them. Such mental presence could be experienced as constant or intermittent, the deceased person putting in unexpected appearances. In other cases narrators emphasised their own role in bringing the person to mind. Presence could be experienced at a more visceral level to the extent of forming part of and living through the self of the bereaved person. People drew on images of embodiment to convey their experience, reflecting the intersubjective nature of self-hood. The sense of embodied connection with deceased loved ones could be a source of comfort.

In making sense of such experiences, my participants drew on certain beliefs about life and death. In so doing, they revealed a spiritual tolerance and pragmatism that in some cases represented such beliefs as comforting possibilities rather than fervent convictions. Some acknowledged how belief in an afterlife provided validation of their continuing bonds. However, for one person the possibility of actually sensing her father's presence was a source of some anxiety. For another, it involved negotiating the competing discourses of rationality and spirituality. In other cases continuing presence was represented as a matter of certainty. For others their continuing bonds were felt to depend, not on belief in an afterlife, but rather on the memory-making activities of the living, and, as such, an imperative.

In locating and sustaining presence more outwardly, the experience of the interview itself demonstrated the active, constructive role of conversation in this process. Accounts further revealed how talking to others served to evoke the deceased person's presence. For some, talking to others was a means of protecting their loved one's memory by countering any misrepresentation or misunder-standing of him or her by others. Deceased loved ones could form part of normal, everyday conversation, something that was perceived as enhancing their presence. However, as noted by one person, such an inclusive approach was not necessarily shared by all, revealing conflicting norms of inclusion and exclusion in relation to the dead. Narrators conveyed how they negotiated these competing discourses through seeking out and spending time with those who were willing to talk, by representing dead loved ones as if they were still living, or by refusing to com-promise the need to talk.

Narratives of rediscovery revealed how the dead could be 'talked to' as well as 'talked about'. In some cases these conversations were frequent, continuing and formed part of day-to-day life, to include trying to resolve issues from the past and sharing day-to-day events. For others such conversations were separated from the ordinary business of living, taking place at the grave-sides of deceased loved ones. In recounting such experiences people would negotiate the competing discourses of rationality and supernaturalism, to include references to the questionable nature of such activity in the light of 'commonsense' rationality.

Presence was materialised through formal and informal ritualisation and memorialisation, destabilising the boundaries between subject and object. For some, viewing the physical remains of the deceased person, rather than providing unequivocal proof of death, evoked, even enhanced, presence. One woman's demonstration of affectionate behaviour towards the remains of her husband was experienced as disturbing and inappropriate by close others, reflecting the modernist imperative to 'let go'. In relation to the emphasis on self-styled funerals, one person drew attention to the sense of responsibility bereaved family members could experience to ensure that the deceased person was not misrepresented.

In relation to more private rituals of disposal some people appreciated the peaceful, private, bounded space of the cemetery away from the hustle and bustle and routine of daily living. Some accounts revealed how such public, communal spaces could be highly personalised through the growing practice of constructing grave displays from consumer goods. Others found alternative memorial spaces to offer more scope for personalisation, such as local beauty spots associated with loved ones or a more natural setting that represented the regenerative power of the natural world. Some appreciated having a focal point for remembering the dead that could be revisited and tended. Such focal points also provided a site for maintaining generational ties. In the absence of a focal point, generational ties could be maintained through entrusting a younger member of the family with the dispersal of the deceased person's ashes. Support could also be taken from a competing discourse that emphasised keeping the person inside as a constant presence. People's concern to memorialise dead loved ones in ways that reflected their unique personhood conveyed an implicit discourse of care.

Places, times, spaces, activities and objects associated with deceased loved ones while they were alive could take on special significance for bereaved people. Activities that provided a source of enhanced connection with them included religious observance and creative pursuits, such as art, music, patchwork and poetry, as well as more ordinary, practical activities, such as using the computer and making the bed. In some cases such activities provided a means of extending the person's social presence both spatially and temporally. The capacity of material objects to mediate continuing bonds was represented through a variety of keep-sakes, which included interview transcripts. Presence could be actively encouraged through the transforming of objects, such as framing and displaying photographs, or placing objects in particular places. Personal possessions of deceased loved ones, such as jewellery and clothing, could evoke an intimate and sometimes sensory experience of presence. Such items demonstrated how dying people may seek to maintain their social significance beyond the grave.

This chapter has revealed how the dead retained a significant social presence and influence in the lives of the living by virtue of bereaved people's continuing attachment to their loved ones. Such attachment encompassed loyalty, care and protectiveness, recognition and appreciation and a sense of common humanity. It reflected an intersubjective exercise of agency that was not dependent on embodiment and could even be enhanced by disembodiment. However, the way that attachments defied the boundaries between the living and the dead, could sometimes be experienced as disturbing. The memory-making activity generated by such attachment represented a celebration of the enduring nature of personhood and relatedness that reached beyond the grave. Such activity and the meanings people gave to this have revealed how continuing bonds are more than products of internal, psychological processes but represent profound, far-reaching and complex social events.

8 Continuing bonds in contemporary society

This book has explored the unique and personal stories of a vulnerable and, to some extent, marginalised group of people, to identify the cultural frameworks through which the experience of losing a loved one may be understood and managed in contemporary British society. As indicated, this exploration presents a view that reflects the interests and concerns or subjectivity of the researcher as much as those of participants. The informal, conversational and interactive approach I took to interviewing enabled my participants' stories to emerge from our shared encounter. The nature of this encounter thus afforded me access to local worlds and the opportunity to capture and illuminate the profoundly sensitive and intimate experiences that participants shared with me. An ongoing, self-reflexive approach has informed my handling, understanding and presentation of these experiences. As a result, it is hoped that what I have revealed of the nature of bereavement as a social and cultural phenomenon, outweighs what has been obscured of the sheer variety and richness of people's individual experiences.

In introducing the research on which this book is based I identified a recent shift in academic approaches to understanding grief and bereavement in which increasing emphasis is being placed upon the social nature of loss. I discussed how that context informed my approach to investigating the way 25 bereaved individuals tried to make sense of the experience of losing a loved one. This shift in focus reflects the inadequacy of scientific, individualised and medicalised approaches which have largely neglected the extent to which grief is socially shaped. Reductionist models have constructed grief as an illness, so that people come to experience their loss as a condition that calls for treatment, for which a visit to the doctor might be the most appropriate response. Constructing grief as a condition of the individual has tended to leave people without sufficient social support (Charmaz, 1980). Such an individualistic conception of grief has inevitably reached an 'impasse' (Bradbury, 1999: 169) since it inhibits any real understanding of the profound nature of loss.

The approach I have taken has enabled me to undertake an in-depth investigation of the discourses people used and the nature and implications of such usage. This investigation has enabled me to identify the cultural connections between individual narratives of grief and contribute a more sociological understanding of bereavement. This final chapter will draw together and present the salient points of this exploration, highlighting their implications for bereavement theory, policy and practice. First, I draw attention to the way my participant's accounts took the form of three interrelated narrative strands that reflected the chronology of events (Reissman, 1993): 'narratives of dying', 'narratives of loss' and 'narratives of rediscovery', the last two being closely intertwined. I go on to consider the way these three narrative strands were linked by a twofold predominant concern to affirm and preserve both the personhood of the deceased loved one and the bereaved person's relationship with him or her. I then discuss the way narratives were characterised by a reflexive negotiation of competing discourses in which a humanising perspective provided a common thread of meaning. Finally, I consider how such understandings might inform social policy and practice in relation to helping people to live with the experience of death and bereavement.

Narratives of dying

In recounting their experiences of a loved one's dying my participants constructed dying trajectories to help maintain a semblance of continuity, normality and control in an otherwise unpredictable and uncertain process. These were characterised by a piecing together of events to negotiate a dying that truly belonged to the individual concerned, taking account of both his or her strengths and weaknesses. In a medicalised context in which dying and death have become institutionalised and routinised, people's narratives reflected an increasing concern with humanising the dying experience. To this end, the potentially competing discourses of medicalisation and individualism were negotiated in creative and idiosyncratic ways.

Experiences of institutionalised dying were reported as ranging from highly supportive to grossly undermining of human value and dignity. The medicalisation of dying did not necessarily serve to depersonalise or routinise, but rather provided a framework in which dying people were perceived to demonstrate their own particular and unique version of dying. Indeed, in some cases a medical setting served to enhance the dying person's characteristic selfhood. Medicalisation was not always inimical to a 'natural death', which could incorporate medical treatment rather than such treatment being considered as only invasive.

Individualism and medicalisation in no way minimised the value given to relatedness, intimacy and mutuality, and norms associated with sociality. Narrators negotiated the tension between 'individualism' and its emphasis on individual rights and responsibilities and the norms associated with relationship and social support in highly creative ways. Dying was thus a social, mutual, intimate and shared, as well as an individual and medical event. The participation of family and close others in a loved one's dying was considered normative, people sometimes questioning whether they or other family members 'could have done more'. A romantic discourse conveyed the intimate connection between narrators and their dying loved ones, to highlight the role of narratives of dying in people's continuing bonds. In particular, dying moments celebrated the enduring nature of both personhood and the social bond.

Discourses of religion and death's timing were also subject to humanisation and personalisation. Narratives conveyed an eclecticism and religious tolerance, with religious belief being treated as a personal attribute that could not be contrived. Thus, any religious beliefs held by the dying person were to be respected. Some participants expressed wishing that they were more religious and able to take comfort from a belief in an afterlife, whilst one person expressed relief at not needing to turn to religion. In relation to death's timing, though 'premature' deaths were considered unfair, perceptions of the deceased person's energy for life and the value attached to the relationship tended to outweigh considerations of age.

A good death depended on the extent to which it was a participatory experience that reaffirmed the social bond as well as the dying person's unique selfhood. Narratives revealed how this was achieved through a linking of individuality and sociality to emphasise the themes of 'agency', 'social support' and 'awareness'. My participants conveyed how their dying loved ones continued to exercise agency and take ownership of their dying through 'negotiating the system', 'showing character' and 'taking charge'. The narrator's role in 'respecting the wishes' and 'protecting the subjectivity' of loved ones further contributed to the dying person retaining some control over their situation, reflecting the relational dimension of agency, or 'empowerment' (Barnes, 2000). For the narrator, exercising agency encompassed taking ownership through 'being constructive' and 'giving voice' to the dying person's needs. It included empowerment through 'feeling needed' and 'having done all one could' in the circumstances.

Narratives demonstrated how the impersonality and indignities of the dying system could be negotiated, manipulated and even defeated by the dying individual's personhood. For example, no two cancer deaths were the same, since either a loved one's dying trajectory was represented as deviating from the norm or else he or she was reported to behave in idiosyncratic ways. Indeed, the extent to which dying reflected and demonstrated the unique character of the individual took precedence over the achievement of any 'acceptance' of dying (Kübler-Ross, 1970). Such characteristic dying included showing courage, defiance, putting up a fight and taking charge.

Attention was drawn to the initiative and foresight shown by dying loved ones in relation to some aspects of their dying, for example giving instructions as to their funeral requirements whilst still able to do so. In some cases the demonstration of initiative was regardless of bodily capacity, such as taking charge of one's dying moments. Final moments were sometimes characterised by an unexpected recovery of personhood in a context in which this had been under threat, representing the triumph of human spirit over the routine, impersonal medical settings in which dying often took place. These examples not only conveyed the dying person's continuing agency and capacity to take charge of their lives, but also his or her concern, support and affection for those they were leaving behind.

However increased vulnerability could obscure continuing agency, social presence and value. My participants conveyed a determination to protect the subjectivity of their dying loved ones, when they were no longer able to act for themselves. Indeed, humanistic values that upheld individual autonomy and dignity provided a context in which narrators were able to make decisions about the dying individual's care needs as well as evaluate their treatment by professionals. This could involve being prepared to respect his or her wishes, even where these went against what might be considered to be in his or her best interests, such as refusing to eat.

My participants' knowledge and understanding of their loved ones allowed them to play an empowering role on their behalf. Failing physical and mental capacities called forth a resourcefulness from narrators that enabled them to engage with their loved ones in imaginative and intuitive ways. Such resourcefulness was an important factor in retaining their sense of agency and empowerment. It also depended on establishing a rapport with and being taken seriously by professionals, as well as feeling valued by dying loved ones. Playing a constructive role in treatment and care allowed close others to stay in touch with and retain some control over the messiness of dying. Where the dying individual was in the hands of professionals, by taking the role of his or her advocate, they were able to help shape the situation. A sense of having done all one could in the circumstances left the narrator with positive feelings, whilst the perception that they could have done more provoked feelings of guilt and regret.

Indeed, the experience of agency had its limitations. Dying people could suffer a loss of ownership of their dying and a sense of disempowerment in the face of their failing capacities, which rendered them increasingly dependent on others. Close others could experience helplessness in relation to the limits of their capacity to support and help relieve the suffering of loved ones. Such helplessness could be further exacerbated by the responses of others, including professionals, family members and dying people themselves. Poor communication by professionals about the nature of the person's condition was experienced as having a negative impact on the family's decision-making and capacity to respond adequately to situations. Depersonalising treatment of the dying person by both professionals and family members could leave the narrator feeling unacknowledged and unsupported. The disengagement of the dying person could leave his or her loved one feeling rejected and at a loss.

In a social context that tended to prioritise the rational, autonomous, unitary, embodied self, my participants struggled to affirm the dying person's continuing social presence in the face of those family members as well as professionals, who failed to appreciate and acknowledge this. In recounting their efforts, people conveyed the way personhood and agency manifested through signals, gestures and facial expressions and the way these were received, interpreted and responded to by others. In so doing, they demonstrated the intersubjective nature of personhood, the multiplicity of embodied experience and the complex and negotiated nature of the relationship between individual agency and the social structure (Hallam *et al.*, 1999; Lawton, 2000).

Participants conveyed how achieving a good death was a social event that was linked to the extent to which care, comfort and reassurance was experienced by those involved. Social and individual considerations did not necessarily conflict, with support for the dying person being directed towards preserving, reinforcing and respecting his or her personhood. To this end, the narrator's 'presence', or simply 'being there' and 'being with' rather than 'doing to', enabled him or her to receive and affirm the verbal and non-verbal gestures that demonstrated the ways in which dying loved ones remained uniquely and characteristically themselves. Such support included normalising the situation for loved ones or maintaining connections with familiar and valued aspects of their lives in an attempt to sustain security and comfort in an uncertain, disruptive and often frightening process. In relation to their own need for support, the presence of trusted professionals provided narrators with both the reassurance of knowing that their loved one was in good hands, as well as that of being able to share the burden of responsibility.

The role of awareness in achieving a good death was represented as far more complex and nuanced than the universalised 'awareness contexts' of Glaser and Strauss (1965). Thus, awareness was conveyed as a process rather than a fixed state and formed a fluctuating, negotiable and ambiguous dimension of people's relationships, encompassing both acknowledgement and denial of death. It included the dying person's 'continued mental capacity' in the face of the physical deterioration of dying, evoking both the concern and admiration of close others for the increased suffering this could entail. In some cases an enhanced awareness at the point of death facilitated an intimate leave-taking that left the survivor with the reassurance that the dying loved one would remain part of his or her ongoing life.

Awareness encompassed other forms of 'knowing' that defied commonsense rational perception and assumptions. For some, the dying person's 'intuitive knowing', was invested with more authority than any professional understanding. It was not only dependent on the availability of information and communication, but had a more subtle, intuitive and relational dimension. It transcended bodily integrity and the capacity for speech. It was ambiguous in that it could entail the burden of increased suffering as much as it could empower (McNamara, 2001: 80–91).

Narrators, too, relied not only on being given sufficient information but on more immediate, intuitive and instinctive forms of knowing, the authority of which was dependent on their relationship and intimacy with the dying person. Such knowing gave them an intuitive understanding of their loved one's needs, a capacity to read the situation and so to respond appropriately. In some cases this capacity enabled them to be prepared for and respond positively to the dying person's final moments, transforming them into a social event of special significance (Kellehear and Lewin, 1988–1989; Kastenbaum, 1990). Indeed, these farewells were represented as profoundly moving and memorable occasions that transformed the defeating and demoralising nature of medicalised dying into examples of 'dying well'. However, as for the dying person, such awareness was double-edged in bringing home the nature of a loved one's suffering and impending death.

Narratives of dying revealed how the piecing together of the events leading up to a loved one's death may form an integral part of making sense of bereavement. They conveyed how bereaved people were able to draw upon their deceased loved ones' continuing individuality and personhood to provide solace and sustain them in their grief. As indicated, the importance that surviving loved ones attached to dying people remaining fully themselves reveals a link between palliative and bereavement care.

Narratives of loss and rediscovery

These two narratives are considered together to reflect the way that narratives of dying were more self-contained, whilst narratives of loss and narratives of rediscovery tended to overlap and interlink, conveying the paradox of the way that the deceased person's absence evoked their continuing presence and vice versa. Indeed, the paradox of absence and presence was evoked through formal memory acts and occasions, such as viewing the body, organising, attending and taking part in the funeral, visiting and tending graves and memorial sites. It characterised more informal, everyday activities and events and the objects, spaces, places and times associated with these. It formed a significant feature of interview conversations in that the sharing of the experience of the death of a loved one inevitably served to recreate and perpetuate that person's identity.

My experience of interviewing bereaved people thus represents a further dimension of the way the dead may become integrated into the lives of the living to reflect an alternative discourse to that which promotes the separation of the living and the dead. In addition to continuing presence forming part of the narratives of bereaved people and the bereavement counselling situation, such presence may form a significant feature of the research interview to the extent of finding a place and a voice in the life of a stranger. This experience raises important methodological and ethical issues about the potential of the research interview to change the bereavement experience and its impact on both researcher and researched.

The experience of loss provided the impetus to 'define' just what the deceased person meant to the survivor, drawing attention to both the 'quality' and 'extent' of such absence. People took the trouble to identify specific attributes of loved ones that they sorely missed, such as joviality, companionship, physical presence, practical and emotional support, guidance and validation. They conveyed how they experienced a diminishment of self through specific aspects of their own personalities and their powers of self-control. The process of defining their loss represented an attempt to negotiate the disruption caused to their sense of selfhood. It revealed the complexity of people's relationships, which were defined less by specific roles, and more by individual characteristics. Participants drew attention to the uniqueness and value of the life that had been lost and its irreplaceable nature. In some cases this was expressed in terms of the lost potential of a valued relationship.

Yet, defining loss formed part of a process of rediscovering presence. Narrators conveyed how they discovered more about their loved ones' lives, and about the nature of their own relationship with them, through coming into contact with their personal effects, and through communicating and engaging with others who had known them (Walter, 1996; Riches and Dawson, 1997). For some people, the experience of the funeral provided them with an enlarged perspective of deceased loved ones, enabling survivors to gain access to their social worlds and appreciate the part they had played in the lives of others. A concern with respecting their wishes emphasised the continuing agency and influence of the dead in the lives of the living, providing grieving loved ones with some guidelines for their own responses and behaviour. However, the sense of 'getting it right' could sometimes involve weighing up mixed messages, as well as provoke family disputing over differing interpretations of the deceased person's wishes.

An emphasis on individuality and diversity, or the 'right to grieve in one's own way', whilst promoting tolerance, in some cases left people feeling insecure in relation to the appropriateness of their own grieving style. Narratives of loss revealed how people negotiated such diversity in relation to the impact of the grief of others on their own grief, as well as the impact of their grief on others, both those who were grieving and those who were not. Their sense of loss could be affirmed, exacerbated or overshadowed by the grief of others. Interpretations of the responses of non-grieving people to their own grief made allowances for the sometimes seemingly insensitive or unsupportive nature of these. Lack of support from others could prompt people to rely on their own resources. Narratives thus emphasised the social, interactive, intersubjective nature of grief whilst at the same time upholding its very personal and individual dimension.

In conveying the personal and multi-dimensional nature of the pain of losing a loved one, people's narratives showed how such loss could not be rationalised. Rather, they relied on images and metaphors, such as the loss of parts or wounding of the body. They materialised their loss, not only through ritualised social practices and the occasions, spaces and objects associated with these, but also the ordinary daily business of living and the domestic and public spaces this encompassed. Yet, in so doing, they evoked presence, conveying how this depended upon sensory, imaginative and intuitive knowing, such as sensing and embodying the deceased person, intuitively knowing that he or she was around and materialising his or her presence.

Such continuing presence was experienced as mutually reinforcing, agency being exercised on both sides. In some cases the deceased person's agency was enhanced by virtue of his or her disembodied status. Thus the dead had a hand in the future direction of the living by providing support, energy and opportunity, whilst the living provided comfort, protection and companionship for the dead. Such mutuality suggests that continuing bonds in a Western context are not necessarily one-sided and only benefiting the living (Klass, 1996). Indeed the way my participants conveyed their experience revealed a discourse of care and reciprocity that reflected a desire to integrate the dead into the lives of the living. A concern to respect the deceased person's wishes revealed a further expression of a discourse of care as an aspect of continuing bonds.

Relationships were represented as highly personal and continuous with the way narrators and their loved ones had related while they were alive. For some, deceased loved ones continued to provide practical, reliable and moral guidance. Such continuity could take the form of encouraging generational ties, or retaining the person's details on a mobile phone. It could be reinforced through realising the extent to which the bereaved person's life had been shaped by the deceased. In some cases the nature of the relationship changed to reflect an increased sensitivity towards the person's memory to reflect a more implicit discourse of care. Relationships could also develop through discovering more about the person after they had died in a way that further enhanced their personhood.

Continuing bonds were not only dependent on the intentions of the living but could be experienced as having been initiated by the dead themselves, sometimes via the senses, such as sensing presence, experiencing his or her touch, hearing his or her voice. They could be shaped by the deceased as much as by the bereaved person, something which could be experienced as disturbing as well as comforting. Narratives conveyed an intersubjective rather than a unitary experience of agency and embodiment, the body of the bereaved person forming the site of both the bereaved and the deceased person's empowerment (Hallam *et al.,* 1999).

In conveying such experiences narrators negotiated the competing discourses of modernist scientific rationality on the one hand and those offered by romantic, religious and spiritual or supernaturalist perspectives on the other (Bennett and Bennett, 2000). In relation to experiences and behaviour that defied rational modes of understanding, such as sensing the deceased person's presence, hearing his or her voice or having conversations with him or her, competing discourses of rationality and supernaturalism were juxtaposed in a way that sought to preserve both the power and significance of the experience, as well as the narrator's own credibility (Kellehear, 1996; Howarth and Kellehear, 2001).

Participants found support from both religious and spiritual beliefs and perspectives, which encompassed belief in an afterlife, and secular wisdom, such as the notion of 'getting on with life' and death as part of the 'natural order of things'. Some drew on the psychological discourse of grief as a series of definable stages through which one must pass in order to 'get over it'. However, such wisdom was frequently questioned and in some cases challenged by a discourse of romanticism that emphasised how intimate bonds between people did not end with death. For some, the experience of bereavement had an impact on their existing perspective on life, provoking a rethinking of values and priorities, such as an increased understanding of other people's suffering, an awareness of the importance of spending time with significant others, valuing one's life and taking pleasure in things.

Traditional religious belief, though offering some comfort, could at the same time prove hard to reconcile with the pain of losing a loved one. Some people expressed uncertainty and ambivalence in relation to afterlife beliefs and tended to oscillate between religious, supernatural and rational explanations of mortality. Others rejected religion altogether to draw on the power of continuing emotional attachment and its expression in acts of loyalty to and celebration of the memory of dead loved ones (Hockey and Kellaher, 2005).

Experiences of absence and continuing presence were materialised through formal and informal ritualisation and memorialisation, challenging the distinction between grief and mourning, or inner feelings and outer behaviour. Narratives conveyed how material culture formed an extension of personhood, destabilising the boundaries between subject and object (Hallam and Hockey, 2001). Though for some, the corpse was a powerful symbol of absence, for others it continued to evoke presence. It could take on different meanings at different times, as well as a double meaning, evoking both the absence of the person who once inhabited it as well as a frightening presence that threatened to come to life (Vincent, 1991: 165, cited in Hallam and Hockey, 2001: 14). For some, viewing the corpse initiated a process of searching for and recovering the loved one's personhood. Such responses conveyed the mutable and contingent nature of the reality of death and demonstrated how the life–death boundary was far from clear cut (Hallam *et al.,* 1999; Howarth, 2000). They revealed how the behaviour of people towards the corpse may contribute to its personalisation and demonstrate how it may acquire agency (Hockey and Hallam, 2001).

Narratives reflected the growing emphasis on self-styled funerals to celebrate the unique personhood of deceased loved ones. One person drew attention to the responsibility this placed on family members to ensure that the dead were not misrepresented. Memorialisation included the creation of spaces that reflected the identity of the deceased person and provided focal points for continuing personal and emotional contact with him or her. In interacting with these physical locations participants conveyed how they became attached to the sites themselves. Some people appreciated the peaceful, private, bounded space of the cemetery away from the hustle and bustle and routine of daily living. Such public, communal spaces could be highly personalised through the growing practice of constructing grave displays from consumer goods. Others found alternative memorial spaces to offer more scope for personalisation, such as local beauty spots associated with their loved ones or a more natural setting that represented the regenerative power of the natural world. In the absence of a focal point, a discourse of romanticism located the deceased person within the bereaved as a constant internal presence.

Participants conveyed how deceased loved ones' continuing presence could also be evoked through a variety of experiences that formed part of the ordinary, everyday business of living. Activities that provided a source of enhanced connection with loved ones ranged from religious observance and creative pursuits, such as art, music, patchwork and poetry, to more mundane activities, such as conversation, driving, tending an allotment, using the computer and making the bed. The capacity of material objects to mediate continuing presence was represented through a variety of keepsakes (Hallam and Hockey, 2001; Gibson, 2004). Such presence could be actively encouraged through the transforming of objects, such as framing and displaying photographs, or placing objects in particular places. Personal possessions such as jewellery and clothing could evoke an intimate and sometimes sensory experience of continuing presence (Lupton, 1998). This could be constant or more hidden and intermittent to allow for the need to both retain and let go of the person. Such items conveyed how deceased loved ones could have a hand in securing their continuing presence in the way they chose to distribute their possessions (Matthews, 1979).

Preserving and affirming personhood and the social bond

In sharing their bereavement experiences, my participants conveyed the extent to which they were engaged in preserving and affirming the unique personhood and continuing social significance of deceased loved ones and their relationship with them. This process produced highly individualised and personalised narratives of the way a loved one died, the impact and meaning of his or her absence and the rediscovery of his or her presence. These narratives called into question the cultural boundaries between the living and the dead, self and other, subject and object. It challenged theories of self-identity that privilege intentional, embodied, performative agency, and any straightforward relationship between agency and the body and between individual agency and society's structures. Indeed, the way that the continuing social presence and influence of dying and deceased people in the lives of close others was so profoundly conveyed, suggests a rethinking of the question of what constitutes social being.

The deceased loved one's continuing personhood was powerfully evoked by the way narrators emphasised his or her idiosyncrasies. Far from being idealised, these intimate details evoked the person's humanity and therefore mortality. Yet, it was not only through interview conversations but also experientially and inter-subjectively that personhood became apparent. For, in the process of sharing their experiences with me, narrators not only reported, but also created a particular social space that was inhabited by the deceased person. As well as demonstrating the active, constructive nature of conversation, this experience afforded me a direct and immediate encounter with the socially constructed and intersubjective nature of personhood. As indicated, this experience has revealed how the dead may gain a presence in the interview encounter.

Reflexive negotiation of competing discourses

The open-ended, conversational style of interviewing that was adopted enabled participants to share experiences that reflected their own rather than the researcher's predominant concerns. In recounting these, people negotiated available cultural frames of reference to produce highly complex, idiosyncratic accounts, reflecting individual and personal priorities and agendas. They shifted between discourses to produce a diversity of narratives that encompassed contradictory and contingent meanings. These narratives revealed the complexity, diversity, uncertainty and unpredictability of the bereavement experience in a way which defied any attempt to present it in terms of an overarching model. Modernist values were juxtaposed with postmodern perspectives to incorporate medicalisation and its accompanying rationalisation and prescriptiveness, an individualism that encompassed both modernist self-sufficiency and postmodern relativity and diversity, a romanticism that privileged emotionality over rationality and emphasised the value of intimate relationships, and a spirituality that encompassed traditional religion, new-age beliefs and supernaturalism.

The presentation and interweaving of these various discourses was subject to a concern to humanise both the manner of loved ones' dying and the way in which their deaths were commemorated. Such humanisation included an emphasis on the deceased person's humanness to encompass not only a celebration of his or her potential but an acknowledgement of vulnerability and frailty. This two-fold emphasis was especially characteristic of dying moments in which their restorative nature was represented as a function of both the defeating as well as the redeeming aspects of the dying experience. It was reflected in the care people took to find the 'right' words to convey their experience and perception of a deceased loved one's humanness in a way that captured the unique and multifaceted nature of his or her character and respected and protected his or her memory.

In attempting to relate their experiences to beliefs about life and death, people drew on religious, spiritual and supernatural discourses, as well as conventional wisdom. Some took support from existing beliefs, whilst others reported that their experience of bereavement changed their perspective on life. Indeed narratives were characterised by a negotiation of various beliefs, reflecting the diversity of lifestyles and circumstances. In most cases people demonstrated a reflexive approach to beliefs about life and death regardless of their own particular adherence. Such reflexivity included an acknowledgement of life's uncertainties and the limitations of any belief system. Considerations of death's timing similarly involved a weighing-up of factors so that timeliness and untimeliness were used in a relative manner and with a consideration of the varying perspectives of those involved.

Indeed, my participants' narratives demonstrated a self-reflexivity that included an appreciation of the changing nature of their experience at different points in time. Such shifting viewpoints entailed trying to remember, recapture and convey to me the quality of the experience at the time it occurred, and then reassess it in the light of the present. This involved a process of 'review' whereby people moved backwards and forwards between various points in time. In so doing, they conveyed an appreciation of the double-edged nature of much of their experience in which life was not fixed, but full of ambiguity and paradox. Thus bad and good, loss and recovery, absence and presence, defeat and triumph were juxtaposed to produce highly ambivalent and contingent narratives.

No dying was represented as wholly good or wholly bad, but rather as full of ambiguity, so that almost as soon as a positive feature was recalled its more negative side would become apparent and vice versa. Ambiguity was also reflected in the way that the same themes could be identified as conveying both what was good and what was bad about the dying. For example, continuing awareness during the process of dying was represented as both a burden and a resource. Treasured reminiscences of a loved one's final moments in which the dying person assumed an enhanced aliveness, presence and relatedness to loved ones, formed only a small part of a bigger picture, which could include a difficult dying experience. Such good moments did not negate or obscure but rather were juxtaposed with the more distressing, demoralising aspects.

Similarly in conveying the experience of grief, negotiating the paradox of absence and presence and the interaction of bereavement with other aspects of life produced complex, ambivalent and contingent narratives. Continuing relationships with deceased loved ones were bitter-sweet, a sense of the person's presence being mixed with an equally powerful sense of their loss. Narrators conveyed how they were able to carry on with their lives without their loved ones whilst at the same time maintaining them as a presence in their everyday worlds. Such complexity encompassed the social and intersubjective nature of the self and how losing and recovering the deceased person reflected the experience of losing and recovering parts of the self. Indeed, narratives revealed the extent to which those who had died formed an integral and crucial part of people's sense of identity and the mutual nature of continuing bonds, which could be initiated by the deceased as well as the bereaved person.

Social policy and practice

My experience of carrying out this research and the findings that have emerged from this have important implications for the way our society treats dying and bereaved people. In Part One it was noted that people's perceptions of a death as good or bad have been found to shape the bereavement experience. The narratives of those I interviewed have revealed that a good death depended on preserving and affirming the continuing social significance of dying loved ones and that this was crucial to bereaved people's capacity to forge memories of them that could be lived with. My participants' preoccupation with their loved ones remaining uniquely themselves reflects and affirms the ideology espoused by the hospice movement. It has drawn attention to the inter-relationship between palliative and bereavement care to suggest that such a link needs to be fostered and developed.

However, an understanding of personhood that is limited to autonomous, embodied, performative agency and fails to appreciate the more subtle and intersubjective dimension of social being can only serve to impede such a process. For it encourages the depersonalising treatment of dying people and fails to reflect, acknowledge and affirm the experiences of close others who strive to maintain contact with their loved ones and sustain their personhood. A more flexible and nuanced understanding of personhood is required to provide a context for developing policy and practices that respect and protect rather than disregard or deny the subjectivities and social value of dying people in the face of their extreme vulnerability and dependence. A more inclusive approach towards those who are dying would in turn validate the experiences of bereaved people and support them in their struggle to find meaning in their loss.

My participants' narratives have revealed the limitations of linear stage-model approaches to conceptualising the dying trajectory and the process of grief by demonstrating a more paradoxical and contingent view of the way people die, how close others experience and reconstruct their loved ones' dying, and how they negotiate their absence and continuing presence. Such a perspective has implications for social policy and practice in relation to supporting people in coping with the messiness and unpredictability of living with dying and bereavement rather than imposing a model of how things ought to be. Indeed, people's narratives reflected the complex, diverse and negotiated nature of an experience that disrupts and challenges the normal, established patterns of social functioning. In the face of such uncertainty people's narratives demonstrated the value of presence and 'being with' rather than 'doing to' as an important but often neglected aspect of social support.

Narrators conveyed how they appreciated a non-intrusive, non-judgemental and 'non-therapeutic' space in which to tell their story and further reflect on the nature and meaning of their experiences. Most participants acknowledged the value of such sharing, some doing so at the time, whilst others contacted me later to convey their appreciation. They indicated how it had been an important process of remembering, reconnecting with, appreciating and discovering how much the deceased person still meant to them, of gaining further perspective on and insight into their experience. For some it was cathartic, providing some release and relief that served to ease their burden. I was also left with the impression that people took pride in introducing me to their loved ones. My experience of interviewing seemed to confirm the importance of having the opportunity to talk at length about the deceased person in order to be able to construct a memory of him or her that can be integrated into one's ongoing life (Walter, 1996). Such talk included recounting the way the person died, as well as the impact of their death. It revealed the diversity of meanings people give to their experiences and therefore the importance of respecting and affirming the bereaved person's own style of grieving and methods of coping. Support may then be focused on fostering and enhancing the person's own resources.

Summary

'Narratives of dying' conveyed the hope and comfort bereaved people may find in remembering and recounting how their deceased loved ones' remained uniquely themselves despite the physical and mental deterioration of the dying process. In some cases narrators experienced their loved ones as demonstrating enhanced selfhood at the very point of taking their leave. These narratives also drew attention to the distressing nature of experiences of loved ones being subjected to depersonalising treatment by others or else no longer being available to the narrator. 'Narratives of loss' were characterised by an appreciation of just who the deceased person was and what he or she meant, and would continue to mean to the survivor. In acknowledging and defining their loss, people affirmed and preserved the personhood of their loved ones, demonstrating how social being does not necessarily come to an end with death. 'Narratives of rediscovery' revealed how the dead retained personhood and agency by virtue of their relationships with the living. Relationships between the vulnerable living and the disembodied dead were represented as providing mutual support, validation and empowerment. They could be initiated by the dead as well as the living. They revealed a discourse of care that encompassed protectiveness, continuity, empathy, respect, identification and an intuitive sense of comforting presence, to shed further light on the nature of continuing bonds in a Western context.

These narratives brought into sharp focus how the self was constructed through social interaction and intimately linked to the selves of others rather than being unitary, exclusive and contained in a bounded body. In some cases a supernatural discourse not only problematised theories of embodied agency, but also conveyed an enhanced presence and agency by virtue of the deceased person's disembodied status. Developing and promoting a more relational and intersubjective understanding of personhood would provide validation and support for bereaved people's attempts to communicate and make sense of their experiences, rather than rationalising or pathologising and thereby marginalising these. Such an intersubjective perspective can allow a consideration of ways of being, acting and contributing to social life other than those based on unitary, embodied performative agency. Indeed, people's narratives demonstrated that the disorientating impact of bereavement could call forth a resourcefulness in finding other ways of engaging in social life, such as those based on a more intuitive, imaginative and sensory awareness.

The continuing personhood and agency of dying loved ones tended to depend on the capacity of close others to recognise, interpret, respond to and affirm their characteristic gestures and maintain their relationship with them. In the absence of the physical body personhood manifested itself through impressions, intuitions, imaginative activity and sensations of presence or forms of 'knowing' other than commonsense, rational explanations and assumptions. It manifested itself through a variety of aspects of material culture that resonated with the deceased person's identity, evoking presence and the bereaved person's relationship with him or her. Certain times, spaces, occasions, activities and objects, including the corpse, could acquire agency by virtue of their emotional impact on bereaved loved ones, representing a destabilising of the boundaries between subject and object (Hallam and Hockey, 2001). Thus my participants' narratives conveyed the diverse and improvised ways in which the dead retained a tangible and active presence and became integrated into the lives of the living.

Such emphasis on the continuing social presence and significance of dying and deceased people revealed an alternative discourse in which personhood was relational, intersubjective and therefore more subtle and fluid than that dependent on bodily integrity (Rose, 1996; Battersby 1998; Hallam *et al.,* 1999). This discourse raises important questions for sociological theory about what it means to have personhood and agency in contemporary British society. My participants' 'narratives of dying' drew attention to the complexity and 'multiplicity' of embodied experience (Lawton, 2000). Their 'narratives of loss' and 'rediscovery' destabilised not only the boundaries of the body but also those between the living and the dead, to convey a richer, more profound and complex experience of social being (Hallam *et al.,* 1999; Howarth, 2000, 2007b).

Bibliography

Anderson, M. (2001) '"You have to get inside the person" or making grief private: image and metaphor in the therapeutic reconstruction of bereavement', in J. Hockey, J. Katz, and N. Small (eds) *Grief, Mourning and Death Ritual.* Buckingham Philadelphia: Open University Press, pp. 135–144.

Ariès, P. (1974) *Western Attitudes to Death from the Middle Ages to the Present.* London: Marion Boyars Publishers.

Ariès, P. (1981) *The Hour of Our Death: Phillipe Ariès*, translated from the French by Helen Weaver. Hammondsworth: Penguin.

Árnason. A. (2000) 'Biography, bereavement, story'. *Mortality*, **5**(2), 189–204.

Ash, J. (1996) 'Memory and objects', in P. Kirkham (ed.) *The Gendered Object*. Manchester: Manchester University Press, pp. 219–224.

Ballard, P. (1996) 'Intimations of mortality: some sociological considerations', in P. Badham and P. Ballard (eds) *Facing Death*. Cardiff: University of Wales Press, pp. 7–28.

Barnes, B. (2000) *Understanding Agency: Social Theory and Responsible Action.* London, Thousand Oaks, New Delhi: Sage Publications.

Batchelor, J. and Briggs, C. (1994) 'Subject, project or self? Thoughts on ethical dilemmas for social and medical researchers'. *Social Science and Medicine*, **39**(7), 949–954.

Battersby, C. (1993) 'Her body/her boundaries: gender and the metaphysics of containment'. *Journal of Philosophy and the Visual Arts*, 31–39.

Battersby, C. (1998) *The Phenomenal Woman*. Cambridge: Polity Press.

Bauman, Z. (1992) *Mortality, Immortality and Other Life Strategies*. Cambridge: Polity Press.

Beck, U. and Beck-Gerhsheim, E. (1995) *The Normal Chaos of Love*. Cambridge: Polity Press.

Beck, U. and Beck-Gerhsheim, E. (2002) *Individualization*. London, Thousand Oaks, New Delhi: Sage Publications.

Bell, R.J. (2005) '"Our people die well": deathbed scenes in John Wesley's *Arminian magazine*'. *Mortality* **10**(3), 210–223.

Bennett, G. and Bennett, K. (2000) 'The presence of the dead: an empirical study'. *Mortality* **5**(2), 139–157.

Berger, A. (1995) 'Quoth the Raven: bereavement and the paranormal'. *Omega* **31**(1), 1–10.

Berger, P. L. and Luckmann, T. (1967) *The Social Construction of Reality*. London: Allen Lane.

Blauner, R. (1966) 'Death and the social structure'. *Psychiatry* **29**, 378–394.

Bloch, M. and Parry, J. (1982) *Death and the Regeneration of Life*. Cambridge: Cambridge University Press.

Boas, F. (1911/1965) *The Mind of the Primitive Man*. New York: Free Press, cited J. Hockey (1996) 'The view from the West', in G. Howarth and P. Jupp (eds) *Contemporary Issues in the Sociology of Dying, Death and Disposal*. Basingstoke: Macmillan, p. 9.

Bowlby, J. (1961) 'Process of mourning'. *International Journal of Psychoanalysis* **42**, 317–40.

Bowlby, J. (1980) *Loss, Sadness and Depression: Attachment and Loss*. Vol. 3. New York: Basic Books.

Bradbury, M. (1996) 'Representations of "good" and "bad" death among deathworkers and the bereaved', in G. Howarth and P. Jupp (eds) *Contemporary Issues in the Sociology of Dying, Death and Disposal*. Basingstoke: Macmillan Press, pp. 84–95.

Bradbury, M. (1999) *Representations of Death*. London and New York: Routledge.

Bradbury, M. (2001) 'Forget me not: memorialization in cemeteries and crematoria', in J. Hockey, J. Katz and N. Small (eds) *Grief, Mourning and Death Ritual*. Buckingham, Philadelphia: Open University Press, pp. 218–225.

Brody, H. (1987) *Stories of Sickness*. London: Yale University Press.

Butler, J. (1990) *Gender Trouble and the Subversion of Identity*. London: Routledge.

Butler, J. (1993) *Bodies that Matter: On the Discursive Limits of 'Sex'*. London: Routledge.

Charmaz, K. (1980) *The Social Reality of Death*. London: Addison-Wesley Publishing Company.

Cook, G. and Walter, T. (2005) 'Rewritten rites: language and social relations in traditional and contemporary funerals'. *Discourse and Society* **16**(3), 365–391.

Craib, I. (1998) *Experiencing Identity*. London: Sage.

Cressy, D. (1997) *Birth, Marriage and Death: Ritual, Religion and the Life Cycle in Tudor and Stuart England*. Oxford: Oxford University Press.

Crossley, M. L. (2000) *Introducing Narrative Psychology*. Buckingham: Open University Press.

Csordas, T. (1994) *Embodiment and Experience*. Cambridge: Cambridge University Press, cited E. Hallam, J. Hockey and G. Howarth (1999) *Beyond the Body: Death and Social Identity*. London and New York: Routledge, p.7.

Davies, J. (1993) 'War Memorials' in D. Clark (ed.) *The Sociology of Death*. Oxford: Blackwell, pp. 112–128.

Davies, J. (1996) 'Vile bodies and mass media chantries', in G. Howarth and P. Jupp (eds) *Contemporary Issues in the Sociology of Dying, Death and Disposal*. Basingstoke: Macmillan, pp. 47–54.

De Beauvoir, S. (1966) *A Very Easy Death*. London: Deutsch and Weidenfeld and Nicholson.

Donnelly, S. M., Michael, N. and Donnelly, C. (2005) 'Experience of the moment of death at home'. *Mortality* **11**(4), 352–367.

Duclow, D. F. (2003) 'Ars Moriendi', in R. Kastenbaum (ed.) (2003) *Macmillan Encyclopedia of Death and Dying*. Macmillan Reference USA. Thomson Gale, pp. 36–41.

Durkheim, E. (1915) *The Elementary Forms of Religious Life*. London: Allen and Unwin Ltd.

Einagel, V. I. (2002) 'Telling stories, making selves', in L. Bondi, H. Alvis, R. Bankey (eds) (2002) *Subjectivities, Knowledges and Feminist Geographies*. Lanham MD, Oxford: Rowman and Littlefield, pp. 224–235.

Elias, N. (1985) *The Loneliness of Dying*. Oxford: Blackwell.

Engel, G.I. (1961) 'Is grief a disease?', *Psychosomatic Medicine* **23**(1), 18–22.

Evans-Pritchard, E. E. (1937/1972) *Witchcraft, Oracles and Magic Among the Azande*. Oxford: Clarendon, cited J. Hockey (1996) 'The view from the West', in G. Howarth and P. Jupp (eds) *Contemporary Issues in the Sociology of Death, Dying and Disposal.* Basingstoke: Macmillan, pp. 3–16.

Featherstone, M. (1995) 'The body in consumer culture', in M. Featherstone, M. Hepworth and B. S. Turner (eds) *The Body: Social Process and Cultural Theory.* London: Sage.

Featherstone, M., Hepworth, M. and Turner, B. S. (eds) (1991) *The Body, Social Process and Cultural Theory.* London: Sage.

Field, D. (1989) *Nursing the Dying.* London: Routledge.

Field, D. (1994) 'Palliative medicine and the medicalisation of death'. *European Journal of Cancer Care* 3(2), 58–62.

Field, D., Hockey, J. and Small, N. (eds) (1997) *Death, Gender and Ethnicity.* London, New York: Routledge.

Field, N. (2006) 'Unresolved grief and continuing bonds: an attachment perspective'. *Death Studies* 30(8), 739–756.

Finch, J. and Wallis, L. (1993) 'Death, inheritance and the life course', in D. Clark (ed.) *The Sociology of Death.* Oxford: Blackwell, pp. 50–68.

Foucault, M. (1972) *The Archaeology of Knowledge.* London: Tavistock.

Foucault, M. (1973) *The Birth of the Clinic.* London: Tavistock.

Francis, D., Kellaher, L. and Neophytou, G. (2000) 'Sustaining cemeteries: the user perspective'. *Mortality* 5(1), 34–53.

Francis, D., Kellaher, L. and Neophytou, G. (2001) 'The cemetery: the evidence of continuing bonds', in J. Hockey, J. Katz and N. Small (eds) *Grief, Mourning and Death Ritual.* Buckingham, Philadelphia: Open University Press, pp. 226–236.

Francis, D., Kellaher, L. and Neophytou, G. (2005) *The Secret Cemetery.* Oxford: Berg.

Freud, S. (1917) 'Mourning and melancholia', in S. Freud (1984) *On Metapsychology, Vol 11.* London: Freud Pelican Library, Penguin Books Ltd, pp. 245–269.

Froggat, K. (1997) 'Rites of passage and the hospice movement'. *Mortality* 2(2), 123–136.

Fulton, G., Madden, C. and Minichiello, V. (1996) 'The social construction of anticipatory grief'. *Social Science and Medicine* 43(9), 1349–1358.

Geertz, C. (1983) *Local Knowledges: Further Essays in Interpretative Anthropology.* New York: Basic Books.

Gibson, M. (2004) 'Melancholy objects'. *Mortality* 9(4), 285–299.

Giddens, A. (1991) *Modernity and Self-identity.* Cambridge: Polity Press.

Glaser, B. G. and Strauss, A. (1965) *Awareness of Dying.* Chicago: Aldine

Glaser, B. G. and Strauss, A. (1967) *The Discovery of Grounded Theory.* Chicago: Aldine.

Glaser, B. G. and Strauss, A. (1971) *Status Passage.* London: Routledge and Kegan Paul.

Goffman, E. (1959) *The Presentation of the Self in Everyday Life.* Hammondsworth: Penguin Books.

Goldsworthy, R. and Coyle, A. (1999) 'Spiritual beliefs and the search for meaning following partner loss'. *Mortality* 4(1), 21- 40.

Goody, J. (1962) *Death, Property and the Ancestors.* Stanford: Stanford University Press.

Gordon, D. and Paci, E. (1997) 'Disclosure practices and narratives: understanding concealment and silence around cancer in Tuscany, Italy'. *Social Science and Medicine* 44(10), 1433–1452.

Gorer, G. (1965) *Death, Grief and Mourning in Contemporary Britain.* London: Cresset Press.

Guillemin, M. and Gillam, L. (2004) 'Ethics, reflexivity and "ethically important moments" in research'. *Qualitative Inquiry* 10(2), 261–280.

Hallam, E. (1996) 'Turning the hourglass: gender relations at the deathbed in early modern Canterbury'. *Mortality* 1(1), 61–82.

Hallam, E. and Hockey, J. (2001) *Death, Memory and Material Culture*. Oxford: Berg.

Hallam, E., Hockey, J. and Howarth, G. (1999) *Beyond the Body: Death and Social Identity*. London and New York: Routledge.

Handsley, S. (2001) '"But what about us?" The residual effects of sudden death on self-identity and family relationships'. *Mortality* **6**(1), 9–30.

Hart, B., Sainsbury, P. and Short, S. (1998) 'Whose dying? A sociological critique of the "good death"'. *Mortality* **3**(1), 65–78.

Hertz, R. (1907/1960) *Death and the Right Hand*. New York: Free Press.

Hochschild, A. R. (1983) *The Managed Heart: The Commercialisation of Human feelings*. California: University of California Press.

Hockey, J. (1990) *Experiences of Death: An Anthropological Account*. Edinburgh: Edinburgh University Press.

Hockey, J. (1996a) 'The view from the West', in G. Howarth and P. Jupp (eds) *Contemporary Issues in Dying, Death and Disposal*. Basingstoke: Macmillan, pp. 3–16.

Hockey, J. (1996b) 'Encountering the "reality of death" through professional discourses: the matter of materiality'. *Mortality* **1**(1), 45–60.

Hockey, J. (2001) 'Changing death rituals', in J. Hockey, J. Katz and N. Small (eds) *Grief, Mourning and Death Ritual*. Buckingham, Philadelphia: Open University Press, pp. 185–211.

Hockey, J. (2002) 'Interviews as ethnography: disembodied social interaction in Britain', in Nigel Rapport (ed.) *British Subjects: An Anthropology of Britain*. Oxford: Berg, pp. 209–222.

Hockey, J. and Kellaher, L. (2005) 'Environments of memory: changing rituals of mourning and their personal and social implications'. ESRC Report.

Hollway, W. and Jefferson, T. (2000) *Doing Qualitative Research Differently*. London: Sage.

Houlbrooke, R. A. (1989) *Death, Ritual and Bereavement*. London and New York: Routledge.

Howarth, G. (1993) 'Investigating deathwork: a personal account', in D. Clark (ed.) *The Sociology of Death*. Oxford: Blackwell, pp. 221–237.

Howarth, G. (1997) 'Is there a British way of death?' in C. Charmaz, G. Howarth and A. Kellehear (eds) *The Unknown Country: Death in Australia, Britain and the USA*. Basingstoke, London: Macmillan, pp. 84–97.

Howarth, G. (1998) 'What's emotion got to do with it? Reflections on the personal in health research'. *Annual Review of Health Social Sciences* **8**, 2–7.

Howarth, G. (2000) 'Dismantling the boundaries between life and death'. *Mortality* **5**(2), 127–138.

Howarth, G. (2007a) *Death and Dying: A Sociological Introduction*. Cambridge: Polity Press.

Howarth, G. (2007b) 'The rebirth of death: continuing relationships with the dead', in M. Mitchell (ed.) *Remember Me: Constructing Immortality. Beliefs on Immortality, Life and Death*. New York and Abingdon: Routledge, pp. 19–34.

Howarth, G. and Kellehear, A. (2001) 'Shared near-death and related illness experiences: steps on and unscheduled journey'. *Journal of Near Death Studies* **20**(2) 71–86.

Huntington, R. and Metcalf, P. (1979) *Celebrations of Death: The Anthropology of Mortuary Ritual*. Cambridge: Cambridge University Press.

Illich, I. (1975) *Limits to Medicine. Medical Nemesis: the Expropriation of Health*. London: Marion Boyers Publishers Ltd.

Ironside, V. (1996) *You'll Get Over It: The Rage of Bereavement*. London: Hamish Hamilton.

James, V. and Field, D. (1991) 'The routinization of hospice: charisma and bureaucratization'. *Social Science and Medicine* **34**(12), 1363–1375.

Jaworski, A. and Coupland, N. (eds) (1999) *The Discourse Reader.* London: Routledge.

Kasterbaum, R. (1989) 'Deathbed scenes', in R. Kastenbaum and B. Kasterbaum (eds) *Encyclopedia of Death.* Phoenix, AZ: Oryx Press, pp. 97–101.

Kastenbaum, R. (1990) 'Deathbed scenes as imagined by the young and experienced by the old'. *Death Studies* **14**, 201–247.

Kastenbaum, R. (1999) 'The moment of death: is hospice making a difference?' *The Hospice Journal* **14**(3/4), 253–270.

Katz, J. (2001) 'Introduction', J. Hockey, J. Katz and N. Small (eds) *Grief, Mourning and Death Ritual.* Buckingham, Philadelphia: Open University Press, pp.1–15.

Kellehear, A. (1989) 'Ethics and social research' in John Perry (ed.) *Doing Fieldwork.* Deakin: Deakin University Press, pp. 61–72.

Kellehear, A. (1996) *Experiences Near Death: Beyond Medicine and Religion.* New York and Oxford: Oxford University Press.

Kellehear, A. (2000) *Eternity and Me: The Everlasting Things in Life and Death.* Melbourne: Hill of Content Publishing.

Kellehear, A. and Lewin, T. (1988–1989) 'Farewells by the dying: a sociological study'. *Omega* **19**, 275–292.

Kellaher, L., Prendergast, D. and Hockey, J. (2005) 'In the shadow of the traditional grave'. *Mortality* **10**(4), 237–250.

King, A. (1998) *Memorials of the Great War.* Oxford: Berg.

Klass, D. (1988) *Parental Grief: Solace and Resolution.* New York: Springer.

Klass, D. (1996) 'Grief in an Eastern Culture', in D. Klass, P. Silverman and J. Nickman (eds) *Continuing Bonds.* London, Philadelphia: Taylor and Francis, pp. 59–70.

Klass, D. (1997) 'The deceased child in the psychic and social worlds of bereaved parents during the resolution of grief'. *Death Studies* **21**(2): 147–175.

Klass, D. (2006) 'Continuing conversations about continuing bonds'. *Death Studies* **30**(9), 843–858. Philadelphia: Taylor and Francis.

Klass, D. and Goss, R. (1999) 'Spiritual bonds to the dead in cross-cultural and historical perspective: comparative religion and modern grief'. *Death Studies* **23**, 547–567.

Klass, D., Silverman, P. R. and Nickman, S. (eds) (1996) *Continuing Bonds: New Understandings of Grief.* London: Routledge.

Kleinman, A. (1988) *The Illness Narratives*, New York: Basic Books Inc.

Komaromy, C. (2000) 'The sight and sound of death: the management of dead bodies in residential nursing homes for older people'. *Mortality* **5**(3), 299–315.

Komaromy, C. and Hockey, J. (2001) 'Naturalising death among older adults in residential care', in J.Hockey, J. Katz and N. Small (eds) *Grief, Mourning and Death Ritual.* Buckingham, Philadelphia: Open University Press, pp. 73–81.

Kübler- Ross, E. (1970) *On Death and Dying.* London: Tavistock.

Kübler-Ross, E. (1975) *Death: The Final Stage of Growth.* Englewood Cliffs: Prentice Hall.

Lakoff, G. and Johnson, M. (1980) *Metaphors We Live By.* Chicago, London: University of Chicago Press.

Laungani, P. (1996) 'Death and bereavement in India and England'. *Mortality* **1**(2) 191–212.

Lawton, J. (2000) *The Dying Process: Patients' Experiences of Palliative Care.* London: Routledge.

Lee, R. and Renzetti, C. (eds) (1993) *Researching Sensitive Topics.* London: Sage.

Lindemann, E. (1944) 'Symptomology and management of acute grief'. *American Journal of Psychiatry* **101**, 141–148.

Littlewood, J. (1992) *Aspects of Grief in Adult life*. London: Routledge.

Littlewood, J. (1993) 'Denial of death and rites of passage in contemporary society', in D. Clark (ed.) *The Sociology of Death*. Oxford: Blackwell, pp. 69–84.

Littlewood, J. (2001) 'Just an old-fashioned love song or a harlequin romance? Some experiences of widowhood', in Hockey, J. Katz and N. Small (eds) *Grief, Mourning and Death Ritual*. Buckingham, Philadelphia: Open University Press, pp. 82–93.

Lock, M. (2002) *Twice Dead: Organ Transplants and the Reinvention of Death*. Berkeley, Los Angeles and London: University of California Press.

Lofland, L. H. (1985) 'The social shaping of emotion: the case of grief'. *Symbolic Interaction* **8**(2), 171–190.

Lupton, D. (1994) *Medicine as Culture: Illness, Disease and the Body in Western Societies*. London: Sage.

Lupton, D. (1998) *The Emotional Self*. London: Sage.

McIntosh, J. (1977) *Communication and Awareness in a Cancer Ward*. London: Croom Helm.

McNamara, B. (2001) *Fragile Lives*. Buckingham, Philadelphia: Open University Press.

Marris, P. (1958) *Widows and their families*. London: Routledge and Kegan Paul.

Marris, P. (1986) *Loss and Change*. London: Routledge and Kegan Paul.

Marwit, S. J. and Klass, D. (1996) 'Grief and the role of the inner representation of the deceased', in D. Klass, P. Silverman and S. Nickman (eds) *Continuing Bonds*. London and New York: Taylor and Francis, pp. 297–308.

Matthews, S. (1979) *The Social World of Old Women: Management of Self Identity*. Beverly Hills: Sage.

Mason, J. (2002) *Qualitative Researching*. London: Sage.

Masson, D. (2002) 'Non-professional understandings of the good death'. *Mortality* **7**(2), 191–209.

Mellor, D. (1993) 'Death in high modernity: the contemporary presence and absence of death', in D. Clark (ed.) *The Sociology of Death*. Oxford: Blackwell, pp. 11- 30.

Mitchell, J. (1998) 'Cross-cultural issues in the disclosure of cancer'. *Cancer Practice* **6**(3), 153–160.

Moller, D. W. (1990) *On Death Without Dignity: The Human Impact of Technological Dying*. New York: Baywood.

Morley, J. (1971) *Death, Heaven and the Victorians*. London: Studio Vista.

Moss, M. and Moss, S. (2001) 'Four siblings' perspectives on parent death: a family focus', in J. Hockey, J. Katz and J. Small (eds) *Grief, Mourning and Death Ritual*. Buckingham, Philadelphia: Open University Press, pp. 61–72.

Mulkay, M. (1993) 'Social death in Britain', in D. Clark (ed.) *The Sociology of Death*. Oxford: Blackwell, pp. 31–49.

Neimeyer, R. (ed.) (2001) *Meaning Reconstruction and the Experience of Loss*. Washington, DC. London: American Psychological Association.

Nunkoosing, K. (2005) 'Problems with interviews'. *Qualitative Health Research* **15**(5), 698–706.

Oakley, A. (1981) 'Interviewing women: a contradiction in terms'. In H. Roberts (ed.) *Doing Feminist Research*. London: Routledge, pp. 30–61.

O'Connor, M. C. (1966) *The Art of Dying Well: The Development of the Ars Moriendi*. New York: AMS Press.

Parkes, C. M. (1972) *Bereavement*. New York: International Universities Press.

Parkes, C. M. (1986) *Bereavement: Studies of Grief in Adult Life*, 2nd edn. Harmondsworth: Penguin.

Parkes, C. M. and Weiss, R. (1983) *Recovery from Bereavement.* New York: Basic Books.

Porter, R. (1989) 'Doctors and Death in Georgian England', in R. E. Houlbrooke (ed.) *Death, Ritual and Bereavement.* London and New York: Routledge, pp.77–94.

Prior, L. (1989) *The Social Organisation of Death: Medical Discourse and Social Practice in Belfast.* Basingstoke: Macmillan.

Prior, L. (1997) 'Actuarial visions of death: life, death and chance in the modern world', in P. Jupp and G. Howarth (eds) *The Changing Face of Death: Historical Accounts of Death and Disposal.* Basingstoke: Macmillan, pp. 177–193.

Radcliffe-Brown, A. R. (1964) *The Adaman Islanders.* New York: Free Press, cited R. Huntingdon and P. Metcalf (1979) *Celebrations of Death.* Cambridge: Cambridge University Press.

Raphael, B. (1984) *The Anatomy of Bereavement. A Handbook for the Caring Professions.* London: Hutchinson.

Rapport, N. (1993) *Diverse World Views in an English Village.* Edinburgh: Edinburgh University Press.

Rapport, N. (ed.) (2002) *British Subjects: An Anthropology of Britain.* Oxford: Berg.

Reason, P. (ed.) (1988) *Human Inquiry in Action.* London: Sage Publications.

Rees, W. D. (1971) 'The hallucinations of widowhood'. *British Medical Journal* **4**, 73–41.

Reimars, E. (2003) 'A reasonable grief: discursive constructions of grief in a public conversation on raising the shipwrecked M/S Estonia'. *Mortality* **8** (4), 325–341.

Reissman, C. K. (1993) *Narrative Analysis.* London: Sage Publications.

Richardson, R. (1987) *Death, Dissection and the Destitute.* London: Routledge and Kegan Paul.

Riches, G. and Dawson, P. (1996a) 'Making stories and taking stories'. *British Journal of Guidance and Counselling* **24** (3), 357–365.

Riches, G. and Dawson, P. (1996b) 'Communities of feeling'. *Mortality* **1** (2), 143–161.

Riches, G. and Dawson, P. (1997) 'Shoring up the walls of heartache: parental responses to the death of a child', in D. Field, J. Hockey and N. Small (eds) (1997) *Death, Gender and Ethnicity.* London: Routledge, pp. 52–75.

Riches, G. and Dawson, P. (1998) 'Families bereaved by murder'. *Mortality* **3**(2), 143–160.

Riches, G. and Dawson, P. (2000) *An Intimate Loneliness.* Buckingham: Open University Press.

Richman, J. (2003) 'Holding public health up for inspection', in J. Costello and M. Haggard (eds) *Public Health and Society.* Basingstoke: Palgrave Macmillan, pp. 3–22.

Rose, N. (1990) *Governing the Soul: The Shaping of the Private Self.* London: Routledge.

Rose, N. (1996) *Inventing Ourselves: Psychology, Power and Personhood.* Cambridge: Cambridge University Press.

Rowling, L. (1999) 'Being in, being out, being with: affect and the role of the qualitative researcher in loss and grief'. *Mortality* **4** (2), 167–181.

Sandman, L. (2005) *A Good Death: On the Value of Death and Dying.* Buckingham: Open University Press.

Schut, H., Stroebe, M., Boelen, P. and Zijerveld, A. (2006) 'Continuing relationships with the deceased: disentangling bonds and grief'. *Death Studies* **30**(8), 757–766.

Seale, C. (1998) *Constructing Death.* Cambridge: Cambridge University Press.

Seymour, J. (1999) 'Revisiting medicalisation and natural death'. *Social Science and Medicine* **44**, 691–704.

Seymour, J. (2001) *Critical Moments: Death and Dying in Intensive Care.* Buckingham, Philadelphia: Open University Press.

Silverman, P. and Klass, D. (1996) 'Introduction: what's the problem?' in D. Klass, P. Silverman and S. Nickman (eds) *Continuing Bonds*. London and New York: Taylor and Francis.

Small, N. (1998) 'Death of the authors'. *Mortality* **3**(3), 215–228.

Small, N. (2001) 'Theories of grief: a critical review', in J. Hockey, J. Katz and N. Small (eds) *Grief, Mourning and Death Ritual*. Buckingham, Philadelphia: Open University Press, pp. 19–48.

Small, N. and Hockey, J. (2001) 'Discourse into practice: the production of bereavement care', in J. Hockey, J. Katz and N. Small (eds) *Grief, Mourning and Death Ritual*. Buckingham, Philadelphia: Open University Press, pp. 97–124.

Strauss, A. (1971) *Anguish: the Case History of a Dying Trajectory*. San Francisco, CA: Sociology Press.

Stroebe, M. and Schut, H. (1999) 'The dual process model of coping with bereavement: rationale and description'. *Death Studies* **23**, 197–224.

Stroebe, M. and Schut, H. (2001) 'Models of coping with bereavement: a review'. In M. Stroebe, D. Hansson, W. Stroebe and H. Schut (eds) *Handbook of Bereavement Research: Consequences, Coping and Care*. Washington, DC: American Psychological Association.

Stroebe, M., Gergen, M. M., Gergen, K. J. and Stroebe, W. (1992) 'Broken hearts or broken bonds: love and death in historical perspective'. *American Psychologist* **47**, 1205–1212. Reprinted in D. Klass, P. R. Silverman and J. Nickman (eds) (1996) *Continuing Bonds: New Understanding of Grief*. London: Routledge.

Stroebe, W. and Stroebe, M. (1987) *Bereavement and Health: the Psychology and Physical Consequences of Partner Loss*. Cambridge: Cambridge University Press.

Sudnow, D. (1967) *Passing On: The Social Organization of Dying*. Englewood Cliffs, NJ: Prentice Hall.

Taylor, J. (1651) *The Rule and Exercises of Holy Dying. In which are described the means and instruments of preparing our selves, and others respectively, for a blessed death: and the remedies against evils and temptations proper to the state of sicknesse. Together with prayers and acts of virtue to be used by sick and dying persons, or by others standing in their attendance. To which are added. Rules for the visitation of the sick, and offices proper for that ministery* . . . London: R. Royston. Cited R. J. Bell (2005) '"Our people die well": deathbed scenes in John Wesley's *Arminian* magazine'. *Mortality* **10** (3), 210–223.

Thompson, N. (1997) 'Masculinity and loss', in D. Field, J. Hockey and N. Small (eds) *Death, Gender and Ethnicity*. London and New York: Routledge, pp. 76–88.

Timmermans, S. (1994) 'Dying of awareness: the theory of awareness contexts revisited'. *Sociology of Health and Illness* **16** (3), 323–339.

Timmermans, S. (1998) 'Resuscitation technology in the emergency department: towards a dignified death'. *Sociology of Health and Illness* **20** (2), 144–167.

Turner, V. (1969) *The Ritual Process*. Harmondsworth: Penguin.

Valentine, C. (2006) 'Academic constructions of bereavement'. *Mortality* **11**(1), 57–79.

Valentine, C. (2007) 'Methodological reflections: the role of the researcher in the construction of bereavement narratives'. *Qualitative Social Work* **6**(2), 159–176.

Van Gennep, A. (1909/1960) *Rites of Passage*. Chicago: Chicago University Press.

Vincent, G. (1991) 'A history of secrets?', in J. Prost and G. Vincent (eds) *A History of Private Life. V. Riddles of Identity in Modern Times*. Cambridge, MA: The Belknap Press of Harvard University Press, cited E. Hallam, and J. Hockey (2001) *Death, Memory and Material Culture*. Oxford: Berg.

Walter, T. (1990) *Funerals and How to Improve Them*. London, Sydney and Aukland: Hodder and Stoughton.

Walter, T. (1993) 'Sociologists never die: British sociology and death', in D. Clark (ed.) *The Sociology of Death*. Oxford: Blackwell, pp. 264–295.

Walter, T. (1994) *The Revival of Death*. London: Routledge.

Walter, T. (1996) 'A new theory of grief?' *Mortality* 1(1) 7–26.

Walter, T. (1997a) 'Secularisation', in P. Laungani, C.M. Parkes and W. Young (eds) *Death and Bereavement Across Cultures*. London: Routledge, pp. 166–187.

Walter, T. (1997b) 'The ideology and organisation of spiritual care'. *Palliative Medicine* 11, 21–30.

Walter, T. (1999) *On Bereavement: the Culture of Grief*. Oxford: Oxford University Press.

Walter, T. (2001) 'Sociology', in G. Howarth and O. Leaman (eds) *The Dictionary of Death and Dying*. London: Routledge, pp. 420–422.

Williams, R. (1989) 'Awareness and control of dying: some paradoxical trends in public opinion'. *Sociology of Health and Illness* 11, 201–212.

Williams, S. J. and Calnan, M. (1996) 'The "limits" of medicalisation?: modern medicine and the lay populace in "late modernity"'. *Social Science and Medicine* 42(12), 1609–1620.

Winter, J. (1995) *Sites of Memory, Sites of Mourning*. Cambridge: Cambridge University Press.

Worden, J. W. (1991) *Grief Counselling and Grief Therapy*, 2nd edn. London: Routledge.

Wright, C. and Coyle, A. (1996) 'AIDS-related bereavement among gay men: implications for care'. *Mortality* 1(3), 267–282.

Young, E., Bury, M. and Elston, M. A. (1999) 'Live and/or let die: modes of social dying among women and their friends'. *Mortality* 4, 269–290.

Young, E. and Cullen, I. (1996) *A Good Death: Conversations with East Londoners*. London: Routledge.

Appendix
Participants' personal profiles

The following brief background sketches are provided to contextualise my participants' narratives. Some of the details have been altered to protect people's identities.

Andy, 19, a second generation Indian Sikh, is an undergraduate student. His father died 13 months ago after a period of intermittent illness, aged 43, just before Andy left home to go to university.

Adrian, 39, a mature student, has a mixed Spanish and French background. He was brought up in England, where he now lives with his English wife and their two children. His Spanish father died unexpectedly, three months ago, aged 65.

Brian, 33, from Scotland, works as a chef in a residential home for the elderly. He is married and lives in England with his English wife. His grandmother died eight months ago, aged 83.

Diane, 58, English, works as a personnel officer in a care home. She is married with a daughter and granddaughter. She lost her mother, aged 83, her aunt, aged 90 and her grandmother, aged 102, during the last two years.

Elisabeth, 52, English, has two children and a granddaughter, and, until her husband's death, six years ago, did not go out to work. Since then, she has worked in bars and restaurants, and more recently in a care home for people with learning difficulties. Her husband, a self-employed builder, died suddenly and unexpectedly of a brain haemorrhage, aged 46.

Fiona, 32, English, is married and works as a secretary in an educational setting. Her father died of cancer three months ago, aged 69.

Ivan, 50, English, works in a care home for people with learning difficulties. He has recently re-married and has two children from his first marriage. His divorced parents died two years ago, within one week of each other, his father at 83 and his mother at 73.

Jane, 19, English, is an undergraduate student. After her parents separated, when she was four, she went to live with her great-grandmother until she was 12. Her great-grandmother died two years ago, aged 85.

Janet, 19, English, is an undergraduate student. Her close male school friend died two years ago, from Leukaemia, aged 17.

Jason, 63, English, works in a care home for people with learning difficulties. His partner died five years ago, aged 50. He has a family background of spiritualists and mediums.

Julian, 40, English, from a traditional working-class background, works in a care home for people with learning difficulties. He is unmarried and lives on a boat. He lost his grandfather four years ago, aged 85.

Linda, 50, Irish, is an academic who travels between her home in Ireland and her current post at an English university. She is married with a son and daughter. She lost her mother almost a year ago, after a long period of illness, aged 79.

Lorraine, 40, Irish, lives and works in England as a university lecturer. She lost her godson two years ago when he was just five months old, her father four years ago and her friend 5 years ago.

Lynne, 57, English, works as an administrator in an educational setting. She is married with children and grandchildren. Her mother died of cancer 21 months ago, aged 89.

Marianne, 32, German, is currently studying at an English university. She has lived and worked in England for several years. Her mother died of cancer nearly three years ago, aged 59.

Michael, 58, English, is married with no children and works as a maintenance person in a care home. His Aunt died of cancer three months ago, aged 82.

Pat, 40, American, lives and works in England as a University lecturer. She lost her only English relative, her aunt, to a stroke, five years ago, aged 91.

Patrick, 21, Irish, lives and studies at an English university. His father died of cancer nine months ago, aged 59.

Roy, 45, English, is married with no children. He is a musician and teaches music part-time to people with learning difficulties. His father died of cancer, just over a year ago, aged 74.

Sandra, 19, English, is an undergraduate student. Her close male school friend and her grandmother died 15 and 18 months ago, aged 17 and 79 respectively.

Sarah, 22, English, is an undergraduate student from a farming background. She lost two grandfathers and her maternal grandmother, between 12 and 18 months ago, all in their 80s.

Stephen, 38, English, left a career in the civil service to engage in full-time study as a mature student. He lost his father to diabetes just under six years ago, aged 79.

Susan, 19, English, is an undergraduate student. She lost her great-aunt, suddenly and unexpectedly from a heart-attack, eight months ago, aged 80.

Tania, 50, English, is a single parent with a teenage son and self-employed as a physiotherapist. She lost her mother to ovarian cancer a year ago, aged 79.

Vivienne, 19, English, is an undergraduate student. Her grandmother died just over two years ago, after a fall, aged 84.

Index